1986

Leaders under Stress

Leaders under Stress

A Psychophysiological Analysis of International Crises

Thomas C. Wiegele

Gordon Hilton

Kent Layne Oots

Susan V. Kisiel

Duke Press Policy Studies

Duke University Press

Durham 1985

© 1985 Duke University Press
All rights reserved
Printed in the United States of America
on acid-free paper
Library of Congress Cataloging in Publication Data
Main entry under title:
Leaders under stress.
(Duke Press policy studies)
Bibliography: p.
Includes index.
1. United States—Foreign relations—1945-   —Case studies. 2. Crisis management—
United States—Case studies. 3. Kennedy, John F. (John Fitzgerald), 1917–1963.
4. Nixon, Richard M. (Richard Milhous), 1913–   . 5. Johnson, Lyndon Baines,
1908–1973. 6. Leadership—Case studies. I. Wiegele, Thomas C. II. Series.
E839.L36 1985   353.03′23′0922   85-6832
ISBN 0-8223-0641-7

To Allan D. Bell, Jr.

Contents

Tables and Figures

Tables

Figures

Acknowledgments

Contemporary social science research is often a team effort with responsibilities divided among numerous assistants and informal consultants. The present study clearly conforms to this pattern. The singular noun "study" is a misnomer, however, because this volume is actually a combination of four distinct research initiatives which have been blended into a unified compendium.

The first of these studies, supported by the Cybernetics Technology Office of the Defense Advanced Research Projects Agency (CTO/DARPA) under contract #MDA903-77-C-0355, explored the feasibility of compiling a collection of audio recordings that could be utilized in voice analyses of key public officials during international crises. With the evidence that a usable audio archive could be compiled for the 1961 Berlin crisis, the crisis in the Dominican Republic, and the Cambodian incursion, a second study, supported by Office of Naval Research contract #N00014-79-C0028, was launched. This effort explored the identification of substantive themes as uncovered in voice data. Building upon this second effort, a third study, supported by subcontract #MDA903-80-C-0265 with KAPPA Systems Inc., was undertaken to determine certain psycholinguistic properties of presidential speeches. Finally, under a grant from the Earhart Foundation, more comprehensive statistical analyses were performed, a theoretical introduction to the study was produced, and integrating efforts were completed. We are most grateful for the financial support from all of these sources.

Special thanks go to Richard H. Cady, director of the Bureau of Institutional Research at the University of New Mexico, and William Shearer, professor of communicative disorders at Northern Illinois University. Each of them read the manuscript numerous times and offered suggestions for improvement that were most helpful.

Gerald Hopple of Defense Systems, Inc. and George Kenney of the U.S. Department of State carefully explored the next to the last draft, and we believe that the final draft is much improved because of their advice.

Various administrative aspects of these complex projects were efficiently handled by Joan M. Flaherty, who always worked with grace and good cheer.

Producing data for this volume was an awesome undertaking, and we are most grateful for the help that we received from Lonna Bury, Patrick Conte, Teodoro Del Mundo, Wasi Haider, Leonard Hirsch, Wendolyn Kirkland, Victoria Kraft, Michael McNeil, Lori Nelson, Richard Payne, Ruben Rozental, Timothy Wilson, Kathy Woulfe, and Linda Young. All of these individuals functioned effectively as a cohesive team and were strongly committed to accuracy in their work.

We profited significantly from the courtesies shown to us by the staff of CTO/DARPA. During the course of this research, in addition to friendly encouragement, Judith Ayers Daly sent us numerous articles and reports which were relevant to our work. We also want to thank two former directors of CTO/DARPA, Robert A. Young and Stephen J. Andriole, for their professional interest and confidence.

Lisa Yuen and Mary Navaez ably typed drafts of sections of various chapters. Shelby Jarczyk and Barbara Parot effectively coordinated the production and typing of the final reports of individual projects. Carolyn Cradduck entered the entire manuscript into our computer and conscientiously oversaw the complex production of innumerable drafts.

Finally, we extend our appreciation to Allan D. Bell, Jr., President of Dektor CIS, Inc., to whom this volume is dedicated. Mr. Bell provided training in voice stress analysis for the senior author, furnished equipment to produce the data for this undertaking, and offered much encouragement along the way. It is not an exaggeration to state that without his initial and enthusiastic support this volume could not have been written.

1. The Study of Elites in International Crises: The Theoretical Context

Imagine that the United States and the Soviet Union are locked into a severe international crisis. Both nations consider their supreme national interests to be at stake, and both are fearful of providing any sign of weakness which could be interpreted as a willingness to compromise or disengage from the conflict. The two nations, in our example, are "eyeball to eyeball" in a major confrontation which could lead to nuclear war.

What is the nature of the decisional environment on each side of the globe? In Washington, D.C., the entire foreign policy community is on a crisis alert. Round the clock watch stations have been set up in all offices which are in any way related to the crisis. High ranking U.S. officials have delayed all other business and are concentrating solely on the crisis at hand. Regular working hours have been ignored, and numerous meetings have taken place during all hours of the day and night. The nighttime meetings, occasioned by Soviet actions taken in a different time zone and requiring immediate responses by the United States, have interrupted normal sleep patterns, thereby creating serious physical and psychological fatigue among American decision makers.

The president and his major foreign policy advisors—the group that bears the responsibility for U.S. decisions in this crisis—are especially fatigued and frustrated. The fatigue results not only from the lack of sleep but also from the demands of the situation. Communications to the Soviet Union must be carefully constructed to avoid possible misinterpretation. Reports to the American people must be presented in such a way as to guarantee national support for all U.S. actions, especially those that might lead to war. Words spoken at press conferences must be carefully chosen to avoid any possible inadvertent disclosure. Though doubt and fear prevail in the decision-making group, confidence and determination must be projected to both the American people and the adversary.

But frustration is also a factor in the inner circle. Information requested from various offices in Washington turns out to be either inaccurate or incomplete, clearly not collected for use in this crisis. Computerized data banks in the Department of Defense regarding previous Soviet crisis behavior seem unsuitable for making accurate predictions about the present crisis. Perhaps most important, the wisdom and insight that the National Security Council and other foreign policy advisors were able to provide to the president during more routine times seem to have evaporated at the height of this confrontation. There are no brilliant proposals being offered to the president; his frustration is complete.

A similar pattern has emerged around the Soviet premier in Moscow. Fatigue, frustration, and heavy role responsibilities have taken a corresponding toll.

At the darkest moment of the crisis, the president remarks to a close associate that "in the final analysis it all comes down to a single person, me. And on the other side, it's got to be the Soviet premier." With this thought in mind, the president takes a new approach during the next meeting of the National Security Council. His remarks are worth quoting:

> Gentlemen, I've studied position papers from various offices in your agencies. I've received more data and reports than I cared to read. And, I've listened to your insights, guesses, and hunches about possible Soviet behavior. No one has given me a magic formula. As an individual, I must make the major decisions about this crisis. As an individual, I might have to order a nuclear strike. And as an individual, what I do may very well dramatically change or end the history of this nation.

Not knowing precisely what the president was leading up to, the members of the NSC were surprised to hear him add the following comments:

> If I, as an individual human being, am under this much stress, the same must be true of the Soviet premier. Why have you not given me information about him as an individual? Where are the assessments about his level of psychological discomfort? What issues are bothering him? Is he close to the breaking point? How far can he be pushed before he responds violently?

> You've given me all kinds of information about Soviet national behavior in past international crises, but I want to know about the Soviet premier himself. What's going on inside of him right now?

This book deals with what "goes on" inside of leaders during international crises. In the fictional example just presented, the president's concluding questions are unlikely to be answered satisfactorily because of a lack of measurement tools to assess individual human beings remotely. Academic political scientists seldom think in terms of individual-level analysis, though they should. Policy makers, recognizing the need for information about individuals, require an operational literature that could be utilized in guiding future appraisals of leaders. We hope that this volume will at least partially address these issues by illustrating how it is possible to "get inside" of leaders during international crises.

This study then, deals with many aspects of international crises: political communication, language, psycholinguistics, and the behavior of political elites under conditions of severe psychological stress. Chapter 1 will lay out the theoretical context in which our work has developed. We will begin with a brief description of international crises, and then we will describe the voice stress analysis (VSA) technique which has been used in this study. Next we will review the literature that has been produced to this point, examining in this discussion a group of research issues associated with voice stress analysis. This will be followed by an examination of several aspects of political communication which are relevant to this work. After presenting a model of stress for studying international crises and describing remote electronic mapping, chapter 1 will conclude with a set of propositions that guided the collection of data and the data analysis for the study.

We are aware that we have adopted an unusual method for studying international crises. We also know that the literature on remote or unobtrusive assessment methodologies and particularly on voice stress analysis is virtually unknown in the discipline of political science and in most of the other social sciences as well. Moreover, the applied literature on voice stress analysis is confusing and often contradictory. This study, therefore, is exploratory, and designed to test the utility of voice stress analysis for examining presidential behaviors during international crisis situations. We are quite conscious of the exploratory nature of our work, but we believe that such efforts always precede more definitive studies. International crises are such serious political events that it would be unreasonable to ignore the exploration of an analytical tool that, combined with standard approaches, could contribute to the development of new knowledge about elite decision making during crises.

Some General Reflections on International Crises

Scholars by no means agree on the definition of an international crisis, but we have no intention of producing yet another review of the many definitions available. Such reviews can be found in Robinson (1972), Snyder and Diesing (1977), Brecher (1978), and Oneal (1982). Among the standard works on international crisis are George and Smoke (1974), Holsti (1972), C. Hermann (1969), Holsti and George (1975), Allison (1971), Paige (1968), Zinnes (1968), and Hopple (1980).

However, how one defines an international crisis affects not only one's orientation to the subject matter but also the level of analysis at which research is conducted. For example, in an early discussion, Charles Hermann (1969:29) defined crisis as "a situation that (1) threatens the high-priority goals of the decision-making unit; (2) restricts the amount of time available for response before the situation is transformed; and (3) surprises the members of the decision-making unit when it occurs." Hermann's definition has been discussed extensively and revised considerably during the past decade, but it had merit because it focused attention on activities and behavior within the foreign policy decision-making unit itself.

Snyder and Diesing (1977:6) provide an orientation at the state level by defining a crisis as "a sequence of interactions between governments of two or more sovereign states in severe conflict, short of actual war, but involving the perception of a dangerously high probability of war." Although this definition does refer to individual-level perceptions, it nevertheless pulls the researchers to the "sequence of interactions" which occur at the state level.

Brecher (1978:6) provides both conceptual and operational definitions of a crisis. Conceptually, "a foreign policy crisis is a situational change in the external or internal environment that creates in the minds of the incumbent decision-makers of an international actor a perceived threat from the external environment to the basic values to which a responsive decision is deemed necessary." Apparently reasoning that his conceptual definition could not be used to study real crises, Brecher (1978:6) put forward the following operational definition: "A foreign policy crisis is a breakpoint along a peace-war continuum of a state's relations with any other international actor(s). A crisis is a situation with four necessary and sufficient conditions, as these are perceived by the highest-level decision-makers of the actor concerned: (1) A change in its external or internal environment which generates (2) a threat to basic values, with a simultaneous or subsequent (3) high probability of involvement in military hostilities, and the awareness of (4) a finite time for response to the external value threat."

Our research necessarily focuses on the individual level of analysis. Though state-level analysis is important to a comprehensive understanding of the phenomenon of international crisis, we believe that the individual level of analysis will tap more accurately the reality of decision making during international crises. Holsti (1976:17–18) has suggested that, in certain situations, individual-level analysis will prove especially appropriate for examining international crises:

(1) Nonroutine situations that require more than merely standard operating procedures and decision rules; for example, decisions to initiate or terminate major international undertakings, including wars, interventions, alliances, aid programs, and the like.
(2) Decisions made at the pinnacle of the government hierarchy by leaders who are relatively free from organizational and other constraints—or who may at least define their roles in ways that enhance their latitude of choice. . . .
(3) When the situation itself is highly ambiguous and is thus open to a variety of interpretations. . . .
(4) Circumstances of information overload in which decision-makers are forced to use a variety of strategies (e.g., queuing, filtering, omission, reducing categories of discrimination to cope with the problem).
(5) Unanticipated events in which initial reactions are likely to reflect cognitive "sets."
(6) Circumstances in which complex cognitive tasks associated with decision-making may be impaired or otherwise significantly affected by the various types of stresses that impinge on top-ranking executives.

In writing about the management of international crises, Merritt (1982:79) asserts, "there is an important gap in our knowledge about the effects of individual and organizational stress in decision-making." However, he laments "the fact that we know little or nothing about the effects of systemic stress on the performance of individuals acting on behalf of national systems."

Merritt, of course, is correct. There are numerous gaps in our knowledge of crises, especially as they relate to the personal behavior of a central leadership during periods of intense emotional stress. What is the precise nature of the psychological environment of the decision-making situation? Does this environment affect the character and quality of decisions? Do the possibilities of the outbreak of war, a frequent component of crisis, distort in important ways the behavior of, for example, heads of states? Can "strong" leaders withstand sudden role-overload demands? How are anxieties and fears communicated to colleagues? Or are they not communicated? Could an adversary who can assess stress in opposing leaders gain a tactical advantage during a crisis?

The literature of social psychology provides some responses to these questions, generated for the most part experimentally. In addition, memoirs provide some nontheoretical insights into certain crisis situations. The lack of intimate and precise information is quite understandable since political leaders normally do not make themselves available for scientific study during crisis confrontations.

Researchers thus face a dilemma. They have a snapshot of information about internal decision processes that they suspect have profound effects on the behavior of leaders, but they cannot study these processes because of their gravity, their critical security implications, and the lack of direct access.

Conceivably, Brecher realized this dilemma, and thus provided both a conceptual and an operational definition of international crisis because he assumed that the conceptual definition could not be used in the study of real crises. We disagree. The individual level of analysis is not only important, it is researchable. Brecher's conceptual definition of international crisis can be operationalized by employing a remote assessment methodology that can overcome the lack of access to central decision makers for political analysis.

The Signal Leakage Conceptualization

The signal leakage conceptualization is critical to our focus on the individual person. As Wiegele (1979b:71) wrote:

> Most social science research on the behavior of elites has dealt with such aspects as operational codes, roles, events, situations, socioeconomic factors, recruitment, perceptions, birth order, style, and so forth. Because they deal with behavioral outputs and with social factors outside of the individual himself, these kinds of researches can be considered as peripheral measures or indices of individual behavior. Granted, many of these aspects are often correlated with individual behavior; nevertheless they do not constitute *in a primary way* the direct measurement of the individual himself. It is in this sense that they might be considered peripheral to the human being.

We need a considerably different research focus to shift the researcher away from peripheral measures to more direct but less intrusive measures.

If elites could be measured during international crises both directly *and* remotely, we could open the door to a range of behavioral indices that might contribute significantly to an understanding of their political acts as well as their psychological states while performing those acts. Furthermore, these direct measurements of individuals can ultimately be built into multi-indicator studies of crisis behavior.

Signal leakage is the theoretical conceptualization which most comfortably fits our research needs. Ekman and Friesen (1969) posit the concept of nonverbal leakage of information that was developed within a context of clues to deception. In a later publication (Ekman and Friesen, 1975), they defined leakage "as the unintended betrayal of a feeling the person is trying to conceal." Certain parts of the human body have specific sending capacities which are indexed by the length of time needed to transmit the information, by the "number of discriminable stimulus patterns which can be emitted," and by visibility or the degree to which the analyst is able to observe the leakage content (Ekman and Friesen, 1969:93–94). Druckman, Rozelle, and Baxter (1982) carry the pioneering work of Ekman and Friesen further by developing a more broadly based theory of verbal and nonverbal behavior which includes linkages between behavior and neurophysiological processes.

This study gives the signal leakage conceptualization a much broader substantive basis than simple deception, which is not even a part of our analysis. Rather, we focus on the leakage of nonverbal voice signals that index internal psychological states such as anxiety or discomfort.

In using signal leakage, a question arises. Must signals be captured with the attachment of some sort of sensor (for example, the placement of electrodes on a person's chest to produce an electrocardiogram) or can remote assessments be made? In a sense, social scientists have always made "remote" assessments by deriving information from printed texts or simply by engaging in deductive reasoning about leaders and their policies. However, we are interested in a different and more precise type of remote assessment—one that results in a direct, unobtrusive, real time measure of a psychological or psychophysiological state of a specific subject. Some examples of such measures are pupil dilation, facial expressions (micro-affect displays), body movements, and voice analysis. These measures have frequently been used to index anxiety, psychological "uncomfortableness," or negative affect. When applied to leaders in specific situations, (for example, international crises) such measures hold the promise of aiding in the management and the successful resolution of crises.

Voice Stress Analysis

Voice stress analysis (VSA) is an attractive research methodology for the study of international crises because it allows the remote assessment of leaked physiological signals of psychological stress that previously had been accessible only through direct sensor attachment to a subject.[1]

Voice stress analysis is possible because a change in muscle micro-tremors takes place in the physiology of the human speech mechanism at times of psychological stress. These tremors are in the range of eight to twelve hertz, are inaudible to the human ear, and thus are not openly detectable. Present-day voice stress analyzers are solid state electronic signal processors that take electronically transduced speech from a special high fidelity (20,000 cps) tape recorder, and use filtering and frequency discrimination techniques to isolate the wave forms and display them on a moving strip of heat sensitive chart paper.[2]

Two types of vocal change can result when individuals find themselves under strong psychological stress. Bell, Ford, and McQuiston (1974) identified one type as a gross vocal change that can be detected audibly by noting variations in rate, volume, voice tremor, change in spacing between syllables, and change in the fundamental pitch or frequency of the voice. Some subjects are capable of exercising conscious control over such variations.

The second type of vocal change is not detectable by the human ear and results when individuals are under psychological stress. This phenomenon is unconscious and subjects cannot control it. It results from a slight tensing of the vocal cords under conditions of stress and produces a dampening of selected frequency variations. Bell, Ford, and McQuiston (1974) state, "when graphically portrayed, the difference is readily discernible between unstressed or normal vocalization and vocalization under mild stress . . . these patterns have held true over a wide range of human voices of both sexes, various ages, and under various situational conditions." Although evidence of frequency dampening in stressful situations is clear, a comprehensive understanding of the voice stress phenomenon is yet to be developed (McGlone and Hollien, 1976). In practice, however, the technique has displayed a number of promising characteristics.

[1] This section has been adapted from Hirsch and Wiegele (1981). Permission to reprint from Jossey-Bass is acknowledged.

[2] Numerous brands of electronic instruments can be utilized in voice stress analysis. The voice stress analysis literature has developed almost exclusively around the device known as a Psychological Stress Evaluator (PSE-101), marketed by Dektor CIS, Inc., Savannah, Georgia. So ubiquitous has been the use of this instrument that voice stress analysis is frequently referred to as "PSE research." Strictly speaking, this is an improper designation.

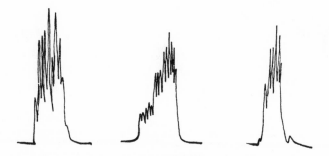

Figure 1.1   Three traces of unstressed words.

Examples of voice stress measurement. Let us examine how stress is represented on a voice stress analysis trace. The normal wave form of a spoken
word under nonstress conditions appears in figure 1.1. Each individual
wave form, or trace, represents a single word. Note the irregularity of the
cycles and that the general configuration resembles a wave; that is, if a line
is drawn connecting the top points of each cycle, an irregular pattern will
be evident.

Figure 1.2 illustrates three examples of the charted responses of a person under considerable psychological stress. As stress becomes stronger,
the undulating wave patterns assume increasingly squarish configurations.
The patterns in figure 1.2 show a degree of rectilinearity believed to be
proportionate to the amount of stress present. Increasing levels of stress
are shown from left to right.

The amplitude (height) of the trace is arbitrarily adjusted to fit the tape
width of the instrument and is not a factor in interpretation. The position-
ing on the strip chart can affect the overall configuration of the trace, however, and some experience with the equipment is necessary to find op-
timum settings.

Review of the Literature

A growing body of literature employs voice stress analysis as a research
tool. The results, for the most part, are inconclusive or positive, depending on the nature of the study. Since the voice stress analyzer is often utilized as a "lie detector," one group of experimental studies tests the validity of this claim. These studies have not found voice stress analysis to be
consistently reliable. The second group of studies examines stress and the
effect of stressors on the individual in both applied and experimental situa-

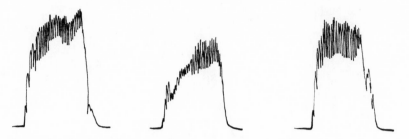

Figure 1.2   Three traces of stressed words.

tions. With some reservations, these studies have generally found voice stress analysis to be a useful tool for certain types of social research.

The deception studies. In a brochure describing its product, Dektor CIS, Inc., the manufacturer of the most frequently used voice stress analyzer, reports on four studies it conducted. In the first validity study, analysts evaluated charts of 75 contestants on "To Tell the Truth" and correctly assigned 71 of them to truth or falsehood categories (94.7 percent). In the second study, Dektor ran a peak-of-tension test with 24 subjects, identifying 22 correctly. A third study describes a Maryland police chief who, in using 162 elements from real-world data culled from the confessions and investigations of felony subjects, found a 100 percent corroboration between voice stress analysis results and guilt and innocence. Finally, Dektor analysts ascertained correct word groupings for traces of "presumed emotion-producing" or "presumed neutral" words in 52 of 53 cases (98.4 percent accuracy).

Variations on the peak-of-tension and emotive/neutral word tests have been repeated by others but with much less successful results. Lewis and Worth (1975) tested for differences in voice-recorded stress resulting from verbal and written stressors. To do this, subjects were asked to react to a series of ten written words and ten spoken words—five neutral (string, shoe, and so forth) and five emotional (blood, coffin, and so on). The five neutral words were spoken normally and as "high-pitched outbursts" (Lewis and Worth, 1975). These observers found no consistent reaction to the written stressors; as often as not, subjects would react more stressfully to a neutral word than to the emotional words. However, they did find substantial difference in the oral experiment. The loud stressors created significantly more stressful responses than the normally spoken stressors, even though the actual words were identical. Of course, this was an experimental situation in which the subjects were not directly involved emotionally.

Horvath (1978) used the peak-of-tension test to compare results from voice stress analysis and galvanic skin response (GSR). Subjects were instructed to choose a number and then conceal it when questioned. With voice stress analysis the researcher could detect the number only 20 percent of the time, no different from chance. Measuring the galvanic skin response, it was possible to detect the chosen number correctly 70 percent of the time. Furthermore, the intercoder reliabilities of the two physiological methods were strikingly different: $r = .38$ for the voice stress analysis and $r = .92$ for the GSR.

However, there are several serious problems with the design of the Horvath study. The first, which the author mentions, is the question of motivation of the subjects. At the low motivation levels that Horvath analyzed with subjective coding, the range of stress within the traces may not have provided sufficient variance for clear delineation. Second, the peak-of-tension test had only five items, perhaps too short an instrument to control for pre- and postdeception anxiety. Third, Horvath did not analyze the trends of the responses or the placement of the deception items within the test. Perhaps those who chose central numbers (2, 3, 4) showed less reliable patterns than those on the ends (1, 5). Last, by asking the questions with the numbers ordered in a manner known to the subjects, the placement of the deception was not random but expected and therefore less stressful. Reeves (1976) has shown that voice stress variation is a measure of reaction to a stressor "presented at the moment," and thus foreknowledge should lessen the effect of the stressor at the moment of deception.

All of these qualifications are valid, but they do not explain the different results obtained from voice stress and GSR techniques. It is possible that GSR is a more sensitive indicator at these levels of stress; however, Horvath's study poses more questions than it can answer about the validity of voice stress analysis.

Like Horvath, McGlone (1975) found that deception could not be identified at low levels of stress, and he designed an experiment to increase the range of stress. Twenty male subjects read "An Apology for Idlers" by Stevenson while experiencing successively increased levels of shock with randomly determined time intervals between trials. Baseline data words were recorded before the administration of the most severe shocks. Under these conditions, voice analysis correctly detected stress 77 percent of the time.

Deception (or fear of discovery) is expected to be a psychological stressor, but stress can obviously result from many other phenomena. Any cause of anxiety or arousal in a person, such as uncertainty, centrality to desires, or anticipation, should be discernible. Analysts who use this technique to detect deception must be sensitive to this.

The nondeception studies. As suggested in the McGlone study, voice stress analysis is apparently more reliable when the stress level is relatively high. Brenner, Branscomb, and Schwartz (1979) performed two experiments that support McGlone's work. The first was a deception study in which they tried to increase motivation, thereby raising the stress level, by offering a reward for concealing a correct response. Subjects were informed of the nature of the study and of voice stress analysis and "were advised that it might be better to produce emotional responses to incorrect items rather than attempt to suppress actual emotional responses to correct ones" (Brenner, Branscomb, and Schwartz, 1979:352). Not surprisingly, Brenner and associates were not able to distinguish the correct items. The study was modeled on earlier GSR research that had resulted in positive identification of correct and incorrect items, and thus it questions the utility of voice analysis at low levels of stress.

In the second experiment, Brenner's group employed a mental arithmetic task where subjects had to perform problems of varying difficulty at a fixed pace. Prior studies had shown that GSR increased with problem difficulty. Traces of the subjects' voice stress analyses showed linear trends, clearly indicating increasing stress with increasing difficulty. As in the McGlone study, when the range in the stress levels was substantial, voice data conformed to the expected pattern and paralleled GSR results.

In another study Brenner (1974) examined the effects of group size on the intensity of stage fright. In an empty auditorium, speech students from the University of Michigan were asked to recite poetry. Then they were split into four groups, and each group was instructed to recite a very difficult poem before a different-sized audience of introductory psychology students—twenty-two, eight, two, and no spectators, respectively. The correlation between voice stress analysis scores and self-reports of arousal was high ($r = .32$). Stress increased as an almost perfect function of group size.

Shearer and Wiegele (1977) asked thirty subjects (fifteen male, fifteen female) to read a list of eight one-syllable numbers. As each subject read the randomly chosen list of words, he or she was presented with a stressor (a burst of high-frequency noise lasting 500 milliseconds in free field 100 db SPL). An independent experimenter performed both GSR and voice stress analyses. The voice analysis traces were correctly chosen for ten of the thirty subjects. This is significantly better than the results of Horvath's comparison of GSR and voice stress.

Smith (no date) conducted two relevant experiments, the first using a multiple question format with control questions and sensitive questions. Twenty subjects were asked to agree or disagree with each question. The two control questions dealt with the days of the week. One question related to test anxiety and was more stressful than the other. The remaining question served as a stressor: the experimenters asked whether the subject had ever stolen office supplies.

It was found that the mean stress on the first control question was significantly higher than the mean stress on the second control ($p = .05$). The combined mean stress of the relevant sensitive questions was also significantly higher than on the second control question ($p = .05$). The second experiment produced similar results.

Psychiatric researchers have also shown interest in voice stress analysis. Using this technique, Wiggins, McCrainie, and Bailey (1975) analyzed recordings of psychiatric interviews of children. They used three major response categories to the children's answers: content of communication, responses to therapist-posed questions, and miscellaneous responses. Content responses included people, ideas, objects, and actions. Subsequently, the children's responses to various people in their environment were analyzed. The difference in stress levels between response to direct questions and child-initiated topics was also analyzed. The study found that stress in the voice could be detected and assessed and that voice stress analysis could lead to new ways of exploring the relationship between psychological stress and content of communication in psychiatric patients.

Borgen and Goodman (no date) designed an experiment to evaluate the responses of eight paid male prisoner volunteers to a Stroop Test. This instrument produces a conflict situation that is assumed to induce stress. Respondents' skin potential, blood flow, and EKG readings were taken during the test while their verbal responses were being recorded. To test for the effectiveness of anti-anxiety drugs, subjects received either ten milligrams of diazepam (Valium), a tranquilizer, or a placebo two hours prior to examination.

The Stroop Test effectively elicited an arousal state that was characterized by significant increases in blood flow, skin potential, and systolic and diastolic blood pressure levels. With a small number of subjects in each group (four), significant differences in stress responses as measured by traditional physiological measures or by voice stress analysis, or both, were not detected. Nevertheless, diazepam reduced the degree of stress as indicated by both types of measurements. All results, however, showed movement in the appropriate directions, thereby suggesting relationships between physiological indicators and voice changes.

Smith (1973) analyzed fifteen hospital outpatients who suffered from general anxiety states. They were asked to respond to questions dealing with common life stressors as well as three phrases about personal life stressors. The subjects were asked to reread the ten items for test reliability. It was correctly hypothesized that there would be a difference between the patient's self-report and the voice stress analysis. Smith concluded that the voice analysis method of identifying particular areas of anxiety would significantly enhance psychological evaluation and treatment.

Smith (1973) demonstrated further that voice stress analysis could be used to reveal significant differences in anxiety states. One experiment contrasted voice stress data of professional broadcasters and of laypersons who called in to a radio talk show. Using both visual schemes and objective rating schemes to analyze voice stress traces, Smith investigated ten responses for each of twenty-two professionals and thirteen members of the public. He found that the public's responses were significantly more stressed than those of broadcasters.

In an experiment with eighteen neurotic outpatients (nine phobic, nine nonphobic), Smith assumed that the phobic group would respond to the experimental situation with a higher anxiety level than the nonphobics (obsessionals, hypochondriacs, and mild depressives). A control group of fifteen student nurses and other medical professionals was also analyzed. Each subject counted aloud from one to ten and was informed that the experimenter was concerned with anxiety levels in the voice. For the visually rated data, it was found that phobics were significantly more anxious than nonphobics. However, this experiment did not yield any significant differences between the nonphobics and the control group. Finally, to measure reliability for both the visual ratings and objective scoring methods, subjects from both experiments were used in a split-half reliability test. By the Brown-Spearman formula, $r = .39$ for visual rating and $r = .61$ for objective scoring. The correlation between both scoring methods was highly significant (Pearson's $r = .61$).

The dental profession has long been concerned with the effects of stress during treatment, and voice analyses have been especially helpful in studying this phenomenon. Johnson (1978) divided eighteen dental professionals into four groups based upon their members' amount of clinical experience and education in pedodontics. Slides of pedodontic situations of varying difficulty were shown to the subjects as stressors. Slide content included traumatic injuries and congenital malformities. The nonstressing slides were simply textures of various colors that contained no cognitive content. The slides were projected onto a screen, and the subject was asked, "Do you see the slide?" The subject's "yes" response was recorded and then analyzed with voice stress techniques.

Johnson hypothesized that the stressor slides would cause most stress to the least experienced groups and least stress to the practicing pedodontists. He found the opposite. Analyzing his results, Johnson suggested that the experienced dental professionals felt more stress because they had a better understanding of the ramifications of what they saw. The overall conclusion was that voice analysis supplied a valid indicator of stress. Johnson's work is consistent with previous research involving the physiological monitoring of anxiety states among experienced and inexperienced parachute jumpers (Tanner, 1976:26–27).

Worth and Lewis (1975) conducted a study in a dentist's office, utilizing the dentist as a stressor. When they asked critical questions about brushing teeth, they did not find significant differences between the answers given in front of the dentist and the answers given without the dentist. However, they did find significantly higher stress levels (chi-square, $p \leq .02$) on the answer to the first question ("Is your name ————?") when the dentist was present.

Voice stress analysis seems to be most clearly validated in studies where the subject is somehow closely tied to the activity that produced the stress and when motivation and centrality are high. These conditions clearly characterize role-responsible, elite political behavior during international crises. Indeed, it is somewhat surprising that the social sciences have not been more sensitive to the development of measures for remotely assessing communicative behavior. After all, much of what we describe as elite behavior is communicative behavior. Thus, a sharper focus on communications could provide a more sophisticated understanding of elite activity, and voice stress analysis can contribute to such an understanding.

Let us proceed, then, to the final voice stress analysis research to be reviewed, politically oriented studies. For the most part, these studies have been nonexperimental and performed in the context of international crises. The crisis milieu was perhaps the safest area in which to begin politically oriented work because it can reasonably be assumed that leaders are indeed functioning under conditions of psychological stress. Furthermore, the issues with which they are dealing are of central concern to them because of their high positions of responsibility.

The first published work to employ voice stress analysis to study international crisis (Wiegele, 1978b) examined the key television and radio speeches of Presidents Truman, Kennedy, and Johnson during the Korean, Cuban, Berlin, Tonkin, and *Pueblo* crises. A single, critical speech for each crisis was analyzed.

Each of the speeches expressed the sentiment that the United States was determined to see its way through to a successful resolution of the crisis. These were labelled determination themes. In crises with a high probability of war (Korea, Berlin, and Cuba), the determination themes displayed very high stress. However, when war did not appear imminent (Tonkin, *Pueblo*), determination themes were substantially lower in stress.

Typically, crisis speeches refer to a precipitating act or set of circumstances that led to the crisis. These precipitating act themes in the speeches were subjected to voice stress analysis. It was found that, since in all likelihood, presidents viewed them as givens of the crisis, they were therefore low in stress level. Only in the Gulf of Tonkin crisis was the precipitating act a theme of high stress, and this was because a North Vietnamese attack in the Gulf was not established beyond doubt when Lyndon Johnson delivered his key address. Consequently, the precipitating act theme was apparently discomforting to the president, resulting in high stress.

Although it did not deal with international crisis, Wiegele's (1978a) study examined the vocalizations of Richard M. Nixon at two stress-laden moments of his public life: his concession speech upon losing the California gubernatorial race in 1962 and his farewell to his staff after he resigned from the presidency in 1974. In his conclusion, Wiegele argued that "events that are traditionally viewed by the electorate as political failures . . . were perceived by Nixon as serious personal failures. Indeed, in the two speeches that were analyzed, Nixon never addressed the broader political consequences of the occurrences" (Wiegele, 1978a : 74). When Nixon alluded to politics in these speeches, he displayed little stress; when he talked about personal failure, his stress levels were exceedingly high.

Research Issues and Assumptions Associated with Voice Stress Analysis

A number of research issues can be raised regarding the use of voice stress analysis in applied political research, and it is important to spell out these issues before beginning a discussion of the project itself.

Preparation of speeches by others. We assume that each speaker that we have subjected to voice stress analysis is rational and conscious of the words he is articulating. There can be little question that when a president speaks extemporaneously he creates his own grammatical constructions; however, we make the further assumption that even in prepared speeches *on international crises* the president has been an active participant in the drafting process. Let us examine this latter observation a bit more closely.

International crises are serious political events. Indeed, the role responsibilities of a head of state in all modern societies are seldom more clearly identified and focused, and therefore more salient, than in an international crisis. It is reasonable to assume that a president plays an active role in the decisional processes associated with the crisis (e.g., see Paige, 1968; Allison, 1971). A frequent outcome of those processes is a prepared statement or report delivered on national radio and television. This form of communication is an intimate part of crisis management because heads of state seek mass support from their citizenry during crises in order to demonstrate national strength and resolve to an adversary. Further, decision makers normally view such documents as devices to signal feelings and positions to adversaries.

Heads of state can write these messages themselves, write them with others, or have them written by others. *Given the seriousness of international crises*, it is appropriate to assume that either the head of state participated directly in the drafting of the statement or he carefully and painstakingly reviewed and often revised the draft(s) of others. Thus, because of the close association of the head of state with the prepared words which he delivers publicly during crisis situations, we assume further that he accepts and understands those words as his own. Therefore, the cognitive processes which are engaged by a speaker in presenting a prepared statement will be reflected in his vocalizations, which can be examined by voice stress analyses.

In addition to formal, prepared statements, a president articulates informal, extemporaneous verbalizations during the course of a crisis, usually in press conferences. We assume that in these remarks the president understands his own verbalizations and that voice stress analysis will accurately assess his cognitions. We further assume that presidential views, especially during nonroutine crisis periods, are important (Graber, 1976:174–212). That is, the words of a head of state are authoritative and accurately reflect national policy positions at the time they are spoken.

Problem of controls. The problem of baseline measurements or controls has been a particularly vexing one for our research. Ideally, some type of clear control should be established for each speaker we examine. What we are assessing, however, is the level of psychophysiological arousal (expressed through stress in the voice) during a particular time period. Such crisis periods are, of course, unique, and it is impossible to recreate them in any meaningful way that involves real role responsibilities.

One way of establishing control would be to measure a single individual in both stressful (crisis) and nonstressful (routine) decision-making situations. Deviations from the "norm" or routine situations could then be assessed on the basis of measurements taken in an international crisis. The major problem with such a design is that the audio record is at best incomplete, and at worst nonexistent. Noncrisis video and audio tapes are made infrequently, and they are not kept for long. Furthermore, presidents seldom make national reports on routine political situations.

A possible way around this problem would be to design a projective study in which the researchers could tape record and analyze all presidential vocalizations prior to a crisis, and then, of course, tape the crisis itself when it occurs. However, this solution is unrealistic. We cannot predict when a crisis will emerge, and most research teams do not have infinite resources to commit to a project in anticipation of a crisis occurring at some indeterminate point in the future.

The problem of controls is related to another problem—the causes of stress in an individual at a specific point in time. For example, during the 45-minute period it might take a president to deliver an important crisis speech, a critic could assert that the president's level of stress (or arousal) was caused by a multiplicity of factors and that therefore it is fruitless to attempt to ascertain precise differential effects.

This criticism appears plausible, but we reasoned quite differently. An international crisis is probably the most severe test of a president's leadership and decision-making ability. International crises occur infrequently during a president's tenure in office, and he therefore recognizes them as unusual events. The international crises that we examined for this study involved *major* decisions for Presidents Kennedy, Johnson, and Nixon. We assume, therefore, that even though the level of stress in an individual may have multiple causes, the *single most powerful cause* will be the international crisis for which the focal person has unique role responsibilities. Therefore, our analyses, though not explaining completely the causes of stress, will nevertheless explain *the major cause* for a specific decision maker at a specific point in time. We do not believe that present-day analytic capabilities can do more than this.

To establish some control or baseline measure of a "normal" stress level given the difficulties of research design, we developed a self-anchoring internal control value for any given audio document under consideration. We selected the mean stress value in a specific document as the speaker's base-line or control value, with deviations above or below the mean represent-ing higher or lower stress respectively for that speaker on that date. Con-ceptually, this selection accounts for the fact that the causes of stress are multiple and changing because it allows the mean baseline value to change for each document under examination. However, it remains our assump-tion that the international crisis itself will be the single most important cause of stress for a president on the date on which he is speaking.

Conscious control of vocalizations. Brenner (1974) found that subjects given knowledge of voice stress analysis were able to conceal deceptions from an analyst. Although this finding might seriously limit the use of voice stress analysis to detect deception, it has no effect on remote use of the technique on naive subjects in analysis of psychiatric exams, group meetings, nondeception experiments, or crisis speeches.

Another virtually unexamined source of concern is the "alternative fac-tors" question. Only Brenner, Branscomb, and Schwartz (1979) have men-tioned this. They found that the stress scores on repeated vocalizations of the numbers zero to nine were not random as expected. Rather, there was a hierarchy of scores, ranging from five (highest) through nine, four, one, zero, seven, three, two, and eight (lowest). Six, as vocalized, did not afford a large enough trace for analysis. Conceivably, voice stress analysis was tapping some unknown, underlying orientation to the numbers.

Limitations of voice stress analysis. There are several limitations in utiliz-ing voice stress methods in remote assessment research. First, if there are no verbalizations, there are no data. Therefore, VSA can be utilized to study only political events in which there are public verbalizations. This rules out numerous research possibilities because many political events are not publicly displayed.

Second, good quality tape recordings must be used. Tapes twice re-moved from the original recording represent no problems in analysis, but beyond this there might be some risks to precision.

Third, the experimental literature on voice stress analysis is growing, but still not especially strong. As Bell (1981:65) points out, the validation studies are confusing and frequently badly designed. At this point in its development, voice stress analysis must be considered to be an emerging technology of potentially great research applicability. As Lykken (1974) observed, voice stress analysis is an important addition to the repertoire of physiologically based research techniques. Its useful applications in socio-political research are only beginning to emerge. The existing literature makes it clear that *voice stress analyses have provided impressive results in real situations involving real challenges to an individual's role, concerns, or situation.* In experimental situations with no controls over the intensity of the stressing stimuli or with no real challenges, results have been mixed.

As indicated above, our use of the voice stress analysis technique to study the behavior of elites in international crises is exploratory. The international crisis is especially conducive to exploratory work given what is known about the characteristics of voice stress analysis. The high stress of international crises falls heavily on heads of state whose role responsibilities demand their direct engagement in resolving the crisis. Moreover, by their very nature, crises are among the gravest of international events: time pressures are evident, the core values of the nation-state are under challenge, and war is highly probable. This type of real situation could not have been better selected as a test of a research technique which, despite its limitations, is most effective in real situations involving important challenges to an individual's role responsibilities. Further, we view the present study as a test of the individual stress model advanced by Hermann and Brady (1972:281–303).

The Study of Political Communication

Because our analysis of the human voice during international crises involves the use of language for the purpose of communication, our work necessarily relates to the literature of political communication.

Virtually every major work on political communication (e.g., Benjamin, 1982; Ealy, 1981; Edelman, 1977; Fagen, 1966; Goodin, 1980; Graber, 1976; Meadow, 1980; Shapiro, 1981) makes the point that communication is central to the study of politics but that political scientists, unfortunately, have neglected it. We agree with this observation, especially as it concerns the study of international crises. Much of what is called crisis behavior is actually communication behavior.

Meadow (1980:4) defines political communication as "any exchange of symbols or messages that to a significant extent have been shaped by, or have consequences for, the functioning of political systems." This definition fits our own work quite well.

Much political communication literature deals with election studies and the effects of certain types of messages on the electorate. Students of speech communication, rhetoric, and journalism have studied campaign literature and the use of mass media in this regard. Even a recent article by Meisel (1982) on communication during international crises limited itself to the effects of the mass media only.

Deutsch's (1963) *The Nerves of Government: Models of Political Communication and Control* represents a considerable theoretical advance over the "applications-oriented" elections studies. However, this volume focuses on cybernetic processes and communication channels, i.e., the macro-communications network. Some recent work on the philosophy and meaning of political language (e.g., Shapiro, 1981; Ealy, 1981) is informative and it illustrates sophisticated linkages to other bodies of theoretical knowledge on communication.

Graber has been especially sensitive to the communication behavior of political elites. She spells out three reasons why their verbal behavior is of "extraordinary" importance. First, "the subject matter which political elites put into words includes topics of great political significance." This leads quite naturally to a second reason: "not only do political leaders discuss vital questions; they also possess, within limits, the power and position to enforce their pronouncements." Finally, "elite verbal pronouncements are also important because of their extremely wide audiences" (Graber, 1976: 178–179).

These three reasons establish the saliency of the communication record for determining the significance of and therefore the signal leakage from elite pronouncements. Graber (1976: 195) is correct in arguing that elite communications are generally recognized as requiring careful scrutiny and interpretation. Indeed, "inferences are made about the antecedents of the messages which caused the political leader to say what he did, about the clues which the message supplies as to the personality and actions of the decision-maker, and about the probable effects of the message" (Graber, 1976: 195).

Graber (1976: 197) argues that "elite views are particularly significant for major, nonroutine decisions" such as international crises. She demonstrates convincingly, moreover, that a speaker's location in a hierarchical power structure appears to correlate comfortably with the individual's credibility. Indeed, "the higher the authority and the greater the reputation for credibility of his office, the more dangerous it would be for the speaker to be caught in a lie" (Graber, 1976: 196). We believe that this observation holds true for the study of international crises, especially given their high probability of war and the possibility of accidental misinterpretation of political messages. Indeed, because of the serious consequences of misinterpretation, decision makers must be conscious of what Edelman (1977:26) calls "the linguistic structuring of social problems."

Cognitive mapping. Students of foreign policy decision making are aware of the cognitive process approach to understanding elite behaviors. According to Shapiro and Bonham (1973:148), a cognitive process takes place "when an individual receives information about an international event, processes it through his belief system (which contains concepts about actors and actions in the international system), and reaches a conclusion about what has happened and what should be done by his nation." Individuals have in their belief systems templates or cognitive maps of their environments and, especially in the case of heads of state, of their political environments. As Holsti (1976:12) has observed, "the beliefs that comprise these maps provide the individual with a more or less coherent way of organizing and making sense out of what would otherwise be a confusing array of signals picked up from the environment by his senses." In constructing cognitive maps scholars have used the assertions of decision makers in order to graphically portray their thought processes (Axelrod, 1976:6). These assertions are then graphically organized by an analyst in order to appraise a speaker's view of a particular element of political reality.

Because cognitive mapping relies upon an analysis of assertions, it is conceptually related to the study of political communication. Our own work in voice stress analysis, based as it is upon spoken messages, can be looked upon as a physiologically based cognitive mapping enterprise. Though quite different from "traditional" cognitive mapping, our work, which is sensitive to psycholinguistics, is nevertheless intimately related to the attempt to remotely assess the mind of foreign policy decision makers through the study of their language behavior. It is also quite compatible with standard cognitive mapping procedures.

Psycholinguistics. Kess (1976) has outlined the various approaches of psycholinguistics to understanding verbal behavior. Psycholinguistics as a field began as a mixture of linguistics and psychology and grew rapidly during the 1950s. Prior to this blending, linguists concerned themselves with the messages transmitted by language, and psychologists, with the individuals receiving and transmitting these messages (Kess, 1976:2–3). Chomsky (1968) argues that linguistics is appropriately viewed as a branch of cognitive psychology (Kess, 1976:2).

Reber (1973) discusses three paradigms used in psycholinguistics research. The associationist paradigm concentrates on learning and learning theory. It focuses on the association between stimulus and response. The process paradigm holds that language results from a set of general cognitive abilities. The context paradigm maintains that human beings have a specific rather than a general set of abilities allowing them to acquire language.

These paradigms have spanned a number of subfields in psycholinguistics. Structural linguistics views language from a systemic perspective. A language is a system with rules of operation. Describing the framework of a language is the core of structural linguistics (Kess, 1976:11). Generative transformational linguistics (cf. Chomsky, 1957) looks at the abilities necessary for the use of language. Chomsky's work moved psycholinguistics toward rationalism and away from an empirical orientation (Kess, 1976:17–19). Another branch of psycholinguistics is behaviorism (cf. Watson, 1924), which treats language as a behavior and is guided by a stimulus-response model (Kess, 1976:33). Functional analysis (cf. Skinner, 1948) holds that language need not be the result of a particular stimulus. Language is operant behavior rather than respondent (stimulus-response) behavior. The acquisition of language occurs in operant conditioning (Kess, 1976:35–36). The mediational approach to psycholinguistics (cf. Osgood, 1963) is basically a stimulus-response model with an intervening variable, the internal state of the respondent. Thus, a stimulus produces a certain psychological state in the respondent which in turn produces the response (Kess, 1976:42). Finally, cognitive psycholinguistics focuses on identifying the cognitive abilities responsible for language behavior (Kess, 1976:42).

Psycholinguistics has made many attempts to assess the internal emotional state of a speaker. Davitz (1969), for example, constructed a "dictionary of emotional meaning." Weintraub (1981) used fourteen categories of speech in order to understand the psychological state of a speaker.

Our own work takes a middle position between the operant conditioning approach and the mediational approach. It is mediational because we are trying to tap the internal state of a speaker as he responds to the stimulus of an international crisis. It also has an element of operant conditioning in that a speaker may respond both to the immediate stimulus, the crisis events, and to a preexisting belief system about the objects of his response. For example, a president's response to a Soviet invasion of a neighboring state may be a result of the act itself and his existing beliefs about the Soviets as well.

Some empirical communications work using language as an analytical orientation. Though most of the previous work in political communication focuses on the general process of communication rather than the act of communicating (a macro- rather than a micro-approach), some interesting empirical studies are relevant to and compatible with our work because they look at the individual level of analysis.

In a carefully designed study, M. G. Hermann (1977) used a three-step model of stress to explore the verbal behavior of elite individual actors during the 1965–1966 New York City transit strike negotiations. In this model stress is present "(1) when there is a threat to a policy or program which a political leader is motivated to achieve or perpetuate, (2) his negative affect (e.g., fear, anxiety, tension, hostility) is aroused, and (3) he tries to cope with his feelings and the threat" (Hermann, 1977:356).

Hermann compared political leaders' verbal behavior in periods of both low threat and high threat. The four individuals who were the subjects of this study were Michael Quill, president of the Transport Workers Union; James O'Grady, chairman of the New York City Transportation Authority; John Lindsay, mayor-elect and then mayor of New York City; and Nathan Feinsinger, chairman of the mediation panel.

Verbalizations during two distinct periods of the strike were assessed—a period of high threat and a period of low threat. Hypothesizing that uncertainty and anxiety would increase as threats increased, Hermann used seven indirect verbal measures of negative affect: the articulation rate, the ah ratio, the use of qualifiers, the type-token ratio, the rate of sentence changes, the rate of repetitions, and speech rate. To assess coping behavior, she measured use of allness terms, self and other references, and negatives.

Hermann reports that Michael Quill was more self-assured in the high threat periods than in the low, but James O'Grady displayed more anxiety and uncertainty as threat increased. Mayor Lindsay exhibited a lack of confidence about the eventual outcome which was not evident in the manifest content of his verbalizations. Feinsinger became more personally involved as threat increased.

In utilizing video film clips of press conferences, Hermann conceptualized these verbalizations as behavioral traces or, in our own terminology, signal leakages. The measures which she used to assess changing levels of stress can be categorized as paralinguistic, i.e., they measure noncontent dimensions of speech. With these paralinguistic measures, Hermann probed beneath the political positions of speakers articulated in public to appraise their internal psychological states.

In a much more narrowly focused study, Osborne (1980) examined the major speeches of President John F. Kennedy by organizing them into four audience types: the nation, colleges, business/professional, and other. Each type was shown to have its own "pattern of arrangement," i.e., its own format for the presentation of topics. Kennedy's nationally televised addresses never began with a humorous comment and never ended with a familiar quotation. By contrast, 50 percent of his addresses to college and business audiences were launched with humor and ended with an appeal based on a quotation.

Osborne (1980:334) comments, "Kennedy clearly followed patterns of organization in structuring his major talks to significant audiences." Furthermore, these patterns differed across audiences or "targeted groups." Osborne wrote to one of Kennedy's major speechwriters, Arthur Schlesinger, inquiring about these patterns. Schlesinger offered no definitive explanation. However, it is clear from Osborne's work that Kennedy was a conscious participant in the speech construction process not only for major national speeches, but for others as well. Further, either consciously or unconsciously, Kennedy was sensitive to the effects his rhetoric and psycholinguistic structuring would have on an audience; therefore he developed a distinctive pattern of organization in his several types of presentations.

A final study by Godden and Maidment (1980), though not empirically rigorous, explores the use of language and anger by President Kennedy during the April 1962 conflict between his administration and the steel industry. Basing their analysis on linguistics and semiotics, Godden and Maidment (1980:325) define a semantic field "as a process of choices within which any text can be understood as the paradigmatic environment of what might have been meant." These writers imply that verbal documents are encoded environments which convey far more meaning than their manifest words impart. For them "implicitudes . . . rest at the intersection of language and event . . ." (Godden and Maidment, 1980:330). It is these "implicitudes" that are explored in an analysis of Kennedy's language. This work interests us because we are committed to delving below the manifest information carried by words. We will treat a speaker's audio record as an encoded environment which can be rigorously assessed by physiological means.

Traditional Crisis Studies

The work just reviewed on political communication, cognitive mapping, and psycholinguistics falls clearly into the realm of the behavioral orientation within the social sciences. We want to point out, however, that the voice stress analyses which are presented in this volume are also quite compatible with traditional crisis studies which have utilized the construction of a historical record based upon interviews, memoirs, and documentary evidence. Indeed, our own work leans heavily on such scholarship. As will be seen, we make frequent references to these traditional and useful sources of information.

Future studies of international crises might comfortably combine intensive traditional scholarship with precise biobehavioral research. Allison's (1971) work on the Cuban missile crisis was pathbreaking in many ways, but certainly one of those was his careful combination of traditional methods of investigation with the application of a behavioral sensitivity to organizational and individual-level theory. Indeed much of the strength of his work is derived from just this combination. In no sense, therefore, should our work be looked upon as a substitute for traditional crisis studies; rather, it should be viewed as an empirical complement to such work, with each intellectual tradition providing its unique strengths in support of the other.

A Model of Stress for Political Analysis

Numerous general models of stress can be utilized in constructing a model of stress for political analysis. Wiegele (1977) has reviewed them in a political context.

Central to our model of stress is the notion of a stimulus which is posited as a situational variable. This is consistent with the stress-oriented research of M. G. Hermann and Brecher's conceptual definition of international crisis. The situational variable is an international crisis situation. The stimulus is in the environment and therefore external to the political decision maker as the role-responsible, individual organism. This conceptualization draws heavily on Selye (1956), who developed the well-known biochemical model of stress, which emphasized the internal biochemical changes that result from stress. These changes are identical regardless of whether the stressor (stimulus configuration) is physical, psychological, or organic. Selye refers to the bodily changes that occur under stress as the General Adaptation Syndrome, a three-stage process consisting of an alarm reaction, resistance, and eventually, though not necessarily, exhaustion.

The effect that the stimulus has on the decision maker is a function of the state of stress in the individual at the time the stimulus is activated, together with the cognitive processes of threat appraisal which are idiosyncratically conducted. Thus, leaning heavily on Holsti and George (1975:257) and Scott and Howard (1970:271–272), we define stress as the negative affect, anxiety, fear, and/or biophysiological change which develops as the internal response of an individual to an external load placed upon him/her by an international crisis (pathogenic agent/stressor) which

| External stimulus configuration (an international crisis) | → | Individual decision maker (as part of an authoritative decisional unit) | → | Generation of psychological stress in individual decision maker | → | Change in vocal characteristics (as evidenced in crisis speech) |

Fig. 1.3   Model of individual-level stress in international crisis.

is perceived to pose a severe threat to one or more values of the political decision maker. The internal condition of stress is then leaked as a signal through the voice, which is used to communicate because of the sociopolitical demands of the crisis situation. This model of stress is diagrammed in figure 1.3.

The Remote Electronic Mapping Sequence

Given our model of individual-level stress during international crises, voice stress analysis can be used to assess tape recordings of crisis verbalizations. There is no general theory of language usage and psychological stress, though it is normal practice for analysts to analyze language intuitively.[3] Such analyses frequently produce excellent insights, but they are not rigorous and they are seldom able to be compared. To correct this situation, content analytic methods have been developed using the printed word as a datum for aggregation and analysis (see, for example, Stone et al., 1966; Carney, 1972; and Holsti, 1969). This work strongly emphasizes frequency counts of various word categories, based on the assumption that the more frequently a topic is mentioned, the more important it is to the speaker. Some content analytic work on psychotic (Paige, 1966; Maher, McKean, and McLaughlin, 1966) and pathological (Laffal, 1965) language is potentially relevant to our work on international crisis, but unfortunately information on these topics is scattered and the dictionaries which have been developed for the analyses are highly individualistic. Of course, Holsti's (1972) landmark volume on perceived hostility during international crises provides a major intellectual foundation for our voice stress orientation.

The present project takes a unique orientation within the general framework of content and psycholinguistic analysis. Instead of employing the *printed* word as the unit of analysis, it uses the *electronic* word. We can refer

[3] However, see Shapiro (1979) and Weintraub (1981) regarding the development of clinical psycholinguistics. See also Schwartz (1982) on schizophrenic language.

Tape record-	→	Production of	→	Production of	→	Thematic and	→	Interpretation
ing of crisis		graphic trace		stress value		psycho-		of stress con-
audio		with voice		scores		linguistic		figurations;
document		stress analyzer				analyses of		psychological/
						trace data		behavioral
								inferences

Fig. 1.4   The analysis of stress through remote electronic mapping.

to this as the remote electronic mapping of an oral text; a diagram of this process appears in figure 1.4.

The mapping procedure begins with a verbalized word as part of a larger oral statement, such as a speech or press conference. We worked with audio tape recordings of the public verbalizations of U.S. presidents, who of course speak English. These recordings were electronically analyzed with a PSE-101 voice stress analyzer, whose output is a graphic trace on a heat-sensitive strip chart. These traces were then scored manually.[4] Next the quantified traces were aggregated and psycholinguistically analyzed in a variety of ways which we describe in chapter 2. After the analysis was complete, inferences were made regarding the psychological and behavioral significance of the organized data.

According to the *New Century Dictionary* (1956), a word is a "sound or a combination of sounds, or its written or printed representation . . . as the sign of a conception." This is a standard definition that would be acceptable to most content analysts.

For us, however, a word is something different. We define a word as an *electronic trace* of a sound or combination of sounds as the sign of a mental conception. This is an important distinction. For example, in this study a long word is *not* one with many letters. Rather, a long word is one which has a large number of pulses (or pen excursions) in its electronic trace. Thus, this study is based on words defined as electronic traces.

Biopolitics and Voice Stress Analysis

Since the early 1970s a growing body of scholars have argued that new knowledge being developed in the life sciences is so insightful and critical to a comprehensive understanding of human behavior, that political scientists risk at least incomplete, if not improper, explanations of political be-

---

[4] For a discussion of a quasi-automated scoring technique see S. G. Schiflett and G. J. Loikith, "Voice Stress Analysis as a Measure of Operator Workload," Technical Memorandum #TM 7-3 SY, Patuxent River, Md.: Naval Air Test Center, March 10, 1980.

havior if they do not begin to build into their work a recognition of the new knowledge from behavioral biology. This case has been made in Somit (1976), Wiegele (1979a and 1982), White (1981), and Corning (1983).

During the past decade and a half numerous studies have been produced which incorporate a biobehavioral perspective into the study of politics; thus, in effect, establishing a new subfield within the discipline.

The present study on international crises is most appropriately linked to political psychophysiology, a subarea of biopolitics. Psychophysiology investigates the physiological bases of behavior which are related to mental functions. Contemporary psychophysiological researchers have been especially interested in the study of the brain and in the measurement and patterning of various physiological responses. Watts (1981) provides an in-depth treatment of several specific physiological approaches to the study of politics, and Wiegele (1985) synthesizes the literature of this orientation in a political behavior context.

Voice stress analysis, based on the physiology of the voice, is most appropriately related to the larger area of psychophysiology. The uncovering of cognitive processes through a specific voice measurement technique is quite consistent with the linkages of mental function and physiology mentioned above.

However, voice stress analysis has unique psychophysiological characteristics: it can be conducted remotely and unobtrusively. Most psychophysiological measurement requires the attachment of some type of sensor to a subject's body, thereby creating the problem of reactivity to the research process. The properties of voice stress analysis, therefore, make it an ideal psychophysiological methodology to remotely assess leaders during international crises.

We are hopeful that the present study will illustrate the usefulness of a psychophysiological orientation to the study of political decision making. Our case is anchored in international relations, but the attractiveness of voice stress analysis extends far beyond this. Reflections on the utilization of voice stress analysis in different analytic environments in both applied and experimental settings will be discussed in the concluding chapter.

General Propositions

Our research was guided by several propositions which, of course, influenced the selection of variables for analysis and the specification of the tests we performed. Stress, as the key variable in the study, is treated as both a dependent and an independent variable. The theoretical justification for our expectations will become clear during the course of the study. However, several propositions that guided our work are briefly outlined.

I. *Perception of threat*

A. The greater the speaker's perception of threat, the higher will be his level of stress.

II. *Perception of control*

A. The greater a speaker's perception of control over a situation, the lower will be his level of stress.

III. *Topics of speech*

A. A speaker's stress level will vary with the substantive topic of the spoken record.

B. The more belligerent the speech, the higher the level of stress.

C. A given topic, when repeated during the course of the crisis, will be marked by a demonstrable pattern of stress each time it occurs.

IV. *Stress level and speech*

A. A speaker's level of stress will vary from speech to speech.

1. Part of this variance will be due to the topic of the speech.

2. Part of this variance will be due to grammatical or linguistic variables.

B. Language behavior across an individual's vocalizations will be idiosyncratic for each speaker.

V. *Baseline measurement of stress*

A. The mean stress level for a given speech will represent the overall state of arousal for a speaker at that time.

B. Variance from this mean will depend on the topics discussed and other variables, such as part of speech, word length, etc.

VI. *Word length and stress*

A. Short words and medium length words, as high frequency verbalizations, will exhibit low levels of arousal.

B. Long words, as low frequency verbalizations, will exhibit high levels of arousal.

VII. *Part of speech*

A. Content words, which carry information (nouns, verbs, adjectives, and adverbs), will be more highly stressed than functional words (filled pauses, prepositions, articles, conjunctions).

B. Qualifying words, which convey the need for precision (adjectives, adverbs) will be more highly stressed than all other parts of speech.

VIII. *Prepared and extemporaneous speeches*

    A. Prepared speeches will differ from extemporaneous speeches in levels of stress.

    B. Two competing expectations regarding prepared and extemporaneous speeches exist:

        1. Extemporaneous speeches will be more highly stressed than prepared speeches because "thinking on one's feet" induces stress.

        2. Prepared speeches will be more highly stressed because they indicate the need for caution and precision.

    C. Differing values between prepared and extemporaneous speeches may provide a measure of psychological stability for a speaker.

2. Methodology

Introduction

This chapter discusses the research design and methods used in the project. First, it spells out how the crises were selected for study and provides some brief descriptive data on each. We also explain the overall design of the project and how this design fits into previous voice stress research. Second, we briefly describe how we produced voice patterns with our instrumentation. In addition, some of the problems associated with organizing our data before the statistical manipulations were undertaken are explained. Finally, the procedure for manually coding voice traces is described, and we provide an example of the coding technique and scoring.

Selection of the Crises

Each crisis selected for this study, Berlin 1961, the Dominican Republic, and Cambodia, had to meet three key criteria:

The crisis had to extend for at least two months.
The crisis had to produce a minimum of ten audio documents which were available for research.
The crisis had to contain at least one major national television or radio broadcast by a U.S. president.

Because a central purpose of this study was to examine the changing levels of stress in individual leaders over time, we expanded the limited time frame that is normally considered to characterize an international crisis. Definitions in the standard literature often focus on the restricted time available for a decision maker to act before the crisis is transformed into a new challenge. Although our definition of a crisis includes the "con-

Table 2.1   Comparative information on Berlin (1961),
Dominican Republic, and Cambodia.

	Berlin 1961	Dominican Republic	Cambodia
Length of crisis, months	14	5	6
Number of available audio documents	22	12	7
Total column inches of spoken text	346.5	434	229.5

stricted time period," we have expanded the definition to include both pre- and post-confrontation events and communications. For us, therefore, crisis is best described as an extended, critical, international situation which includes but is not limited to the traditional sharp confrontation over high-priority national goals. This conceptualization allows the development of longitudinal data regarding the physiological reactions of individual human beings (presidents) to the external situational stresses which their roles require them to bear.

Table 2.1 provides some aggregate descriptive information about the three crises. With only one exception all of our cases met all of the criteria listed above. Only the Cambodian crisis, with seven documents, lacked the desired minimum of ten; however, this was not serious enough to jeopardize our analysis of the data. With almost 230 column inches of text on the Cambodian episode to analyze, we felt that we had enough information from which to generate data. No other cases in the post-1945 period approached the selection criteria.

In each crisis a different individual occupied the office of president: John F. Kennedy during the 1961 Berlin crisis, Lyndon B. Johnson during the Dominican crisis, and Richard M. Nixon during the Cambodian crisis. Our desire to work with different individuals was quite intentional. The study focuses on the interplay between the objective demands of a situation (the crisis) and the psychophysiological reaction of the person responsible for his nation's international behavior. Thus, we sought to develop insights and knowledge about each individual's idiosyncratic cognitive processing of perceived situational demands.

The Documentary Record

We constructed a documentary record for each crisis by consulting the appropriate volumes of *The Public Papers of the Presidents*. We examined these volumes in detail, identifying all oral documents which dealt exclusively with each crisis. We also scrutinized all press conferences in which a question or questions dealing with a specific crisis might have been raised. All documents cited in the text are taken from the appropriate volumes of *The Public Papers of the Presidents*. Most researchers consider these documents to be primary sources, but we do *not* because minor editing often occurs before publication, especially for extemporaneous press conferences. Thus, if voice stress analysts adhere to the printed text of a presidential utterance, they will miscalculate frequency counts and sequences of words. As a result, the audio documents are considered primary in this study.

The Audio Record

A printed, documentary record of a crisis situation can be constructed virtually from a single source; however, this is by no means true when developing an audio record. There are several reasons for this, and they illuminate some of the inherent difficulties involved in performing voice stress research using historical materials.

The primary difficulty lies in the fact that until January 19, 1955, television and radio broadcasts of presidential news conferences were not permitted, and, except in isolated instances, the media made no official record of them. This is unfortunate, since news conferences offer one of the few candid glimpses into the decisional process from the point of view of the voice stress researcher; i.e., they provide *extemporaneous* data in response to relatively unanticipated questions.

Before 1955 the U.S. Signal Corps recorded certain national addresses and other formal presidential presentations, but these events did not include the extensive media questioning that occurs during present-day press conferences. Audio recordings of selected speeches are thus available for many of the international crises which took place after 1945, but they tend to be isolated from the broader crisis context. Therefore, the supporting audio documents which would provide a glimpse into patterns for the longitudinal development of a crisis are often not available.

Questioning styles of the press differed substantially in the early years from what is common practice today. Questions have become more pointed and hostile; answers appear to be more open and candid. This change seems to have occurred around 1960, perhaps because of the widespread interest in the presidential debates of that election year and the rapidly increasing infusion of television into American homes. Also, around this time various recording sources began to take an interest in creating a comprehensive audio record of a president's tenure in office. The result is that audio records after 1960 are much more useful and fleshed out for research than those before 1960. For the above reasons, therefore, the crises discussed below all occurred after 1960.

Availability of Audio Records

Although the historical audio record improved after 1960, it is neither complete nor centrally located. Unfortunately, unlike the public printing of the written record, oral records are widely scattered. They have no central repository or acceptable and useful indexing system. Further, the need to preserve these valuable audio resources is not even recognized.

The production of an audio record for a president is at best idiosyncratic and at worst irrational. For example, the tape recording of a given news conference may not exist in the appropriate presidential library, but a statement given over national television the same day might be readily available in the same library. Other audio recordings from the same week, for example, might be found in the National Archives or one of the three national broadcasting networks. On the other hand, they might be held only by one of the networks and not by the National Archives. In some instances, for unknown reasons, a speech might not be recorded at all. The magnitude of this problem of scattered records cannot be exaggerated, and the difficulties that it causes can only be appreciated when one actually attempts to assemble a coherent audio record of an international political event.

But the difficulties are even more complex. As a matter of course, we were forced to contact the three national broadcasting networks, requesting searches of their audio archives. Erratic, conflicting, and unclear corporate policies, combined with the vagaries of copyright law, make the networks an unreliable, though sometimes necessary source of audio information. Oral repositories and collections were usually less useful; they often contained only the remembrances of minor figures in a given political period. All of the oral documents referred to in this study and listed on the time lines in succeeding chapters have been located and are obtainable.

Design of the Study

Previous voice stress research (Wiegele, 1978a, 1978b) focused on the key speeches of presidents during international crises. Key speeches are those central and comprehensive addresses delivered by a president to a national radio and television audience in which he carefully lays out the

Crisis	Chronology
Berlin	P P S(k) P S P S P P P P P P P P P P P P P
Dominican	P S S S(k) S S S P P P P
Cambodia	S S(k) P S S P P

Key: S = Speech, P = Press conference, (k) = Key vocalization of the crisis.

Fig. 2.1 Chronology of presidential vocalizations.

causes of the confrontation, describes the actions which he has ordered to meet the immediate challenge, asks for national support for his actions, and expresses the determination of his nation's citizens to see the crisis through to a successful conclusion. In short, there exists a rather clear and consistent rhetorical format in key crisis presentations; they are not difficult to identify. Much traditional scholarship on international crises has focused on the "key" speeches as expressive of national positions and presidential prerogatives while at the same time neglecting the rich content of other forms of information.

The key speeches exist in contrast to the "normal" verbal manifestations of a president during a crisis. These include numerous responses to crisis-oriented questions at press conferences, special reports to Congress, sections of speeches devoted to other topics which present information relevant to the crisis, and brief "updating" reports during the course of the crisis itself. As indicated above, previous voice stress research has focused only on the key speeches. This strategy ignores longitudinal information. Figure 2.1 diagrams the chronological design of the research undertaken in the present project.

In this design each verbalization serves as a point of measurement for amassing evidence about stress in a speaker's voice. Thus, by examining multiple documents in each crisis, it is possible to generate information regarding the changing manifestations of stress in a speaker as he proceeds through the resolution of a crisis. Verbalizations, of course, do not necessarily coincide with a chronology of crisis events. Later on in this study we juxtapose, in tabular form, the chronology of presidential verbalizations and events so that readers can judge for themselves how the two fit together.

Overview of the data. For the three crises studied, we put 21,000 words from 38 speeches and press conferences into machine-readable format. We considered taking a sample of the 21,000 words but rejected this strategy because we felt that a sample would seriously distort the character of our analyses. Stress values are not distributed randomly across an entire oral document. As we will demonstrate, they cluster around critical substantive themes. Thus, our pool of data represents the entire body of publicly vocalized words that were available for analyzing each president in each crisis.

Operation of the Voice Analysis Equipment

Quality of audio recordings. Central to the entire voice stress analysis process is a high quality tape recording with certain audio attributes. First, it is desirable that background noises, such as machine humming, crackling sounds, or distant voices, be held to a minimum. Second, to avoid an indistinguishable overlay of voices, it is important that only one person be recorded at any one time. For example, it has been our experience when using tapes of presidential press conferences that the president may begin answering a question before a journalist has finished asking it. The overlapping words must be excluded from the analysis. Third, the speaker's voice should be clear and understandable. The electronic isolation of words is easier in more slowly paced speech. Fourth, speech disturbances by a speaker should not be eliminated from analysis. For example, stuttering or mispronunciation of words may be a manifestation of stress, and such traces increase the precision of the analysis even though they are normally edited out of most printed texts.

General equipment needs. The necessary equipment for voice stress analysis consists of an electronic voice stress analyzer and a tape recorder. These two machines must be electronically compatible since they function together in generating data. A computerized scoring system, expected to be available in the near future, would of course require additional hardware designed to incorporate a computing capability into a voice analysis system. A number of commercial firms manufacture voice stress analysis equipment. Each product, of course, has its own design characteristics.

The Voice Stress Analysis Procedure

A complete discussion of the voice stress analysis procedure can be found in appendix 1. This section is intended to familiarize the reader with the basic procedure so that the remainder of the study will be more readily understandable.

Equipment. This study utilized a Uher 4000 Report-IC tape recorder and a PSE-101 voice stress analyzer. The PSE-101 is manufactured by Dektor CIS, Inc. of Savannah, Georgia, and marketed under the trade name of "Psychological Stress Evaluator" (PSE). It is also essential that the VSA operator have a written text of the speech being analyzed. Because speakers mispronounce or run words together, the written text helps to clarify these problems. In addition, the written text delineates the beginning and ending of paragraphs. The importance of this function will become evident in the study itself.

Scoring and coding

Once traces have been produced (see appendix 1), they must be scored and coded. We developed a manual coding procedure which gives a numerical (interval level) score for each word. Voice stress analysis produces a trace for each word such as those in figures 1.1 and 1.2 in the previous chapter.

Much previous work on voice stress analysis has used two- and five-point scales (Wiegele, 1978b). The five-point scale poses problems because coders find it difficult to distinguish stress levels visually. The two-point (stress/no-stress) scale is easily coded and reliability is high. However, a crude two-point scale is not sensitive to varying levels of stress; it can be used only to determine that stress exists.

To overcome these coding difficulties and to increase the richness of our data, we devised an objective scale for stress scoring based on the physiology of the voice. It is a tedious manual procedure, but it captures subtle differences in stress level that the previous scales do not tap.[1]

Researchers have attempted to resolve reliability problems in coding but with varying degrees of success. Smith (1977), for example, used a rating system designed to eliminate experimenter bias and achieve precise measurement. A trace is scored by measuring its height and then finding its midpoint. Coders determine the total time for the trace (y) and the time during which the trace is above the midpoint (x). Dividing x by y yields a percentage score. We found this process to be prone to error given the need to measure very short distances. Smith's (1977) procedure is illustrated in figure 2.2.

In Dektor's discussion of traces (1972), the center of the mass is used to demonstrate the dampening of the frequency modulated (FM) signal in the trace. If this line is quantified, we can eliminate the problem of subjective coding. Two methods were explored—one dealt with the degree of the

---

[1] Efforts to automate the scoring process are complicated by the fact that the electronic equipment needed apparently distorts the nature of the signal. A further complication involves knowing where words begin and end. Currently, only a human operator can make such a determination.

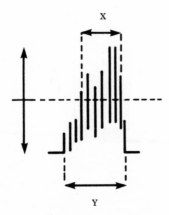

Figure 2.2   Illustration of Smith's coding procedure.

slopes of this line, the other with changes in slope direction. These methods produced several problems which are discussed in appendix 1.

The most efficient method is to use the top points of the pen excursions (pulses) for scoring. This judgment is based on the rationale that the fluctuations in a trace will dampen as stress increases, thus leading to the "squarish" configuration discussed earlier. This reasoning led us to believe that the number of changes in slope direction (with the length of the trace controlled) would be a good indicator of the frequency modulation, or lack thereof. We developed explicit coding rules and then tested for the validity of the coding scheme. The formula for calculating a stress score for a word is:

$$\text{Stress} = \frac{\text{number of slope direction changes per word}}{\text{number of pulses per word}}$$

Some additional examples will illustrate this procedure. Assume that the voice stress analyzer has produced traces such as those shown in figure 2.3.

In example 1 there are eight pulses. Segment a-b is the first slope and is scored +1. Segment b-e is the second slope and is also scored +1, as is e-f. Segment f-g represents no change and is scored −1. Segment g-h is the last slope and is thus scored +1. The score for this example is

$$\frac{4-1}{8} = .38.$$

In example 2 there are nine pulses. Segment a-b is the first slope and receives a score of +1. Segment b-c scores +1, as does c-e. Segment e-f

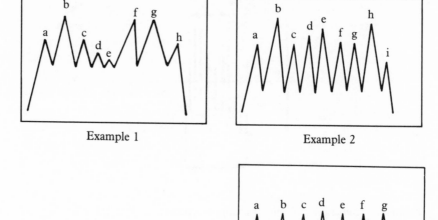

Example 1

Example 2

Example 3

Figure 2.3   Examples of actual word traces.

again scores +1, but f-g scores −1 since there is no slope in segment f-g. Segments g-h and h-i are each scored +1 since they are slopes. The score for example 2 is

$$\frac{6-1}{9} = .56.$$

In example 3 there are no slopes. Therefore, segment a-g, the entire trace, scores −1. So the score for example 3 is

$$\frac{-1}{7} = -.14.$$

Once these traces have been produced, we have an inverted measure of stress. That is, the higher the stress, the lower the score. Because this complicates the analysis, we reversed the scores by subtracting each score from 1. We then had a value which was directionally consistent with the intensity of stress. Carrying out the procedure with examples 1, 2, and 3 yields final scores of: 1 − .38 = .62, 1 − .56 = .44, and 1 − (−.14) = 1.14. Finally, the decimals were eliminated to make the scores more usable.

After developing this scheme we tested the procedure for reliability.

The tests for reliability are discussed fully in appendix 1 and reviewed briefly here.

Five coders first ranked 300 pairs of traces (25 words in all combinations) according to which word was the most highly stressed. For each coder the 25 words were then ranked on a continuum so that tests for reliability could be performed. Substantial differences were evident in these tests.

Within-coder reliabilities were derived by applying a Guttman scale to the paired ranks. The coefficients of reproducibility (*Cr*) ranged from .83 to .93. These *Cr* values are high, but they show enough inconsistency to cause concern. Intercoder reliabilities derived from the Guttman scale scores ranged from .69 to .88 (all significant at $p=.001$).

Next, objective scores were calculated for each word and correlated with the coders' Guttman scores. These correlations ranged from .59 to .74 (all significant at $p=.002$ or better). These scores are lower than the intercoder reliability scores. However, after careful examination of the traces, we were satisfied that the objective coding scheme is valid. The intercoder reliability score for the objective coding scheme was .95, a sufficient level for reliable analysis.

The Data

The data, derived from the coding procedures outlined above and in appendix 1, consisted of two sets of observations for each speaker: a first set at the paragraph level and a second set of word-level observations.

Within the paragraph-level data sets, there are 243 paragraphs for Kennedy (109 prepared and 134 extemporaneous), 146 paragraphs for Johnson (126 prepared and 20 extemporaneous), and 187 paragraphs for Nixon (109 prepared and 78 extemporaneous).

The variables in the paragraph file are described below.

Variable	*Name*	*Value/Description*
V1	Speaker	1-Kennedy
		2-Johnson
		3-Nixon
V2	Speech Number	Chronological
V3	Paragraph	Paragraph number within speech
V4	Prepared	0-Not prepared
		1-Prepared

V5	$\bar{X}$ Noun	Raw stress score for nouns
V6	$\bar{X}$ Verb	Raw stress score for verbs
V7	$\bar{X}$ Adjective	Raw stress score for adjectives
V8	$\bar{X}$ Adverb	Raw stress score for adverbs
V9	$\bar{X}$ Pause	Raw mean stress score, filled pauses
V10	$\bar{X}$ Preposition	Raw mean stress score, prepositions
V11	$\bar{X}$ Article	Raw mean stress score, articles
V12	$\bar{X}$ Conjunction	Raw mean stress score, conjunctions
V13	$\bar{X}$ Stress	Raw mean stress score for paragraph
V14	Percent Noun	Percentage of paragraph consisting of nouns
V15	Percent Verb	Percentage of paragraph consisting of verbs
V16	Percent Adjective	Percentage of paragraph consisting of adjectives
V17	Percent Adverb	Percentage of paragraph consisting of adverbs
V18	Percent Pause	Percentage of paragraph consisting of filled pauses
V19	Percent Preposition	Percentage of paragraph consisting of prepositions
V20	Percent Article	Percentage of paragraph consisting of articles
V21	Percent Conjunction	Percentage of paragraph consisting of conjunctions

V5 through V13 are raw average stress scores for each part of speech within a given paragraph and a paragraph's mean stress score. As just described, these scores are actually inverted so that a low stress score indicates high stress. To make the data readily understandable, these variables were all reversed so that a higher score indicates higher stress.

The word-level data are organized into 15 variables.

Variable	Name	Values/Description
V1	Word 1	First four letters of the word
V2	Word 2	Next four letters of the word
V3	Word 3	Next four letters of the word

V4	Word 4	Next four letters of the word
V5	Word 5	Last four letters of the word
V6	Crisis	1-Berlin-Kennedy 2-Dominican-Johnson 3-Cambodia-Nixon
V7	Speech	Speech Number
V8	Prepared	0-Prepared 1-Not prepared
V9	Paragraph	Paragraph within the speech in which the word appears
V10	Word Number	Sequential number by paragraph
V11	Word Length	Derived length of word
V12	Stress	Raw stress score for the word
V13	Part of Speech	1-Noun 2-Verb 3-Adjective 4-Adverb 5-Filled Pause 6-Preposition 7-Article 8-Conjunction
V14	Place I	Place of word within speech 1-Beginning 2-Middle 3-End
V15	Place II	Place of word within paragraph 1-Beginning 2-Middle 3-End

V12, "stress," is actually an inverted score for word stress. Therefore, we again reversed the stress score by subtracting it from 1 in order to facilitate analysis. V8, "prepared," is a binary variable which was coded contrary to convention. This variable has been reversed; a 1 indicates a prepared speech and a 0, an extemporaneous speech.

The size of this data base made it possible to perform a variety of statistical manipulations with confidence. Since these data contained virtually every word spoken by the three presidents during public pronouncements on the crises, the question of the representativeness of the sample is irrelevant.

Tests

The development of voice stress analysis has made possible an objective measure of the psycholinguistic stress being experienced by a given speaker as well as a physiologically based measure of word length. Our stress and word length measures are at the interval level; most of our other variables are nominal. Our selection of tests was designed to take account of this fact. Thus we selected techniques such as ANOVA, which allowed us to test interval-level dependent variables against nominal- or ordinal-level independent variables. In other instances we collapsed certain nominal-level variables into binary categories. This allowed us to perform several linear tests on what was essentially nonlinear data. Although we thereby lost some information, we selected these procedures in order to make use of tests which are robust enough to handle some of the weaknesses inherent in nominal data.

To sum up, guided by the propositions spelled out in chapter 1, this study is concerned with analyzing the signals leaked by presidential speakers during extended international crises. Three cases have been selected for detailed examination with physiologically based voice stress analysis procedures. In general, we shall demonstrate that it is feasible to remotely assess elite vocalizations during crises for the purpose of determining negative affect or concern regarding the substantive issues being discussed. It will also be possible to construct psychophysiological and psycholinguistic profiles of U.S. presidents. These profiles will be useful both to investigators and crisis managers as they attempt to assess individual-level behavior during international crises.

3. John F. Kennedy
and the 1961 Berlin Crisis

Twenty of President Kennedy's vocalizations during the Berlin situation were subjected to voice stress analysis. A stress value score for every word in all of the documents was developed. We then calculated the mean stress value for each paragraph and document. As we stated in chapter 1, the mean score for a document is used as an indicator of the general level of stress exhibited by the speaker during a specific vocalization. This document mean score can be conceptualized as a baseline measure of the overall state of negative affect of the speaker at the time of the speech. A chronology of Kennedy's speeches and the events of the crisis is presented in table 3.1. What follows is a brief review of Kennedy's public vocalizations during the crisis. Readers unfamiliar with the history of the Berlin crisis will find a brief historical description of this event as well as the Dominican Republic and Cambodian crises in appendix 4.

Overview of President Kennedy's Verbal Statements during the Berlin Crisis

President Kennedy first discussed the deteriorating situation in Berlin at his news conference on June 28, 1961.[1] When questioned by reporters at that news conference, Kennedy revealed that the Western allies had met, but had not decided on a course of action in response to what he called the "Soviet-manufactured" crisis in Berlin. In his opening statement, made from a prepared text, Kennedy reiterated the American position of support for Berlin and warned the Soviets against supposing that "allied unity and determination can be undermined by threats." He concluded the

[1] The texts of all official documents in this study can be found in the appropriate volume of the *Public Papers of the President.*

Table 3.1   Chronology of the Berlin Crisis and John F. Kennedy's public pronouncements.

Date	Chronology	Kennedy's pronouncements
(1961)		
February 17	Khrushchev delivers aide-mémoire	
May 19	White House announces Vienna Conference	
June 3	Vienna Conference	
June 28		News conference
July 1	50,000 refugees leave East Berlin	
July 8	Khrushchev announces military buildup	
July 19		News conference
July 25	Key Kennedy speech on Berlin	Radio and TV address on Berlin crisis
August 1	Checkpoints established by East Germany	
August 10		News conference
August 13	Division of Berlin begins	
August 19	U.S. Army group ordered to West Berlin	
August 21		Remarks following the Vice-President's report on the Berlin situation
August 23	Moscow threatens air accessibility to West Berlin	
August 24	White House warns Soviets	
August 30	USSR resumption of nuclear testing	News conference
September 15	U.S. resumption of nuclear testing	
September 25		Address before UN General Assembly
October 11		News conference
October 17	First stage of negotiations—Rusk & Gromyko—Khrushchev withdraws insistence on settlement	
November 8		News conference
November 29		News conference
(1962)		
January 2–	Second stage of negotiations	

Table 3.1 (Continued)

March 6		
January 15		News conference
January 31		News conference
February 9–	Aerial harassments	
March 29		
February 14		News conference
February 21		News conference
March 11–	Third stage of negotiations	
March 29		
March 14		News conference
March 21		News conference
March 29		News conference
April 11		News conference
April 13	West Germany refuses to endorse negotiations	
April 16–	Fourth stage of negotiations	
May 30		
April 18		News conference
May 9		News conference

prepared statement by calling for the right of self-determination for all Germans.

Two weeks later, after an increased stream of refugees entered West Berlin and the Soviets undertook a military buildup, Kennedy addressed the Berlin situation at another news conference. In his prepared statement at this second news conference, Kennedy repeated his charge that the Soviets had caused the crisis, arguing that the Soviets were violating international agreements and attempting to take advantage of an "abnormal" situation to absorb West Berlin into a totalitarian East Germany.

On July 25, 1961, Kennedy delivered a televised address on the U.S. military posture. The Berlin crisis weighed heavily in his remarks. He requested an additional three billion dollars for defense, larger call-ups in the draft, and an improved state of readiness for American tactical forces. He pledged a U.S. commitment to freedom in West Berlin and Southeast Asia and called on the American people to support his strong stand against the Communists.

At his news conference on August 10, 1961, Kennedy appeared much less antagonistic toward the Soviets, calling for peace through negotiation in the coming months. However, he reiterated his concern for the freedom of West Berlin. In response to a question on refugees, Kennedy stated that the United States had no policy either to encourage or discourage the flight of individuals from the East.

Three days later the construction of the Berlin Wall was begun in an effort by the East Germans to stop the flow of refugees to the West. Up to August 30, 1961, Kennedy made no substantive public comment on the construction of the Berlin Wall. His first remarks were quite moderate.[2] Again, rather than enunciating a "hard line," Kennedy repeatedly mentioned the need for negotiations, and, for the first time, he spoke of Khrushchev's sensitivity to the horrors of nuclear war. Kennedy defended the movement of U.S. troops to West Berlin as a demonstration to both the Berliners and the Soviets of the American commitment to the perpetuation of freedom of access to West Berlin. Kennedy was cautious in dealing with a question on the "barriers" between East and West Berlin. While he commented that the situation was unsatisfactory, he pointed out that "communication does exist." The president also expressed concern over the reluctance of the NATO allies to exercise their full responsibilities in Berlin.

Kennedy did not comment on the situation in Berlin again until almost a month later at a memorial service for Dag Hammerskjold on September 25. He reiterated that it was the responsibility of the United States to uphold the freedom of West Berlin and indicated that the United States saw the need to maintain freedom wherever it was threatened.

Kennedy was vague about the Berlin situation in answering questions at his news conference on October 11. Though he was not sanguine about the prospects for settlement and was slightly more belligerent toward the Soviets, he admitted, for the first time, that the Soviets had a de facto right to construct the Berlin Wall since it was in an area "which the Soviet Union has held since the end of World War II for over sixteen years." Kennedy again called for peaceful negotiations on the Berlin situation.

On November 8, the president answered questions concerning Chancellor Adenauer's upcoming visit to the U.S. He praised the Chancellor for his policies and mentioned the possibility of rearming Germany.

On January 15, 1962, Kennedy presented his most definitive statement on why the U.S. did not "tear down" the Berlin Wall. The reasons he gave were: de facto Soviet control over the Wall area, the possibility of provoking war, and the fact that the Soviets had not abrogated the right of access to West Berlin by the NATO allies and the West Germans.

---

[2]The president's remarks of August 21 (Document #335) were simply thanks to Vice-President Johnson for undertaking a trip to West Berlin.

At his November 29, 1961, news conference, Kennedy answered questions concerning the possibility of instituting UN supervision of the autobahn which connected West Berlin with West Germany. He also discussed the complaints of American reservists about boredom.

On January 31, 1962, Kennedy reported that no progress had been made in the Berlin negotiations but urged that "the means of communication and the channels of communication . . . [would] be kept very wide open."

In a series of press conferences through the late winter and early spring of 1962, Kennedy spelled out further details of the administration's position. On February 14, 1962, the president indicated that the crisis was still "real" and that the reservists were needed until another division could be outfitted. A week later Kennedy denied the need for a four-power meeting because "so far the results have been comparatively minor or miniscule." On March 14, 1962, Kennedy reiterated the need to overcome obstacles at the conference table, thereby emphasizing a diplomatic perspective. The question of the bored reservists came up again on March 21, and Kennedy's answer was similar to his previous response: he stated that the crisis remained critical and that the reservists were needed until new divisions could be formed.

On March 29, in response to a question on Khrushchev's "casual urgency" on Berlin, Kennedy repeated his warning not to underestimate the dangers of the situation or the need for continued negotiations. On April 11, Kennedy again announced that no progress had been made in the negotiations on Berlin. During an April 18, 1962, news conference, questions concerning the possible displeasure of the European allies were raised. Kennedy expressed assurances that the allies were informed of all proposals and that if preliminary discussions were fruitful, all of the interested parties would be included in the final negotiations. The president also declined to take a stand on a possible role for the East German government after the ultimate conclusion of the crisis.

The last vocalization was a news conference on May 9, 1962. At that time Kennedy defended the American role in the preliminary talks, quoting Winston Churchill: "It is better to jaw, jaw, than to war, war." A question was also raised concerning the acceptance of the American proposals by the Adenauer government; Kennedy skirted the issue by stating that he knew of no differences between the two governments.

Figure 3.1 shows a plot of the mean stress values for each public vocalization made by Kennedy during the course of the Berlin crisis and outlined above. The curve, overall, constitutes a graphic presentation of the changing values of stress or physiological arousal experienced by Kennedy during the course of the Berlin crisis. Using figure 3.1 as a guide and checking the descriptions presented above, we note a distinct difference between Kennedy's belligerent and conciliatory speeches.

In the early documents (June 28, July 17, and July 25), the president outlined the American position on the crisis. All of his subsequent vocalizations deal with one or more of the issues raised in those early pronouncements: the NATO position, the defense buildup, Soviet belligerency, and the American response. As one would expect in the early stages of an unfolding crisis, Kennedy's stress level is relatively high during this period.

On August 10, Kennedy's tone is conciliatory and his stress level is lower. Not once during the August 10 news conference does Kennedy mention a "Soviet threat" or discuss military matters. However, on August 21, while reporting on Vice-President Johnson's trip to West Germany, Kennedy repeatedly mentions American determination to keep Berlin free. While his short statement is not hostile, the tone is decidedly different from that of August 10. The August 21 conference comes one week after the beginning of construction work on the Berlin Wall.

On August 30, Kennedy probably was as politically moderate as he could be on the issues of Soviet demands and the military threat. His level of stress was not high during this conference. One month later, at the United Nations, Kennedy's tone is more self-righteous and his attacks on Soviet policy more exacting. The high stress level during his UN address may be in part a result of the placement of the Berlin material within the document. The portions of the speech on Berlin are near the end of a very long address and are embedded in a section on threats to peace. This section includes a discussion of Southeast Asia and, to the extent that this topic also stresses the president, the value for Berlin may be somewhat inflated.

In the remaining high stress speeches (October 11, January 15, January 31, February 14, March 21, and April 11), the president deals primarily with three issues: the lack of an overt American response to the construction of the Berlin Wall, the question of the reservists, and the lack of progress in the negotiations. These can be contrasted with the remaining lower stress vocalizations (November 8, November 29, February 21, March 14, March 29, April 18, and May 9), in which Kennedy discusses primarily the Western alliance and the need for negotiation. The differences between the two types of statements about the negotiation process, i.e., the need for

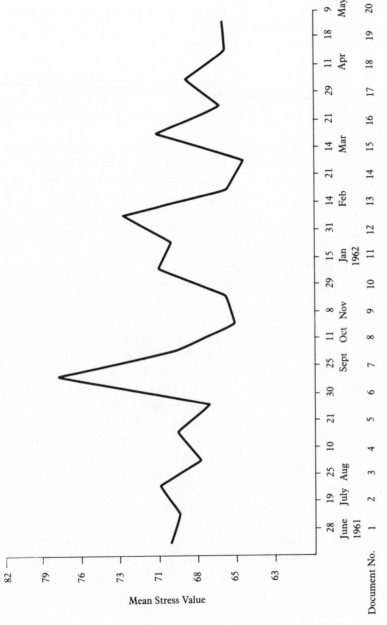

Figure 3.1   Stress levels by speech in John F. Kennedy during the 1961–1962 crisis in Berlin.

negotiation and the lack of success in the negotiation process, are clear both within and between speeches.

This second examination of the documents helps to explain Kennedy's seemingly random stress levels portrayed in figure 3.1. Rather than being randomly determined the stress levels appear to be reflections of the forcefulness of his speeches. In those documents where danger, threat, or controversy are primary, the stress level of the president is high. Conversely, when he discusses negotiation, conciliation, and the alliance, his mean stress levels are lower. This provides a good first test of the face validity of the mean stress levels as they relate to the substance of the vocalizations.

It is important, however, to go beyond aggregate stress levels to understand more clearly the issues in a crisis. In order to do this, the next section will develop a further cut in the analysis by taking a step down from the aggregate to the level of the paragraph.

Stress Themes within the Documents

The data presented and analyzed below are stress value scores for paragraphs or, more properly, themes within the vocalizations on the Berlin situation as articulated by Kennedy. A theme was established for each paragraph within a vocalization before coding. Theme labels are a shorthand attempt to develop a description of each paragraph's dominant substantive thought. Where possible, an effort was made to incorporate words or phrases from the original paragraph in the theme label or designation in order to reflect accurately the flavor of the spoken words. So that we might make comparisons across speeches, we standardized the stress scores for each paragraph. We detrended the stress scores by computing Z-scores for each paragraph. Thus, the mean score for each speech forms a baseline measurement with which to compare changes in the level of stress experienced by the speaker. The Z-scores were stratified as follows: above 1.96 ($p=.025$) equals extreme stress; 1.64 to 1.95 ($p=.025$) equals heavy stress; 1.05 to 1.63 ($p=.1$) equals moderate stress; -1.04 to 1.04 ($p=.70$) equals average stress; -1.05 to -1.63 ($p=.1$) equals low stress; -1.64 to -1.95 ($p=.025$) equals slight stress; and 1.96 or below ($p=.025$) equals minimal stress. The reader should recognize that the Z-score assigned to a particular paragraph is dependent upon the mean and standard deviation for the speech within which it appears. Thus, it is necessary to compare both the Z-scores and the absolute stress values of a particular theme.

The Z-scores for each theme within each speech are presented in table

3.2. The cell positions indicate both the standardized stress score and the dates on which the theme was discussed by the speaker.

It is important to point out that we view table 3.2 and similar tables in the following two chapters as the centerpieces of voice stress analyses of international crises. Each table must be examined carefully and with considerable attention to detail. These tables provide a means of disaggregating presidential vocalizations on any given day of a crisis, and then rank ordering those vocalizations by stress level of substantive topics. It is possible, for example, to read across the top stratum to ascertain the substantive concerns producing the most negative affect in a speaker, or to read across the bottom stratum to observe those issues which are of little concern.

Students of crisis management should be aware that stress values are plotted during an ongoing crisis on a day-to-day basis. Therefore, a graphic description such as presented in table 3.2 will unfold slowly during a crisis. Each day's rank ordering, however, could provide critical information which could be used in decision-making analysis. More will be said about the information in these tables in the analytic conclusion to each chapter and in the comparative analysis in chapter 6.

In examining the themes for each paragraph, we also sought to collapse the many substantive issues into larger composite themes. To accomplish this we looked for multiple representations of the themes across speeches. In developing the composite themes, each paragraph theme was typed on a single index card. The collection of cards was shuffled and given independently to four individuals. Two of these individuals were not acquainted with the project. The other two individuals were the principal investigator and a project research assistant. Project knowledge had no effect on theme designation. The four individuals were instructed to form as many categories of composite themes as they believed existed among the paragraph themes and to name each category, i.e., establish a composite theme designation. The cards were reshuffled and presented to each individual in turn. In performing this task, we were looking for agreement across the coders as well as for unique and insightful combinations in the data. We found both.

After the four coders separated the cards, we analyzed the group placement by the codes on the back of each card. Each card now had four numbers, one for each coder. Those cards which had four identical numbers (i.e., perfect correspondence) were taken to be the core composite themes. Next, the groups which had an agreement rate of three out of four were added to the extant groups or placed in new groups. At this point, 75 percent of the cards had been assigned to a category. The remaining cards were then placed into the existing categories or into new categories by

Table 3.2   Stress stratification of paragraph themes, John F. Kennedy, Berlin Crisis, 1961–1962.

Z-Scores	Date
	June 28, 1961
Extreme stress	2.35 Soviets campaigned in 1958 to force West out
1.96 and above	2.21 Soviets repudiating their commitments
	2.14 Threat is grave
	1.96 Allied exercise of treaty rights
Heavy stress	
1.95 to 1.64	
Moderate stress	1.58 West proposed permanent treaty
1.63 to 1.04	1.44 Allied unity and determination strong
	1.42 Soviets ask U.S. peace treaty with East Germany
	1.31 West Berlin is developing
	1.19 Soviets charge East German control over West
	1.09 U.S. and Western security involved
	1.06 Soviets responsible for disturbing peace
Average stress	.81 Don't underestimate Western will
1.03 to −1.04	.60 Soviets should recognize Western commitments
	.59 Soviets aim to end Allied rights in Berlin
	.57 West will discuss new proposals
	.51 Self-determination must be accepted in Berlin
	.23 Peace, security, and commitments involved
	.01 Soviet proposals undermine freedom
	− .26 East to eliminate freedom in West Berlin
	− .93 Treaty will permanently partition Germany
Low stress	−1.19 Unilateral action cannot alter rights
−1.05 to −1.63	−1.40 No current plans for partial mobilization
	−1.62 1948–1958 relatively peaceful in Berlin
Slight stress	−1.71 Soviets created Berlin crisis
−1.64 to −1.95	
Minimal stress	−2.34 Soviets and East Germans raising tensions
<−1.96	−3.50 Multilateral Western discussions possible
	July 19
Extreme stress	5.06 Soviets aim to absorb West Berlin
1.96 and above	4.42 People of West Berlin are free
	3.48 Soviets cannot unilaterally end Western rights
	3.44 NATO consultations under way
	3.18 Soviets may cause crisis
	3.07 Soviets urged to reconsider policies
Heavy stress	1.91 West Berlin is a free city
1.95 to 1.64	1.91 Consultations being held among West

Table 3.2   Kennedy (Continued)

Moderate stress
1.63 to 1.04

Average stress	.53	If peace is broken, Soviets responsible
1.03 to −1.04	.49	Deficits should not build up
	− .81	U.S. considering declaration of emergency

Low stress
−1.05 to −1.63

Slight stress
−1.64 to −1.95

Minimal stress	−2.29	Economic proposals under consideration
<−1.96	−2.36	Soviet aide-mémoire unsatisfactory
	−2.46	Consultations must improve
	−2.63	NATO entering difficult period
	−4.60	Statement on Berlin to be made
	−4.77	U.S. has worldwide commitments
	−5.27	U.S. to honor commitment on Berlin
	−6.98	Budget figures will be released
	−7.13	This is administration's position
	−8.50	Past statements on intervention stand

July 25

Extreme stress	2.81	Commitments must be kept
1.96 and above	2.80	More nonnuclear weapons needed
	2.74	Berlin must remain peaceful
	2.51	We will not abandon our duties
	2.49	U.S. will not be driven out of West Berlin
	2.42	West successful in challenge
	2.04	Challenge must be met

| Heavy stress | 1.80 | Further sea and air buildup necessary |
| 1.95 to 1.64 | 1.75 | General economic outlook is good |

Moderate stress	1.24	Important to protect citizens from attack
1.63 to 1.04	1.17	Request for increases in Navy and Air Force
	1.15	Soviet defensive concerns legitimate
	1.07	Soviets cannot end U.S. presence

Average stress	.94	Civil defense funds requested
1.03 to −1.04	.88	Request for increased number of troops
	.84	Noncritical expenditures must be contained
	.78	We share responsibility for defense
	.70	Serious responsibilities ahead
	.66	Possibility of a tax increase
	.65	Western position in Berlin legitimate
	.54	Berlin linked to Allied security
	.54	W. Berlin more than symbol of freedom

Table 3.2   Kennedy (Continued)

	.47 U.S. ready to explore peaceful solutions
	.46 Soviets stirred up Berlin crisis
	.18 Requests to be sent to Congress
	.09 Misjudgments have been made
	.04 Additional powers may be requested
	− .26 Burdens must be borne for freedom
	− .28 U.S. prepared to defend its rights
	− .30 U.S. determined to sustain peace and freedom
	− .49 West must coordinate efforts
	− .51 Crisis can be surmounted
	− .53 Support president in days ahead
	− .62 Draft calls increased; reservists activated
	− .70 Financial burden can be carried
	− .85 No easy solutions
	− .91 Berlin a testing place of Western courage
	− .97 Do not assume West is weak
Low stress −1.05 to −1.63	−1.07 Freedom of Berlin not negotiable
	−1.10 Source of world trouble is Moscow
	−1.21 All aggressor pressures will be met
	−1.32 Deactivation of ships and planes delayed
	−1.33 Worldwide response capacity maintained
	−1.41 Map makes situation clear
Slight stress −1.64 to −1.95	−1.67 Immediate threat in West Berlin
	−1.70 Serve country/support president
	−1.80 U.S. rights in Berlin clear and deep
	−1.90 We shall not surrender
Minimal stress <−1.96	−2.00 West Berlin behind Iron Curtain
	−2.15 Dangers of Nuclear Age
	−2.32 U.S. defense buildup under way
	−2.43 Achievement of NATO goals should be hastened
	−2.55 More funds for armed forces requested
	−2.66 Burdens on president are heavy
	−2.70 U.S. cannot accede to Khrushchev's threats
	−3.00 U.S. preparations under way
	−3.75 U.S. determined to defend West Berlin

	August 10
Extreme stress 1.96 and above	2.32 Groundwork necessary before summit
Heavy stress 1.95 to 1.64	
Moderate stress 1.63 to 1.04	

Table 3.2 Kennedy (Continued)

Average stress	.70	Equitable solution desired
1.03 to −1.04	.45	Peaceful solution sought
	− .45	Khrushchev asks U.S. negotiations with East Germany
	− .97	Movement of refugees not influenced by U.S.
Low stress	−1.45	Seek every means for peaceful solution
−1.05 to −1.63		
Slight stress		
−1.64 to −1.95		
Minimal stress		
<−1.96		

	August 21	
Extreme stress		
1.96 and above		
Heavy stress		
1.95 to 1.64		
Moderate stress		
1.63 to 1.04		
Average stress	1.01	Freedom to be maintained in West Berlin
1.03 to −1.04	− .05	Thanks to Vice-President
	− .78	Vice-President has reported
Low stress		
−1.05 to −1.63		
Slight stress		
−1.64 to −1.95		
Minimal stress		
<−1.96		

	August 30	
Extreme stress	2.37	McNamara correct to decline answers
1.96 and above		
Heavy stress	1.94	Grateful to Clay
1.95 to 1.64	1.91	General Clay to be personal representative in Berlin
Moderate stress	1.55	Clay to maintain contacts
1.63 to 1.04	1.47	Not sanguine about settlement
	1.40	Tempo of negotiations satisfactory
	1.17	Military and foreign policy overlaps
	1.14	Responses on important questions immediate
Average stress	.80	Letter from Adenauer confidential
1.03 to −1.04	.51	U.S. urges NATO to increase forces
	.34	Troops represent U.S. commitment

Table 3.2   Kennedy (Continued)

.26 Some response problems remain
.24 U.S. concerned about access to West Berlin
.09 Warning to Soviets: Don't take advantage
.08 Hopeful for a negotiated settlement
− .00 NATO Allies positions not known
− .09 Communication open between East and West Berlin
− .45 U.S. willing to discuss equitable solution
− .63 East Berlin situation unsatisfactory
− .68 Definition of access, etc., necessary
− .76 U.S. and Allies should meet responsibilities
− .96 Intimate communication on Berlin necessary

Low stress −1.05 to −1.63	−1.05 McNamara's responsibilities are military −1.20 U.S. aware of seriousness −1.60 Force should not be used in Berlin
Slight stress −1.64 to −1.95	−1.75 U.S. seeking solution
Minimal stress < −1.96	−2.01 Berlin untenable militarily −4.82 Areas of negotiation not to be stated

September 25

Extreme stress 1.96 and above	2.89 Negotiation a possibility—crisis unnecessary
Heavy stress 1.95 to 1.64	
Moderate stress 1.63 to 1.04	
Average stress 1.03 to −1.04	.72 Peace threatened in Berlin .32 Closing of frontiers in Russian literature .32 West not threatening war over Berlin .02 Crisis is unnecessary − .57 U.S. not committed to rigid formula
Low stress −1.05 to −1.63	
Slight stress −1.64 to −1.95	
Minimal stress < −1.96	−2.03 West cannot yield on interests and commitments −3.56 West will defend and guarantee access −5.77 West Berlin has chosen freedom

October 11

Extreme stress 1.96 and above	6.36 Nuclear forces increased 4.65 Nonnuclear forces increased 4.57 Clarifications developing in talks 3.29 Germany is new government to participate

Table 3.2   Kennedy (Continued)

Heavy stress 1.95 to 1.64	1.75 U.S. should be stronger

Moderate stress 1.63 to 1.04	1.34 Solution not yet in sight
	1.33 Talks proceeding
	1.08 Nuclear period is dangerous

Average stress 1.03 to −1.04	.89 Journalists have problems
	.23 Political and economic viability of West Berlin important
	.16 Common Western position being developed
	.11 Soviets have described their positions
	− .11 Increase in defense budget
	− .15 No clear solution on Berlin yet
	− .27 East European politics unsatisfactory
	− .33 Americans concerned over war
	− .40 U.S. to protect vital interests
	− .52 Explorations, no negotiations, under way
	− .83 Soviets controlled East Berlin and Germany since 1947

Low stress −1.05 to −1.63	−1.32 Collision of opinions over Berlin
	−1.40 No negotiations yet

Slight stress −1.64 to −1.95	−1.74 Some privacy needed in talks
	−1.82 Soviet challenge is serious
	−1.93 Settlement won't be easy

Minimal stress < −1.96	−2.16 New Western position to be considered
	−2.23 Additional information on national security
	−2.32 Most dangerous time in history
	−2.60 U.S. to meet its commitments
	−3.72 No true negotiations yet
	−3.85 Western positions emerging
	−3.93 Eastern Europe held by Soviets for 16 years
	−6.66 Stories on JFK-Gromyko meeting
	−8.34 U.S. to protect interests without war

November 8

Extreme stress 1.96 and above	

Heavy stress 1.95 to 1.64	1.71 Forthcoming discussions with Adenauer

Moderate stress 1.63 to 1.04	

Average stress 1.03 to −1.04	.18 No summit planned/Adenauer coming to U.S.

Low stress −1.05 to −1.63	

Table 3.2   Kennedy (Continued)

Slight stress
−1.64 to −1.95

Minimal stress   −2.37 Remilitarization of West Germany
<−1.96

                        November 29
Extreme stress   3.08 Reservists contributing to security
1.96 and above   2.75 Reservists demonstrate commitment
                        1.96 Service of reservists is valuable

Heavy stress
1.95 to 1.64

Moderate stress
1.63 to 1.04

Average stress   1.22 Hope of less than one-year duty for reservists
1.03 to −1.04   1.00 Options provided by callup
                        1.00 Reservists are a deterrent to war
                         .78 U.S. commitments must be kept
                         .37 Reservists maintaining peace
                         .09 Reserve duty not to exceed one year
                         .03 Distortion in press
                        − .21 Training and equipment important
                        − .40 Need for free access to West Berlin
                        − .70 Camps not prepared
                        − .75 U.S. involved in major problem area

Low stress   −1.50 Reservists' lives upset
−1.05 to −1.63

Slight stress
−1.64 to −1.95

Minimal stress   −2.07 Form of international authority undecided
<−1.96   −2.39 U.S. has insufficient conventional forces
                        −2.48 Meeting with Adenauer delayed
                        −2.60 Possible international authority

---

                        January 15, 1962
Average stress   .78 Soviets controlled East Berlin since 1940s
1.03 to −1.04   − .55 No suggestion to tear down Berlin Wall

Low stress   −1.16 Tearing down Wall could have led to violent reaction
−1.05 to −1.63

                        January 31
Extreme stress
1.96 and above

Heavy stress
1.95 to 1.64

Table 3.2   Kennedy (Continued)

Moderate stress
1.63 to 1.04

Average stress   .00 No progress on Berlin/danger remains
1.03 to −1.04

Low stress
−1.05 to −1.63

Slight stress
−1.64 to −1.95

Minimal stress
<−1.96

                          February 14

Extreme stress
1.96 and above

Heavy stress
1.95 to 1.64

Moderate stress
1.63 to 1.04

Average stress   .00 Need for troops continues
1.03 to −1.04

Low stress
−1.05 to −1.63

Slight stress
−1.64 to −1.95

Minimal stress
<−1.96

                          February 21

Extreme stress
1.96 and above

Heavy stress
1.95 to 1.64

Moderate stress
1.63 to 1.04

Average stress   .35 Conflicting diplomatic signals from Adenauer
1.03 to −1.04   − .42 Interference in air and ground movement dangerous

Low stress
−1.05 to −1.63

Slight stress
−1.64 to −1.95

Table 3.2   Kennedy (Continued)

Minimal stress < -1.96	-2.86	Hope for Soviets to desist

March 14

Extreme stress 1.96 and above		
Heavy stress 1.95 to 1.64		
Moderate stress 1.63 to 1.04		
Average stress 1.03 to -1.04	.38 $-$ .44	Harassment makes perfect solution Provocative incidents to be avoided
Low stress -1.05 to -1.63		
Slight stress -1.64 to -1.95		
Minimal stress < -1.96		

March 21

Extreme stress 1.96 and above		
Heavy stress 1.95 to 1.64		
Moderate stress 1.63 to 1.04	1.57 1.33	Reservist callup strengthened U.S. Inequities exist in life
Average stress 1.03 to -1.04	$-$ .33 $-$ .87	Calling back of reservists Release of reservists not to be quick
Low stress -1.05 to -1.63	-1.06	Talks on Berlin continuing
Slight stress -1.64 to -1.95		
Minimal stress < -1.96	-4.11	Two new divisions needed

March 29

Extreme stress 1.96 and above		
Heavy stress 1.95 to 1.64		
Moderate stress 1.63 to 1.04		

Table 3.2 Kennedy (Continued)

Average stress 1.03 to −1.04	.83 − .77	Dangerous and difficult problem in Berlin Vital and urgent problem in Berlin
Low stress −1.05 to −1.63		
Slight stress −1.64 to −1.95		
Minimal stress <−1.96		

	April 11	
Extreme stress 1.96 and above		
Heavy stress 1.95 to 1.64		
Moderate stress 1.63 to 1.04		
Average stress 1.03 to −1.04	.91	Clay's service in Berlin valuable
Low stress −1.05 to −1.63	−1.21	Gold flows must be corrected
Slight stress −1.64 to −1.95		
Minimal stress <−1.96		

	April 18	
Extreme stress 1.96 and above		
Heavy stress 1.95 to 1.64		
Moderate stress 1.63 to 1.04		
Average stress 1.03 to −1.04	.94 .33	Diplomatic probes continue West Germans will make own positions known
Low stress −1.05 to −1.63	−1.14	Status of East German regime on access unclarified
Slight stress −1.64 to −1.95		
Minimal stress <−1.96		

Table 3.2 Kennedy (Continued)

	May 9
Extreme stress	2.70 Participation is not recognition
1.96 and above	2.60 Unity of West critical
Heavy stress	
1.95 to 1.64	
Moderate stress	1.34 U.S. carries major burdens
1.63 to 1.04	
Average stress	.95 Talks will continue
1.03 to −1.04	.74 Western unity improved
	.26 Not optimistic about talks
	.02 Negotiations might be better handled
	− .19 Confusion over recognition of East Germany
	− .39 Organization of access authority
	− .56 Different positions on access authority
	− .62 Proposals to East Germans not recognition
Low stress	
−1.05 to −1.63	
Slight stress	
−1.64 to −1.95	
Minimal stress	−2.73 Unity in West now strong
<−1.96	−3.30 No de facto recognition of East Germany

agreement among the coders. All groups were then reviewed for coherence and named. Finally, these groups were then reviewed by the project staff.

We attempted to make groups of ten or more cards (i.e., paragraphs) but at times we believed there were good reasons for keeping some of the groups small. During the course of the task, both of the independent coders constructed a composite "nuclear mention" category which the internal coders had assigned to a military grouping. When we reviewed these paragraphs, we agreed that the paragraphs were sufficiently unique to merit a special category. When we aggregated the Z-scores for each theme, these paragraphs turned out to have a much higher level of stress than either the "reservists" or "troop buildup" categories into which the remainder of the military group was divided. Overall, thirteen composite categories were created. These categories and the Z-scores for each of them are presented in table 3.3.

The rank ordering of the themes in terms of stress shown in table 3.3 represents a hierarchy of the president's concerns or negative affect as felt by Kennedy during the course of the Berlin crisis. The data in table 3.3

show the composite themes across all speeches, with those having the highest positive values producing the greatest amount of concern in the president and those with negative values representing the least stressful issues. Contrary to traditional content analysis, note that frequencies of occurrence of a theme (N on table 3.3) do *not* correlate with the hierarchy of concern or negative affect. For example, the "description of events/situation" appeared 58 times, the highest frequency for the crisis, but it is rather low in the hierarchy of Z-scores and mean stress values.

Further, differences in table 3.3 reflect the certainty/ambiguity differences noted in previous research. Wiegele (1978b) found that past events are viewed by presidential decision makers as "givens" and, therefore, are less stressing than are the future needs and actions caused by these events. Thus, this finding that the category "description of events/situations" is lower in stress for the president should not concern us. Indeed, we would be very surprised to find the reverse.

During the Berlin crisis, President Kennedy did not appear to be significantly stressed by the need for a military buildup; rather, in a military sense it was the nonroutine circumstances of the nuclear question, the Soviet challenge, and the reservists that aroused him. During the crisis, Kennedy's discussion of the nuclear/nonnuclear distinction in the arms buildup pointed to a strong concern for the dangers of nuclear weapons

Table 3.3   Composite theme hierarchy across stress strata, John F. Kennedy, 1961–1962.

Theme designation	Summed Z-Scores	N	$\bar{X}$	Z-Scores for composite themes
Mention of nuclear/nonnuclear distinction	13.81	3	4.6	8.12
Talks proceeding/solution distant	11.62	14	.83	1.78
Western unity and actions	10.77	14	.77	1.68
Soviet challenge	12.56	17	.74	1.63
Reservists	10.35	15	.69	1.55
Berlin freedom	1.71	6	.29	.87
U.S. position	−18.15	31	−.59	−.61
Economic/financial concerns	−6.23	10	−.62	−.66
Need for/call for negotiations	−19.24	30	−.64	−.69
Description of events/situation	−44.92	58	−.77	−.91
Troop buildup needed	−10.10	13	−.78	−.92
General Western position	−15.45	16	−.97	−1.24
Burden on the president	−4.89	3	−1.63	−2.35

and an attempt to control this danger. That he was so stressed when he mentioned his choice of the nonnuclear options probably indicates that either he was not convinced that this was the right choice or he feared that his decision might not be popular. The rhetoric of his speeches leads to the latter explanation on intuitive grounds: Kennedy made the less dramatic, but safer, nonnuclear moves.

The nuclear question was apparently of grave concern to Kennedy for several reasons (cf. Sorensen 1965:588). The inadequacy of American forces in Europe concerned the president. Thus, he saw the troop buildup as crucial because the Soviets may have believed that if no strong American response other than a nuclear response was feasible, there would be no American response at all. The Soviets would see an American defense of Berlin as unlikely and might attempt to slowly strangle West Berlin. A conventional troop buildup, however, would demonstrate to the Soviets that the United States was ready to meet its commitment in Berlin (Sorensen, 1965:588). Sorensen's account demonstrates that the nuclear/nonnuclear distinction was of great importance to Kennedy.

The question of the reservists was a sensitive domestic problem for Kennedy. To show the nation's determination, he called up many reservists during the early phases of the crisis to serve until two new divisions could be assembled, outfitted, and trained. The problem was that the reservists were not well outfitted (some were "training" with broomsticks) and, having been called up on short notice, were separated from their families. As the months went by and the shoddy training conditions of the reservists became known, the reservist question, which was raised at virtually every press conference, became a thorn in Kennedy's side. His high stress scores on this issue probably reflect this.

Referring again to table 3.3, the hierarchy of composite themes divides into conflict-reactive (as the highest) and maintenance-descriptive (as the lowest) groups, with an ambiguous category, Berlin freedom, straddling the two. To find that across speeches with significantly varying general levels of stress we can isolate specific types of topics with consistent stress levels seems to bode well for future foreign policy analysis. Obviously, we have barely begun to scratch the analytical surface.

Word-Level Analysis

In this section we move from thematic (or paragraph) analysis to the individual word as our unit of observation. Our data set consists of 9,713 words spoken by Kennedy during the twenty Berlin crisis speeches. We

Table 3.4   Stress and word length, mean and standard deviation: John F. Kennedy.

	Mean	SD	N
Stress	67.112	15.934	9,713
Length	20.778	9.826	9,713

have interval-level measurements of both stress and electronically derived word lengths. Table 3.4 presents the means and standard deviations for these two variables. We also wish to test for the effects of stress on speech, part of speech, word length, and the prepared/extemporaneous dichotomy. We therefore produced a breakdown of our stress scores by each of these variables (see table 3.5).

The word-length variable (designated simply as "length") for table 3.5 has been recoded based on the mean and standard deviation of the variable. All words within plus or minus one-half of one standard deviation from the mean are coded as medium, those more than one-half of one standard deviation greater than the mean are coded as long, and those more than one-half of one standard deviation less than the mean are coded as short.

Table 3.5 reveals some interesting findings. Kennedy exhibits a broad range of mean stress values across his twenty speeches, reaching a minimum of 59.25 on March 14, 1962, and a maximum of 82.36 on September 25, 1961. Tanter (1974:85ff) divides the Berlin crisis into three phases, precrisis (June 4–July 24, 1961), crisis (July 25–September 12, 1961), and postcrisis (September 13–October 17, 1961). Based on a scaling process, Tanter (1974:85) finds that the highest intensity of interaction occurred during the "crisis" phase (mean intensity=27.51 versus 4.62 during the precrisis phase and 9.73 during the postcrisis phase). In our work, Kennedy's point of highest stress occurs during Tanter's postcrisis phase (September 25, 1961). Overall, the president's mean stress level appears unrelated to Tanter's phases of the crisis and to his *subjectively* scaled mean intensity of interaction. Quite possibly, Kennedy's perceptions of the intensity of the crisis were not the same as Tanter's. Indeed, it may be that Tanter's intensity scale differs from the personal "internal intensity scales" used by decision makers in times of crisis.

We also find that Kennedy's mean stress value for prepared speeches is much higher than that for his extemporaneous pronouncements. Kennedy exhibits the highest stress value on long words and is the least stressed by

Table 3.5   Stress breakdown for Kennedy.

| | Grand mean = 67.11 | |
Stress by	Mean	N of words
Speech		
1. (6-28-61)	68.33	609
2. (7-19-61)	67.25	981
3. (7-25-61)	69.76	2,760
4. (8-10-61)	64.66	288
5. (8-21-61)	67.84	69
6. (8-30-61)	63.24	919
7. (9-25-61)	82.36	385
8. (10-11-61)	68.04	817
9. (11-08-61)	60.31	131
10. (11-29-61)	61.42	635
11. (1-15-62)	70.05	102
12. (1-31-62)	68.42	93
13. (2-14-62)	74.87	52
14. (2-21-62)	61.37	173
15. (3-14-62)	59.25	92
16. (3-21-62)	70.40	235
17. (3-29-62)	62.47	129
18. (4-11-62)	66.89	230
19. (4-18-62)	61.69	297
20. (5-09-62)	61.85	714
Prepared		
Prepared	70.87	4,368
Extemporaneous	64.03	5,342
Length		
Short	64.75	3,620
Medium	67.52	3,664
Long	69.98	2,426
Part of speech		
Noun	67.44	3,515
Verb	67.89	2,020
Adjective	68.80	1,956
Adverb	68.72	745
Filled pause	58.37	400
Preposition	64.23	511
Article	61.97	264
Conjunction	63.83	299

short words, an expected result. Kennedy also exhibits a higher level of stress on the major parts of speech or content words (nouns, verbs, adjectives, and adverbs) than he does on the minor or functional parts of speech (filled pauses, conjunctions, prepositions, and articles). Qualifying content words (adjectives and adverbs) are the most highly stressed.

Each of these variables will be discussed and tested for their effects on stress in the following sections. The effects of speech, part of speech, and the prepared/unprepared dichotomy will also be tested for their possible effects on word length.

Speech

The variable "speech" is designed, in this instance, merely as a number designating each of the twenty speeches in chronological order so that we can compare the mean stress values among Kennedy's speeches. Speech is, in reality, an aggregate variable, under which are subsumed a variety of characteristics. Speech may include the prepared/extemporaneous dichotomy, and a number of "circumstantial" characteristics such as the speaker's general level of arousal because of the crisis itself or as a result of other, external factors.

Table 3.6 presents the results of a one-way analysis of variance (ANOVA) with stress dependent and speech independent. The F-value is fairly high (45.58), which is statistically significant at $p \leqslant .001$, with 19, 9691 degrees of freedom.

It is rather difficult to interpret these results. Speech is an aggregate variable composed of a number of contextual variables. We have not broken speech down, and do not have a list of contextual variables which make up the aggregate. Nonetheless, this finding is of substantive significance because it should lead us to ask what sort of contextual variables (as opposed to thematic or linguistic variables) may affect a speaker's stress level during

Table 3.6   One-way analysis of variance on stress with speech independent: John F. Kennedy.

Source of variation	Sum of squares	DF	Mean square	F	Significance of F
Main effects	201949.250	19	10628.906	45.581	0.000
Speech	201949.250	19	10628.906	45.581	0.000
Explained	201950.000	19	10628.945	45.581	0.000
Residual	2259815.000	9691	233.187	—	—
Total	2461765.000	9710	253.529	—	—

one speech as compared to another. However, recall that in chapter 1 we made the assumption that, of the potential multiple causes of stress in a decision maker, the international crisis itself will be the single most powerful. We remain comfortable with that assumption.

Word Length, Part of Speech, and Prepared/Extemporaneous Speeches

In order to get a better picture of Kennedy's linguistic behavior, we performed an ANOVA on his stress level using our recoded length variable, part of speech, and the prepared/unprepared dichotomy as the independent variables. The results of this ANOVA are shown in table 3.7.

We can see from table 3.7 that the two-way and three-way interactions among the variables are modest. This leads us to believe that each of the three variables may have had an independent effect on Kennedy's stress level.

Hierarchically, the prepared/unprepared dichotomy seems to be exerting the most influence, followed by length and part of speech. The F-value for the prepared/extemporaneous dichotomy is very strong, and we have little doubt that it is exerting a major influence on Kennedy's level of stress. We will take up the effects of each of these three variables in greater

Table 3.7   ANOVA on stress with word length, part of speech, and prepared independent: John F. Kennedy.

Source of variation	Sum of squares	DF	Mean square	F	Significance of F
Main effects	161978.750	10	16197.875	68.526	0.000
Part	26777.527	7	3825.361	16.183	0.000
Prepared	80032.500	1	80032.500	338.580	0.000
Length	15273.902	2	7636.949	32.308	0.000
2-way interactions	12312.500	23	535.326	2.265	0.000
Part Prepared	4324.578	7	617.797	2.614	0.011
Part Length	6823.766	14	487.412	2.062	0.011
Prepared Length	612.079	2	306.040	1.295	0.274
3-way interactions	2577.625	14	184.116	0.779	0.693
Part Prepared length	2577.648	14	184.118	0.779	0.693
Explained	176869.000	47	3763.170	15.920	0.000
Residual	2283873.000	9662	236.377	—	—
Total	2460742.000	9709	253.450	—	—

detail in the following sections. We will also discuss word length as a dependent variable.

Prepared vs. Extemporaneous Vocalizations

Figure 3.2 displays the distribution of prepared and unprepared documents across the eleven-month period of the crisis. Six of the first seven documents are either entirely prepared or contain prepared statements which were read at the start of a news conference. These mixed or "hybrid" vocalizations will be examined shortly. At present, however, the important point is that Kennedy's prepared vocalizations are positioned at the beginning of the crisis. We attribute this tendency to the need to keep the American public informed of the changing situation as it evolved and the desire to achieve precision in publicly articulating U.S. policy positions.

The first seven vocalizations occur during the initial three months of the crisis, i.e., from June through September, 1961. During this time period the situation in Berlin was deteriorating rapidly. To stop the massive flow of refugees from East Germany into West Berlin, the East Germans set up checkpoints on August 1 and began construction of the Berlin Wall on August 13. Following this, both the United States and the Soviet Union began to reinforce their respective theatre capabilities. In addition, both countries resumed the testing of nuclear weapons in early September. This action-reaction process, which was seen as a serious threat to world peace, culminated in President Kennedy's most highly stressed vocalization of the entire crisis, his September 25, 1961, address to the UN General Assembly.

Recalling our supposition that in a prepared statement the speaker in all likelihood is more fully aware of his role as a spokesman for his nation, the extremely high stress score here appears to be justified. In the September 25 speech, Kennedy was speaking not only as the President of the United States, but also as the leader of the Western alliance at a time when world peace was being threatened by Soviet aggressiveness. Kennedy, as an individual, could not have failed to realize the symbolic and material importance of this speech, to which the entire world was witness. Given these circumstances, Kennedy saw to it that his address was a strong statement of the Western position on the Berlin Wall episode. In such a critical situation, therefore, one might expect a speaker to exhibit an extraordinarily high stress level.

The remaining documents (our numbers 8 through 20) are extemporaneous vocalizations made at news conferences. During this eight-month

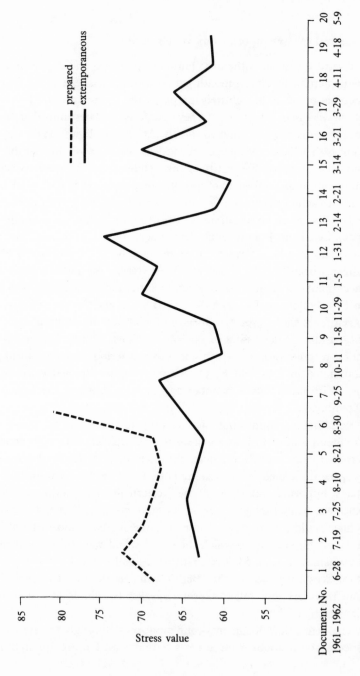

Figure 3.2   Mean stress scores for prepared and extemporaneous pronouncements, chronological: John F. Kennedy.

period (October 1961 to May 1962), negotiations on the Berlin situation passed through four stages. These are delineated in table 3.1. Kennedy's continuing pattern of high and low stress again reflects his alternating belligerent and conciliatory postures during the negotiations.

Figure 3.3 indicates most clearly that Kennedy's prepared vocalizations are more highly stressed than his unprepared vocalizations, with mean stress scores of 70.87 and 64.03, respectively ($t=21.60$, $df=9711$, $p=.000$). This can be attributed to the speaker's concern, in prepared speeches, for asserting his position clearly, forcefully, and precisely, and to the speaker's awareness of the important role he is occupying as spokesman for his nation. These scores are ordered from the highest stressed speech to the lowest, i.e., detrended from their normal chronological order.

One factor distinguishes Kennedy from both Johnson and Nixon (who are both discussed in the following chapters), and that is the presence of mixed or hÿbrid vocalizations, consisting of a prepared statement followed by responses to questions at a news conference. Documents 2 and 6 fall into this category. In figure 3.3 these two documents dramatically illustrate the difference in mean stress scores of prepared and extemporaneous speech outlined above. This may be attributed to the different thematic content of each type of vocalization.

In the prepared portion of document 2, a July 19, 1961, news conference, Kennedy informed the American people of the Soviet threat to world peace then unfolding in Berlin. He repeatedly emphasized the dangerous character of the situation; the resulting mean stress score for this segment of the document was quite high at 72.28. In the extemporaneous portion of the same news conference, Kennedy answered questions from reporters concerning the U.S. position, consultation with allies, possible future courses of action, and economic concerns. Once the president had delivered his prepared message, he could relax a bit and deal with some of the more "ordinary" aspects of the problem. The result was a considerably lower mean stress score, 63.07, for the unprepared portion of the document.

In a similar manner, the August 30, 1961, news conference, document 6, consisted of a prepared statement followed by queries from reporters. In the prepared portion, which was comprised of only three paragraphs, Kennedy announced the appointment of General Lucius Clay as his personal representative in Berlin and stressed the importance of having a competent person in that position. Kennedy was attempting to inspire confidence in Clay's ability to handle the crucial situation in Berlin, which resulted in a mean stress score of 68.61, a score higher than the 63.25 mean

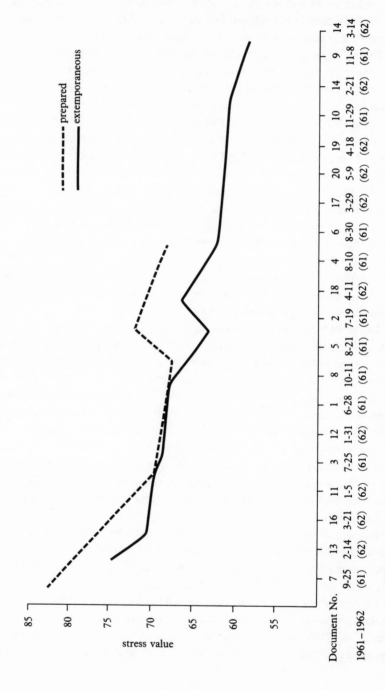

Figure 3.3   Detrended mean stress scores for prepared and extemporaneous pronouncements: John F. Kennedy.

stress score for the document as a whole. In the unprepared section of the document, Kennedy's comments centered around the political attractiveness of a peaceful solution to the problem in Berlin. The mean stress value here is a much lower 62.60.

Part of Speech

The next relationship which we examined was that between stress and part of speech. The psycholinguistic literature presents a dichotomy which we found useful to adopt. The four main parts of speech, generally considered to be nouns, verbs, adjectives, and adverbs, are known as content words (Miller, 1951). They represent the core of language and give meaning to speech. According to Brown (1973), children initially learn to communicate through the use of content words, which make up about 95 percent of the words in one's vocabulary. The other four parts of speech, or the minor parts of speech, are prepositions, articles, conjunctions, and interjections. We found no interjections in any of the pronouncements studied, so the category has been deleted from the analysis. We did, however, note the presence of filled pauses (see appendix 1), and because they do contribute to stress scores, they were included in the analysis. These minor parts of speech are known as function words (Brown, 1973); and they are learned and used in the later stages of a child's linguistic development. Brown also postulates that these function words in some instances express psychological meaning.

Recalling the distinction made above between content words and function words, and the fact that content words make up the overwhelming majority of one's vocabulary (Brown, 1973), the breakdown in table 3.8 is easy to understand. Here, Kennedy's content words account for 84.8 percent of his vocabulary during the Berlin crisis, while function words comprise the remaining 15.2 percent. These figures are consistent with Miller's (1951) work.

Figure 3.4 displays the mean stress scores for each part of speech in Kennedy's vocalizations in detrended order. In general, function words tend to fall below the mean, while content words fall both above and below the mean. The one notable exception to this trend is the line for prepositions. In four different vocalizations (documents 5, 12, 13, and 19), prepositions are the most highly stressed part of speech, and, as seen in the data for the thirteenth document, prepositions account for the highest absolute mean stress score in a document for the entire crisis with a mean of 87. This will be treated more fully below. Table 3.9 illustrates the break-

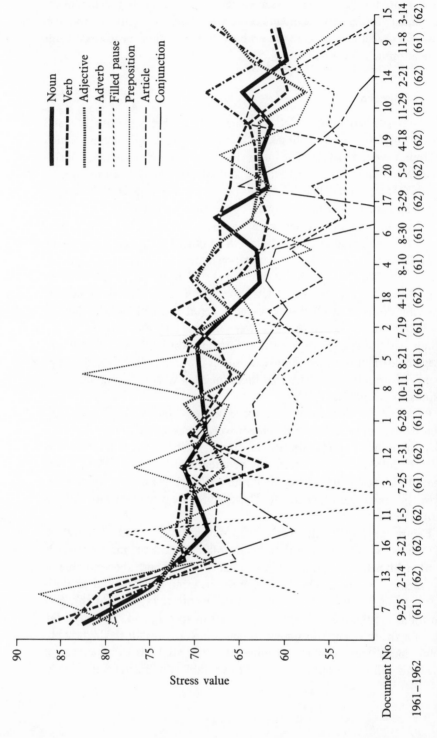

Figure 3.4 Detrended mean stress scores for parts of speech: John F. Kennedy.

Table 3.8   Frequency distributions of parts of speech: John F. Kennedy.

Part of speech	Relative frequency (%)
Noun	36.2
Verb	20.8
Adjective	20.1
Adverb	7.7
Filled pause	4.1
Preposition	5.3
Article	2.7
Conjunction	3.1
Total	100.0

down of mean stress scores for each part of speech across all of Kennedy's vocalizations. Kennedy's main parts of speech, or content words, are more highly stressed than the minor parts of speech or function words. We will discuss the content words first and then proceed to an analysis of the functional parts of speech.

Figure 3.5 shows the mean stress scores of the main parts of speech. As table 3.9 shows, adjectives and adverbs are the most highly stressed, followed by verbs and nouns. Generally, for Kennedy, adjectives and adverbs stay above the mean, while nouns and verbs are found both above and below the mean. An interesting trend is seen if one first examines the nine most highly stressed vocalizations, i.e., those on the left-hand side of figure 3.5, then the eleven lower stressed speeches, those on the right-hand side. In the most highly stressed vocalizations, verbs and adverbs exhibit the highest stress values. In the less stressful speeches, however, adjectives and adverbs are the most highly stressed. The higher scores of verbs and their modifiers (adverbs) during the most highly stressed of Kennedy's vocalizations may be attributed to Kennedy's perception of the gravity of the situation in these instances and his desire for precision. The thematic content of these vocalizations centered around the Soviet threat to world peace and the actions that the United States would take to assure freedom of access to West Berlin. In the lower stressed vocalizations, Kennedy usually described events or discussed the steps necessary to attain a peaceful diplomatic solution, which may account for the high stress levels of descriptive words, adjectives and adverbs.

Returning to figure 3.4, we can examine function words, or the minor parts of speech. As seen in table 3.9, prepositions are the most highly stressed of the function words. In figure 3.4, this is seen most clearly in documents 5, 12, and 13, where prepositions have stress scores that are

Table 3.9   Mean stress scores for parts of speech: John F. Kennedy.

Parts of speech	$\bar{X}$ Stress scores
Main	
Adjective	68.81
Adverb	68.75
Verb	67.88
Noun	67.44
Minor	
Preposition	64.24
Conjunction	63.83
Article	61.97
Filled pause	58.38

much higher than those of any other part of speech within each document. Prepositions are also the most frequent of the functional parts of speech, comprising 5.3 percent of Kennedy's words in the data pool. Recalling Brown's (1973) work on the development of language in children, the high stress scores for prepositions may indicate subtle psychological discomfort. It is possible that, in the absence of filled pauses, anxiety may be expressed by Kennedy through high stress scores on function words. Filled pauses are a normal part of Kennedy's speech, however, comprising 4.1 percent of his words during the Berlin crisis. Only 0.5 percent of Kennedy's words during prepared statements are filled pauses, while during extemporaneous vocalizations this frequency jumps to 7.1 percent. Filled pauses occur in all but two of Kennedy's speeches and have the lowest mean stress score of any part of speech, 58.37. It is apparent that filled pauses are not indicative of stress in Kennedy's speech. Thus, for Kennedy psychological discomfort is manifested at times through high stress on another category of function word, the preposition.

Part of Speech in Prepared Speeches and Statements

Figure 3.6 displays the mean stress scores for each part of speech in Kennedy's prepared vocalizations. Among the content words here, adverbs are the most highly stressed (70.37), followed by verbs (69.85), adjectives (68.25), and nouns (68.24). Among the functional parts of speech, conjunctions have the highest mean stress score (68.22), while filled pauses have the lowest (57.00). It is interesting to note that the scores of verbs and adverbs are very close together, as are those of nouns and adjectives. In

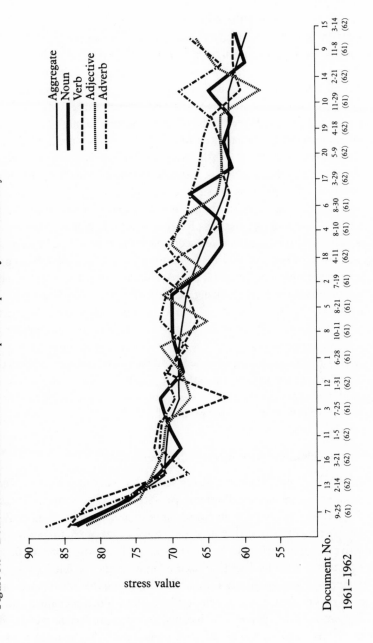

Figure 3.5   Detrended mean stress scores for main parts of speech: John F. Kennedy.

both cases the scores of the modifiers are higher than the scores of the words they modify, though these differences are slight.

In document 7, however, the difference between verbs and adverbs is larger. We also note that the difference between adjectives and nouns is larger in document 7, Kennedy's speech to the UN General Assembly. In adjective/noun combinations like "international rights," "peaceful circulation," "deep commitments," "Western powers," and "free city," the adjectives are all more highly stressed than the nouns they modify. In adverb/verb combinations such as "genuinely suffocate," "freely expressed," "calmly resolved," and "now explored," the adverbs are more highly stressed than the verbs they modify. This may be attributed to a particular characteristic of prepared speeches which was discussed earlier in this study. That is, in prepared speeches the speaker is concerned with conveying his message as accurately and forcefully as possible; and while doing so he attempts to present a good image in order to inspire the audience's confidence in him as a leader. Conscious emphasis is placed on adjectives and adverbs, sometimes called words of emotion, to accomplish this purpose; and this probably accounts for the higher stress levels for adjectives and adverbs in prepared vocalizations. Furthermore, nouns (naming persons and things) and verbs (identifying action or being) frequently can be looked upon as givens, while adjectives and adverbs involve questions of language choice and precision as a speaker cognitively searches for the correct qualifier to convey his message.

Figure 3.6 also shows that Kennedy's filled pauses had very low stress levels. Filled pauses account for only 0.5 percent of Kennedy's words in prepared speeches and, therefore, were not a significant factor in determining his overall stress level for prepared speeches.

Part of Speech in Extemporaneous Pronouncements

Figure 3.7 displays the mean stress scores for parts of speech in Kennedy's extemporaneous vocalizations. As with the content words in prepared speeches, discussed in the previous section, adverbs and adjectives are the most highly stressed, with mean stress scores of 66.39 and 66.41, respectively, while verbs and nouns are less stressed with scores of 64.41 and 64.32, respectively. Kennedy used a large number of filled pauses in his extemporaneous vocalizations, perhaps indicating that filled pauses are a normal part of Kennedy's speech profile. As mentioned previously, filled pauses comprise 7.1 percent of Kennedy's extemporaneous words. As Kennedy answered questions at news conferences, he frequently used

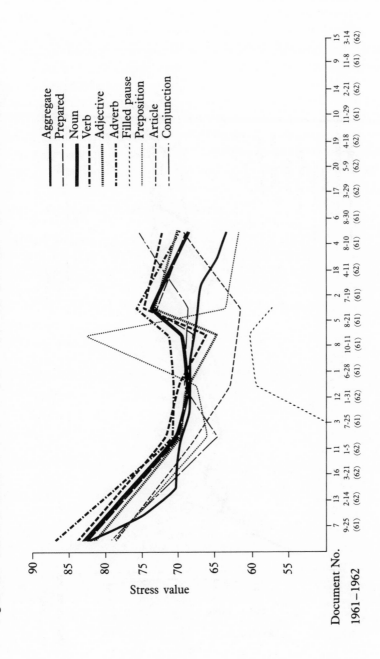

Figure 3.6 Detrended mean stress scores for parts of speech, prepared pronouncements: John F. Kennedy.

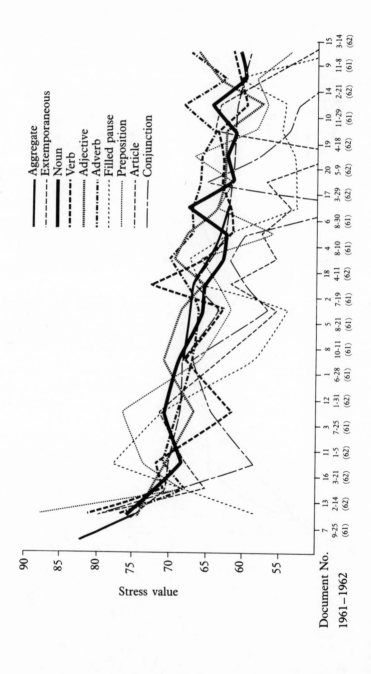

Figure 3.7 Detrended mean stress scores for parts of speech, extemporaneous pronouncements: John F. Kennedy.

filled pauses to give himself time to formulate the next phrase or sentence. The overall effect of filled pauses on the aggregate stress level of his extemporaneous speech, therefore, was to lower it.

Derived Word Length

Word length in prepared speeches and statements. After exploring the feasibility of using various methods to determine word length (see appendix 1), we decided to utilize the number of pulses produced by a word on a voice stress chart as the criterion. This choice had two clear advantages over other methods. First, data for each word were readily available. The words already had been coded during a previous manipulation; and it was only necessary to determine the boundaries of short, medium, and long words (see appendix 1). Second, using the number of pulses for each word rather than the number of letters to determine word length firmly anchored our research in a voice stress orientation, thus distinguishing it from traditional forms of content analysis. We will use the phrase "derived word length" to designate electronically determined word lengths.

The analysis of stress scores for Kennedy broken down by word length produces results which conform to our expectations. The mean stress score for long words was 69.98, for medium length words 67.52, and for short words 64.75. Figure 3.8 displays the mean stress scores for word length broken down by speech.

In all but three cases long words are the most highly stressed. Two of the three exceptions, the fifth and eleventh speeches, have short words as the most highly stressed, followed by long words and then medium length words. In the fourth speech, medium length words were the most highly stressed followed by long words and then short words. The hierarchy of stress scores for long, medium, and short words was broken three times, in speeches 9, 13, and 16. In speech 9, the stress score for short words actually went above the mean, but in speeches 13 and 16, the low stress scores for medium length words seem to be responsible for the deviation.

Overall, long words tend to raise the aggregate stress level for Kennedy's speeches while short words tend to lower the aggregate mean. Medium length words, on the other hand, exert a mixed influence on Kennedy's stress level.

Figure 3.9 displays derived word length information for Kennedy's prepared pronouncements. The data follow the same basic trend as the aggregate data, with long words the most highly stressed (72.68), followed by medium words (70.77), and then short words (69.10). In both cases where

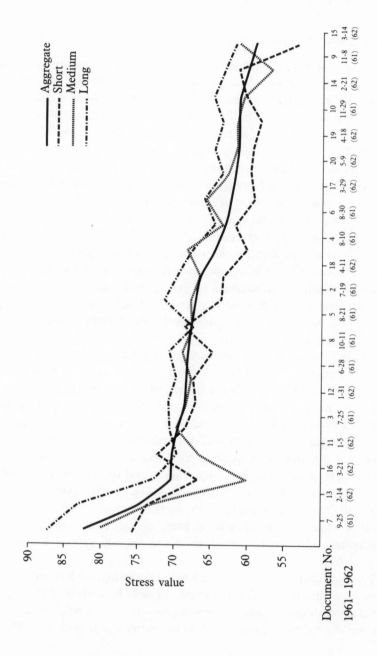

Figure 3.8   Detrended mean stress scores for derived word lengths: John F. Kennedy.

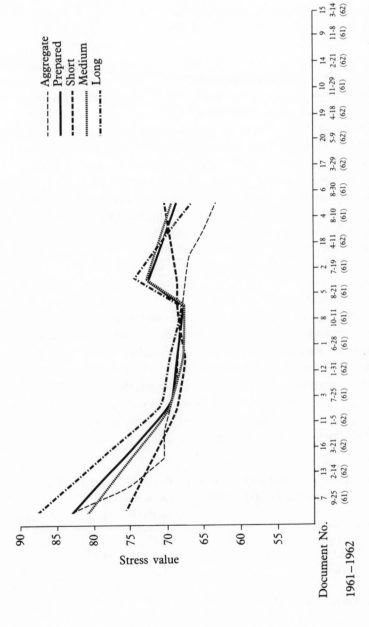

Figure 3.9 Detrended mean stress scores for derived word lengths, prepared pronouncements: John F. Kennedy.

the data deviate from this tendency, speeches 5 and 6, short words are the most highly stressed. In addition, in speech 6 the normal hierarchy of derived word length and stress is completely reversed. Not only were short words the most stressed, but long words were the least stressed. Looking into the content of the paragraphs for an explanation of this reversal was not helpful. We will return to this point in our comparative analysis.

In sum, Kennedy's mean stress scores for word length in prepared vocalizations clearly followed the trends in the aggregate data. Long words were the most highly stressed and raised the mean stress value, while short words tended to lower the mean stress level. Medium words again had little influence on the mean stress score.

Word length in extemporaneous pronouncements. In figure 3.10 one can see that the mean stress scores for word length in Kennedy's extemporaneous speeches conform to our previous observations. Long words are the most highly stressed and short words the least stressed. Speeches 4 and 11 deviate from this trend: medium words were the most highly stressed in speech 4 and short words were the most highly stressed in speech 11. These anomalies cannot readily be explained by reference to situational factors during the crisis. It may be that the length of the crisis (fifteen months) prevented any pattern of identifiable deviations from being established because the crisis itself was not the sole focus of Kennedy's attention during those fifteen months.

The range of stress scores based on word length for Kennedy is shown in table 3.10. Prepared speeches exhibit a fairly narrow range of stress scores for Kennedy (3.58), while extemporaneous speeches have a slightly broader range (4.20). The aggregate, however, has a range of 5.23. The differences which a speaker exhibits are generally a function of the psychological idiosyncracies of the individual. As will be discussed later, the normal pattern is for long words to be the most highly stressed and short words the least. However, the exact range of the difference between word

Table 3.10   Ranges of mean stress scores for derived word lengths in prepared vs. extemporaneous pronouncements: John F. Kennedy.

	All speeches	Prepared	Extemporaneous
$\bar{X}$ Stress	67.11	70.87	64.03
Short	64.75	69.10	62.27
Medium	67.52	70.77	64.77
Long	69.98	72.68	66.47
Range—highest/lowest stress	5.23	3.58	4.20

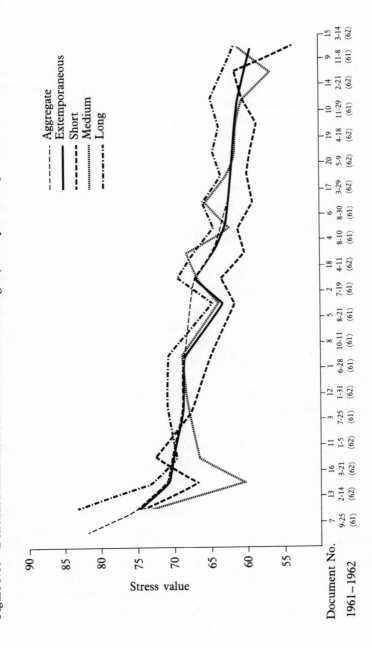

Figure 3.10   Detrended mean stress scores for derived word lengths, extemporaneous pronouncements: John F. Kennedy.

lengths is an idiosyncratic factor. This observation will be relevant in the comparative chapter when we spell out clusters of idiosyncrasies for each president.

Determinants of Word Length

The next task is to find out whether word length is related to such factors as the aggregate variable speech, part of speech, and the prepared/unprepared dichotomy. Overall, Kennedy's mean word length, measured in terms of pulses, was 20.78 and the standard deviation was 9.83. To test the effects of speech on word length we performed an ANOVA on word length with speech independent. The results of this ANOVA are shown in table 3.11.

We found that the differences in word length that can be attributed to speech are significant, but neither large nor of much theoretical value. Speech, to repeat, is an aggregate variable and may affect word length in several ways depending upon the exact components of the aggregate variable.

The effects of part of speech and the prepared/unprepared dichotomy are more striking. Kennedy's prepared speeches had a mean word length of 22.53, while his unprepared speeches had a mean of 19.35. Nouns tended to be the longest words in Kennedy's vocabulary with a mean of 22.35, followed by adverbs (22.11), adjectives (20.87), and verbs (20.83). Filled pauses were the longest of the minor parts of speech (17.78), followed by prepositions (16.14), conjunctions (15.67), and articles (14.52). Thus the major parts of speech tended to be longer than the minor parts of speech, and this is not unusual.

In order to test the significance of part of speech and our prepared/extemporaneous dichotomy on word length we performed a two-way ANOVA, the results of which are shown in table 3.12.

Table 3.11   ANOVA on word length with speech independent: John F. Kennedy.

Source of variation	Sum of squares	DF	Mean square	F	Significance of F
Main effects	34043.906	19	1791.784	19.237	0.000
Speech	34043.906	19	1791.784	19.237	0.000
Explained	34043.938	19	1791.786	19.237	0.000
Residual	902649.688	9691	93.143	—	—
Total	936693.626	9710	96.467	—	—

Table 3.12   ANOVA on word length with part and prepared independent:
John F. Kennedy.

Source of variation	Sum of squares	DF	Mean square	F	Significance of F
Main effects	63358.762	8	7919.844	88.240	0.000
Part	39065.563	7	5580.793	62.179	0.000
Prepared	20550.910	1	20550.910	228.970	0.000
2-way interactions	2908.551	7	415.507	4.629	0.000
Part Prepared	2908.574	7	415.510	4.629	0.000
Explained	66267.313	15	4417.820	49.222	0.000
Residual	870072.688	9694	89.754	—	—
Total	936340.001	9709	96.440	—	—

The F-values for both variables are high and significant at $p \leq .001$. We must conclude that all three of the independent variables discussed in this section appear to exhibit effects on word length.

Word length, as we have measured it, may be dependent upon both the specific word and the manner of pronunciation for a given speaker. That is, word length is probably an idiosyncratic factor which is partly affected by cultural determinants and/or regional patterns of pronunciation.

Frequency Distributions of Derived Word Lengths

In order to test the relative frequencies of words of varying lengths a recoding scheme was developed based on the number of pulses for each word. It should be noted that the recoding scheme for word length used in this section differs from that used in the previous sections in that it is not based on standard deviations. Such a recoding scheme would not be appropriate for these measures because frequencies would simply be determined. Thus, the words in our file were recoded for this purpose as follows: 10 through 14 pulses equals short, 15 through 22 pulses equals medium, and over 25 pulses equals long. The frequencies of these lengths are shown in figure 3.11.

Overall, Kennedy used more medium (34.7 percent) and long (33.3 percent) words than short (32.0 percent) words, though the difference between the highest and lowest frequencies does not provide a clear picture of Kennedy's usage of short, medium, and long words. Despite his aggregate tendencies to use more medium length words, we find that in 11 of 20 speeches Kennedy used short words the most frequently.

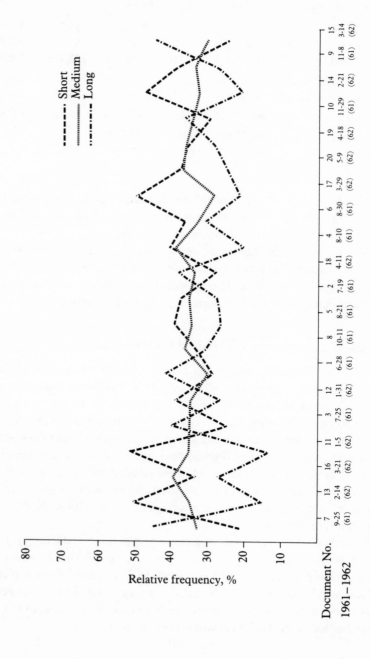

Figure 3.11   Detrended percentage distribution of derived word lengths: John F. Kennedy.

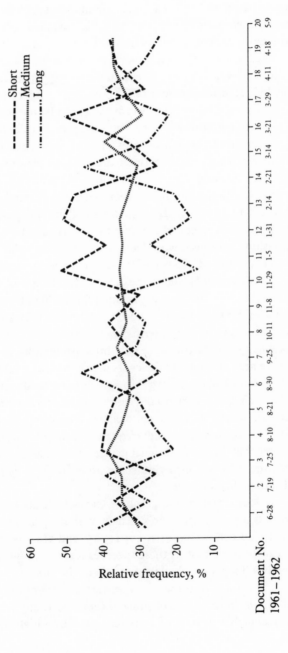

Figure 3.12 Percentage distributions of derived word lengths, chronological: John F. Kennedy.

Zipf (1949) and Miller (1951) have found that the frequency of usage for a word is associated with phonemic word length, or, in this case, electronically derived word length. Specifically, these two analysts found that the more frequently a word is used, the shorter it is likely to be. This trend shows up clearly in Kennedy's verbalizations, although our definition of word length, of course, differs from the traditional.

To determine whether there may have been any situational factors linked with derived word length we replotted the frequencies for word length in chronological order. These data are presented in figure 3.12.

Kennedy's medium length words appear to be the stabilizing influence in his speech pattern, while short and long words exhibit an inverse floating relationship. In only three cases (speeches 8, 16, and 19) are Kennedy's medium words not situated between the short and long words. In each of the three cases medium words are the most frequently used. In eleven of the remaining pronouncements, short words are the most frequently used.

Figure 3.13 compares figure 3.12 with a chronological arrangement of mean stress scores derived from figure 3.8. A high frequency/high stress relationship for derived word lengths is present in eight speeches (1, 3, 5, 7, 10, 11, 15, and 18). In two of these cases (5 and 11), the correspondence is seen on short words, and in the other six, on long words. There does not appear to be any situational explanation for the high frequency/high stress relationship for short words in documents 5 and 11. However, the two pronouncements are similar in terms of context.

Speeches 5 and 11 consist of only three paragraphs, and both treat topics which are peripheral to the crisis per se as well as exhibit a stress score which is slightly above average. In speech 5, Kennedy tells the nation that he has received a report from Vice-President Johnson on the situation in Berlin. In speech 11, he mentions the possibility of tearing down the Berlin Wall. Although the high frequency of short words may be attributed to the generally noncontroversial nature of the speeches, we must observe the picture as a whole to gain some understanding as to why the short words are highly stressed.

If one looks back at the graph of chronologically plotted mean stress scores and compares the scores visually with the pronouncements in question here (speeches 1, 3, 5, 7, 10, 11, 15, and 18), one notices that in all cases except document 15 these speeches represent higher stress points in Kennedy's fluctuating rhythm throughout the course of the Berlin crisis. Only in document 10 is the total mean stress score of the speech below the mean for the entire range of pronouncements. It appears, therefore, that when Kennedy was in what he perceived to be a high stress situation, he

Figure 3.13   Mean stress scores of derived word lengths, chronological: John F. Kennedy.

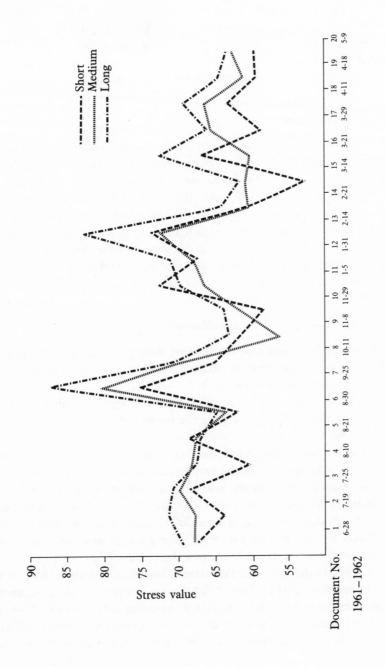

tended to use more long words and these long words accounted significantly for the high stress values. Exceptions to this have already been noted. The fluctuations themselves are indicative of Kennedy's shifting from strong to conciliatory statements throughout the crisis.

Kennedy exhibits a consistent tendency toward high frequency/high stress correlations. These correlations span the entire crisis and correspond to highly stressed pronouncements throughout the crisis.

Place in Paragraph

Figure 3.14 shows the mean stress scores for paragraph positions across Kennedy's 1961 Berlin crisis. A slight trend toward lower stress at the ends of paragraphs was detected for Kennedy. The mean stress score for ends of paragraphs was considerably lower than those of the other two paragraph positions in Kennedy's utterances (end 66.15 vs. 67.44 beginning and 67.67 middle). This is illustrated in figure 3.14 by the position in 11 of the 20 pronouncements studied. It is not possible to infer much from this pattern in Kennedy's verbalizations, i.e., that words at the ends of paragraphs tend to be lower stressed.

General Analyses of President Kennedy

What is the meaning of the data we have presented about President Kennedy? Our conclusions are divided into two sections: thematic analysis and psycholinguistic analysis.

Thematic analysis. If a researcher were engaged in performing voice stress analyses of Kennedy during the Berlin crisis, what clues to his behavior and what insights regarding policy might be obtained as a result? In order to answer these questions, we must again look at table 3.2. We will focus our observations on the two highest strata: "extreme stress" and "heavy stress," which we will refer to collectively as "severe stress." Keep in mind, at this point, that an analyst could acquire this information *only on a day by day basis* as the crisis unfolds. The question an analyst would be likely to ask, therefore, is: what *issues* are causing severe stress (i.e., concern or negative affect) in the president today?

On June 28 there is no configuration among the severe stress themes that might provide a clue to Kennedy's behavior. On July 19, however, the severe stress themes of "Western rights," "freedom in West Berlin," and "allied consultations" appear to indicate concern with the legalistic and nonviolent aspects of the crisis. It is conceivable that, though Kennedy spoke

Figure 3.14　Detrended mean stress scores for paragraph positions: John F. Kennedy.

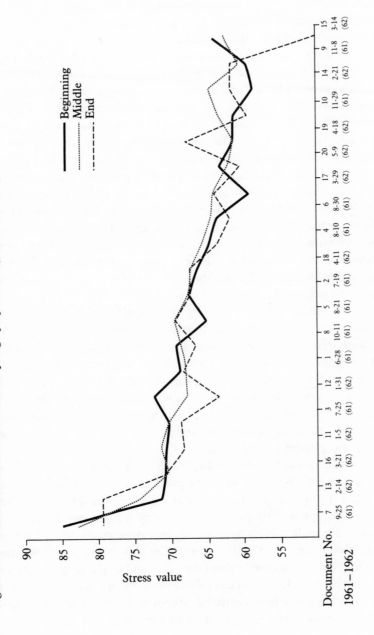

of these topics, he may have harbored strong reservations regarding a legally based and nonviolent solution to the crisis or he may have felt strongly about what he perceived to be the firm legal right of the West in Berlin. Either interpretation suggests caution about further concrete actions which could have drawn harsh counterreactions.

This latter conclusion is reinforced by an examination of the severe stress themes of July 25. Of the nine paragraph themes that reached the severe stress level, five dealt with the American determination to maintain its commitments. This is consistent with previous work on the Korean and Cuban missile crisis decisions, which found that when the "mean for the determination theme . . . exceeds the overall mean for the crisis speech, it is not unreasonable to infer that the speaker is viewing the situation as critical, dangerous, and possibly leading to war. On the other hand, when the converse holds, it is likely that the speaker perceives the situation as less threatening to his nation and that he is therefore less willing to run risks that could lead to war" (Wiegele, 1978b:504). Despite the lack of firm U.S. action "on the ground" in Berlin, an analyst should have interpreted the cluster of severely stressed determination themes on July 25 as indicative of the gravity with which Kennedy viewed the situation. Indeed, it is conceivable that the United States was closer to the outbreak of hostilities than is generally assumed.

A further interpretation of the July 25 determination themes relates to the possible selection of an option to escalate the confrontation. If such an escalation were under consideration, a researcher performing voice stress analyses might have determined that escalatory behavior on the part of the Soviets would have resulted in a high probability of a strong and violent American response. In short, escalation was not likely to succeed (unless the Soviets were willing to run successively higher risks), given Kennedy's frame of mind as revealed in the leakage of psychological information through the physiology of the voice.

The oral documents of August 10, 21, 30, and September 25 provide an analyst with little in the way of meaningful information. Of the five severe stress themes of October 11, three dealt with U.S. strength and military forces. Although in these paragraphs Kennedy is reporting that both nuclear and nonnuclear forces have been increased, he also indicates the need for additional strength. The likely conclusion to be drawn from this is that Kennedy felt uncomfortable about the status and readiness of U.S. forces in the fall of 1961. This conclusion is reinforced by the voice stress data for November 29, which indicate that all three of the severe stress themes dealt with the reservists who were called up for the crisis.

From November 29 through May 9 of the following year, very little information is available at the severe stress level; and, therefore, few insights could be generated by an analyst with regard to specific issues. However, the lack of data at this level does appear to indicate that during this period the cognitive saliency of the crisis for Kennedy had declined significantly.

Psycholinguistic analysis. Let us turn now from conclusions based upon thematic analysis to the word level, where we can develop a psycholinguistic profile of John F. Kennedy. Seven major characteristics of Kennedy as a language processor in international crisis situations can be identified.

(1) Kennedy's prepared statements and speeches were more highly stressed than his extemporaneous pronouncements. In mixed vocalizations, the prepared portion is more highly stressed than the extemporaneous portion.

(2) Across all verbalizations, Kennedy exhibited the highest stress on adjectives.

(a) In prepared statements and speeches, Kennedy exhibited the highest stress on verbs.

(b) In extemporaneous vocalizations, Kennedy exhibited the highest stress on adverbs.

(3) Across all crisis verbalizations, the three highest stressed parts of speech for Kennedy were adjectives, adverbs, and verbs.

(4) Across all crisis verbalizations, the three lowest stressed parts of speech for Kennedy were conjunctions, articles, and filled pauses.

(5) Kennedy's electronically derived long words were consistently the most highly stressed, followed by medium, then short words.

(a) A clear difference in the range of stress scores in derived word lengths was greater in the aggregate than in Kennedy's prepared and extemporaneous vocalizations.

(b) Kennedy's range of stress scores for derived word lengths for extemporaneous speech was wider than that for prepared speech.

(6) Derived medium length words were the most frequently used by Kennedy, followed by long words, then short words.

(a) In Kennedy's vocalizations, medium words have a narrower, more consistent range of derived word length mean stress values than either short or long words.

(b) In Kennedy's most highly stressed vocalizations, the word lengths that are the most stressed are also the most frequent. This occurs for both long and short words.

(7) Kennedy's words in the final third of a paragraph (or theme) tend to be lower stressed than other words.

Thematic analyses and psycholinguistic profiles will be presented for Lyndon B. Johnson and Richard M. Nixon in succeeding chapters. However, we will not provide the full range of detail on the psycholinguistic variables during the Dominican and Cambodian crises because this information is very similar to that just presented for the Berlin crisis. Thus, rather than present these data in redundant detail, we will simply provide a brief summary. (The complete, detailed analysis of the psycholinguistic data for the Dominican and Cambodian crises is available from the senior author upon request.) We will then offer some general conclusions in a comparative chapter, and will present additional information in tabular form which was not presented for Presidents Johnson and Nixon when their specific crises were discussed.

Summary

We have shown in this chapter that voice stress analysis provides a way to distinguish the thematic, substantive concerns of a speaker. Kennedy's stress level varies according to the topics of his presentations.

We have also demonstrated that Kennedy's prepared speeches, which dealt with crucial issues, were more highly stressed than were his extemporaneous vocalizations. Furthermore, other variables, such as part of speech and word length, were also indicators of Kennedy's level of psychological arousal.

Part of the reason for Kennedy's zigzag stress configuration across time, we have argued, is the fact that the 1961 Berlin crisis was an embedded crisis. It was in this sense part of a larger continuous confrontation, i.e., the Cold War. Thus, his stress level appears to be a combination of his reaction to the crisis itself and his feelings toward the larger issues of the Cold War. As a result, he alternates between belligerent and compromising stances in order to appear both peaceable and determined, rather than taking positions simply in response to the crisis events themselves.

Finally, the issue which concerned Kennedy the most was the possibility of a military confrontation with the Soviets. He was especially concerned over the possibility of a nuclear conflict growing out of the Berlin crisis.

4. Lyndon B. Johnson
and the Crisis in the
Dominican Republic

The Dominican crisis appears to be a "typical" crisis in that it involved a short, intense period of confrontation over high priority national goals. However, much like the 1961 Berlin crisis, the events in the Dominican Republic can be looked upon as an extended, critical international situation. As will be seen, a chronology of critical events spans a period of at least two years. But more precisely, President Johnson's vocalizations regarding the crisis cover a period of some four months. We now turn to a brief review of the substance of these vocalizations.

Overview of President Johnson's Verbal Statements
during the Dominican Crisis

Refer to table 4.1 in which the chronology of the Dominican crisis is plotted juxtaposed to the public pronouncements of President Johnson. It should be clear that our data have been gathered at discrete points during the crisis continuum of events and that they do not precisely match a comprehensive chronology.

Figure 4.1 plots the general stress values of each public utterance listed in the right-hand column of table 4.1. Overall, this curve constitutes a graphic presentation of the changing values of stress or physiological arousal in Lyndon Johnson when he speaks about Dominican events during the course of the crisis.

At an April 27 press conference, the president expressed his concern with the developing situation in the Dominican Republic. He called the situation "grave," and spoke of the continuing breakdown of public order in Santo Domingo. Further, he directed "the evacuation of those who wish to leave." At this point, the president expressed the hope that order could

Table 4.1   Chronology of the Dominican Crisis and Lyndon B. Johnson's public pronouncements.

Date	Chronology	Johnson's pronouncements
(1962)		
December	Free elections, Bosch elected	
(1963)		
(1964)		
September	Bosch removed from office/Reid Cabral new head of state	
(1965)		
January–April	Social and political conditions deteriorate	
April 24	Reid attempts arrest of junior officers/Confusion over occurrence of coup/First critical message received	
April 25	Johnson orders naval ready group/Reid arrested, Molina new head of state	
April 26	Wessin and de los Santos request U.S. troops/U.S. embassy achieves partial cease-fire/Evacuation procedures initiated	
April 27	Anti-Bosch leaders deliver ultimatum/American citizens endangered/Negotiations break down	News conference
April 28	Bennett informed Americans can't be protected/Benoit requests 1,200 U.S. troops/Johnson orders 400 troops to D.R.	Statement ordering troops into Dominican Republic
April 29	Bennett requests additional troops/OAS establishes international security zone	
April 30	Formal cease-fire signed/Three battalions dispatched/Three more battalions land	Statement on situation in D.R.
May 1	Cease-fire broken/2,000 troops arrive/OAS committee arrives in D.R.	
May 2	6,500 troops land in D.R.	Report to American people on situation in D.R.

Table 4.1   (Continued)

May 3		Remarks on Dominican situation
May 4		Request for additional appropriations
May 5	OAS negotiations cease-fire	
May 6	OAS creates peace force	
May 7	Benoit junta resigns/Troop deployment totals 21,000/Barreras assumes control	
May 27	600 U.S. Marines leave D.R.	
May 28		Remarks on Dominican situation
May 29	Johnson withdraws 1,700 troops	
June 1		News conference
June 3	Johnson announces all Marines to leave	
June 4	Last U.S. Marines leave D.R.	
July 4	Additional 1,400 removed; 10,900 still left	
July 9	300 troops leave	News conference
July 13		News conference
August 29		News conference
September 3	Garcia-Goday becomes head of state	
September 25	United States removes 2,100 troops	
October 21	Another 300 troops withdrawn	
(1966)		
June 1	Free elections held	
June 29	3,200 U.S. troops removed	
September 20	Last U.S. troops leave	

be restored in the Dominican Republic and that a peaceful solution to the problems could be found.

By the evening of the following day (April 28), however, the momentum of events had increased to the extent that the president felt obliged to deliver a nationally televised address to the American people. Johnson reported that authorities in the Dominican Republic could no longer guarantee the lives of U.S. citizens. Given this situation, the president stated that "I have ordered the Secretary of Defense to put the necessary American

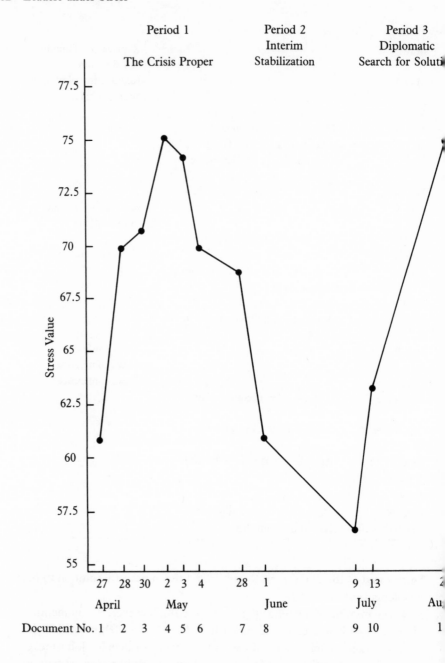

Figure 4.1   Stress levels by speech in Lyndon B. Johnson
during the 1965 crisis in the Dominican Republic.

troops ashore in order to give protection to hundreds of Americans who are still in the Dominican Republic and to escort them safely back to this country. . . . Pursuant to my instructions 400 Marines have already landed." Johnson called for a cease-fire among the contending forces, and indicated that the U.S. government would keep the Organization of American States (OAS) informed about the situation.

Two days later (April 30), in still another national TV broadcast, the president reported that violence and disorder had increased and that 200 Americans and other nationals had been evacuated. The president emphasized that "people trained outside the Dominican Republic are seeking to gain control," and that if they should be successful, they would thwart the aspirations of the Dominican people for social justice. In announcing that OAS representatives were leaving for the Dominican Republic, Johnson pointed out that the United States would "give its full support to the work of the OAS."

On May 2 the president delivered the key oral document of the Dominican crisis. In this lengthy speech, he presented the details of the turmoil of the previous weeks as perceived by the U.S. government. He apparently viewed the events in the Dominican Republic as a major crisis for the United States when he stated: "there are times in the affairs of nations when great principles are tested in an ordeal of conflict and danger. This is such a time for the American nations."

He described, again with great detail, the urgent communications between the U.S. embassy in Santo Domingo and the White House. In asserting that the U.S. officials in the Dominican Republic unanimously recommended urgent military intervention, Johnson stated that, "I knew there was no time to talk, to consult, or to delay." It is possible that the president viewed the situation as a personal challenge to himself: "I do not think that the American people expect their president to hesitate or to vacillate in the face of danger just because the decision is hard when life is in peril."

It should be emphasized that in this speech Johnson announced that 2,000 more troops had been landed and that he had ordered an additional 4,500 to be put ashore as soon as possible. This action represented a significant military commitment for the United States.

As is evident in figure 4.1, the speech of May 2 contained the highest level of stress of any speech in this crisis. The vocalizations of April 27, 28, and 30 produced progressively higher stress levels leading up to the key speech. These physiological data bear a good deal of resemblance to the increasing intensity of political developments in the Dominican Republic:

events progressed until it was necessary for the president on May 2—Sunday evening at 10:00 P.M.—to present a major national address which announced a significant increase in U.S. troop commitments, from 400 on April 28 to 6,500 on May 2, five days later.

From this high point in the stress data, stress levels declined progressively through five measurement points to July 9. On May 3 Johnson spoke at some length of the Dominican crisis in his "Remarks to the 10th National Legislative Conference, Building and Construction Trades Department, AFL-CIO." His comments here were essentially a review of previous positions, but stress levels, though lower than those of the key speech, remained quite high.

This downward trend continued on May 4, when the president spoke to a joint meeting of the House and Senate Appropriations, Foreign Relations, and Armed Services Committees. He again recounted the crisis events as a prelude to asking for an additional appropriation of $700 million to fund operations in Vietnam and the Dominican Republic. At the conclusion of his remarks, he reported that rooftop snipers were shooting at the U.S. embassy in Santo Domingo, but he indicated that he was hopeful that the OAS might achieve a satisfactory solution of the crisis.

Three weeks later, in a commencement address at Baylor University, Johnson's stress level, when discussing the Dominican Republic, had subsided somewhat from the May 4 level. The continuation of this trend is important because Johnson apparently perceived, or at least he announced, that the crisis had been concluded: "A cease-fire was achieved, bringing an end to the threat of wholesale bloodshed." Further, the president reflected that "for the first time in history the Organization of American States has created and sent to the soil of an American nation an international peace-keeping force. That may be the greatest achievement of all."

As an indication that the situation was apparently calming down, Johnson announced that 1,600 U.S. troops had been withdrawn during the previous two days as contributions from Latin American nations had been incorporated into the OAS peacekeeping force. The president authorized an additional withdrawal of 1,700 men in anticipation of a further "cooling off."

At a news conference on June 1, Johnson deemed the situation in the Dominican Republic to be serious and called upon the OAS to intensify its efforts to reach a peaceful settlement. Nevertheless, the president authorized a further withdrawal of 2,000 military personnel.

The lowest stress level exhibited by Johnson during this crisis occurred at his news conference of July 9, in which he was asked to evaluate the current situation in the Dominican Republic. He replied that "there is a minimum of disorder. There is some economic dislocation and some strikes that have given some difficulties, but under all the circumstances we have made remarkable progress." He reported that he was encouraged by the work of the OAS, which appeared to be moving toward a solution.

Thus, the low stress period from June 1 to July 9 corresponds to Johnson's apparent perceptions that, while the situation had not yet fully stabilized, it was clearly moving toward stabilization and that the most acute crisis period had passed. A concrete index of this perception was the continuing withdrawal of U.S. troops from the Dominican Republic.

Nevertheless, again referring to figure 4.1, how is it possible to explain the rather substantial increase in stress levels at the measurement points of July 13 and August 29? Johnson's (1971) memoirs appear to provide a plausible explanation for the seeming anomaly. The president (1971 : 202) recounts that the major problem to be solved after the cease-fire had been negotiated was "to encourage Dominicans to find the men and formula to lead them from stalemate to an interim government and elections." This was a frustrating exercise which resulted in three major initiatives and several minor ones. As a group, these included U.S. efforts to send individuals and teams of emissaries to find a solution for the restoration of orderly processes of government as well as special visits to the same end by the papal nuncio, the governor of Puerto Rico, and Abe Fortas, a personal friend of President Johnson. None of these were successful, but as Johnson (1971 : 203) relates:

> The third initiative finally succeeded. A special committee of the OAS, made up of Ambassadors Ilmar Penna Marinho of Brazil, Ramon de Clairmont Duenas of El Salvador, and Ellsworth Bunker of the United States, arrived in Santo Domingo on June 3, 1965. On June 18 the special committee issued a Declaration to the Dominican Republic. This document urged popular support for its proposal: peaceful free elections, a general amnesty, and a provisional government under Garcia Godoy, widely respected civilian who had been Foreign Minister under Bosch. Elections were to be held within nine months. This proposal, called the Act of Dominican Reconciliation, was finally accepted and the Garcia Godoy government was installed on September 3.

It was probably the ambiguity of that searching process, which stretched through the summer of 1965, that elevated the levels of stress in Johnson when he spoke of Dominican events on July 13 and August 29. On July 13 the president reported that there remained an urgent need for a peaceful solution in the Dominican Republic, but that compromise was clearly possible. By August 29 the OAS committee appeared on the verge of an agreement, and Johnson stated that the United States would support the ultimate arrangement. However, from the point of view of the president, if an agreement were not forthcoming it was possible that the situation might have deteriorated, with renewed disorder and violence, thereby requiring a further American response, including the possible reintroduction of U.S. troops. These possibilities must have been known to Johnson and presumably contributed to the high levels of stress at the two final measurement points.

Thus, figure 4.1 displays three separate psychophysiological situations. The first is the crisis proper, extending from April 27 through June 1. During this period Johnson reached a stress peak with the key national address of May 2, which announced a major U.S. troop commitment. The second, from June 1 to July 9, comprises a low stress period of diplomatic search for a lasting solution to the problems confronting the Dominican people. It is likely that the data for the third period, July 13 to August 28, are incomplete, and that we have analyzed only the *initial* increasing levels of stress relating to this situation. Further probing, which is not necessary for the present analysis, would provide a complete picture.

Stress Themes within the Crisis Documents

In figure 4.1 we plotted the stress values for each oral document in the crisis. These numbers represent the mean of all stress values of individual words for an entire document. We now want to look at data which sum the word stress values for standardized paragraphs. Put differently, we again want to drop down in our analysis from the document level to the paragraph level.

The data presented in table 4.2 are stress value scores for paragraphs or, more properly, themes within documents. A theme was established for each paragraph in a document before coding. These themes express the dominant, substantive thought of the paragraph, as explained in chapter 3.

In table 4.2 Z-scores are reported for each paragraph theme that is identified. Each cell position indicates both the stress level and the date on which the themes were publicly presented. It should be clear that the May 2 to June 1 period witnessed the greatest concentration of high Z-score themes. This period, therefore, represents the period of highest physiological arousal in the president's voice and thus in all likelihood indicates a period of intense stress and concern for him as a person. Johnson experienced no heavy or extreme stress during the April 27 to 30 time span, lead-

Table 4.2   Stress stratification of paragraph themes, Lyndon B. Johnson, Dominican Crisis, 1965.

Z-Scores	April 27
Extreme stress 1.96 and above	
Heavy stress 1.95 to 1.64	
Moderate stress 1.63 to 1.04	1.26 Grave situation in D.R./evacuation ordered
Average stress 1.03 to −1.04	
Low stress −1.05 to −1.63	−1.26 Grave situation/hope for order
Slight stress −1.64 to −1.95	
Minimal stress <−1.96	

	April 28
Extreme stress 1.96 and above	
Heavy stress 1.95 to 1.64	
Moderate stress 1.63 to 1.04	
Average stress 1.03 to −1.04	.26 Troops ordered ashore to protect Americans .15 Congressional leaders informed of president's decision .05 President appeals for cease-fire again/OAS to be kept informed − .14 Congress supports decision/American lives are in danger − .35 400 Marines have landed
Low stress −1.05 to −1.63	
Slight stress −1.64 to −1.95	
Minimal stress <−1.96	

	April 30
Extreme stress 1.96 and above	
Heavy stress 1.95 to 1.64	

Table 4.2   (Continued)

Moderate stress 1.63 to 1.04	1.11 Aspirations of Dominicans threatened
Average stress 1.03 to −1.04	.85 The world watches the OAS .82 U.S. supports principles of OAS .62 OAS representatives go to D.R. − .17 Shaky cease-fire achieved
Low stress −1.05 to −1.63	
Slight stress −1.64 to −1.95	
Minimal stress <−1.96	−2.28 American troops in D.R. for last 2 days

	May 2 (Key)
Extreme stress 1.96 and above	3.16 No more Communist governments in Western Hemisphere 2.77 All revolutionaries in D.R. not Communist
Heavy stress 1.95 to 1.64	1.66 No desire to interfere
Moderate stress 1.63 to 1.04	1.59 Revolution hindered government
Average stress 1.03 to −1.04	1.01 Ambassador Bennett recalled .91 Change should be peaceful: non-Communist .72 Communist-inspired revolutionary disorders .71 Report of danger from ambassador .68 Some might have waited to send troops .54 Vacillation would be dangerous .44 Appeal for order ignored .42 U.S. efforts for peace .40 U.S. has alerted other nations .35 Additional forces ordered to D.R. .25 U.S. to keep commitments .16 Report to OAS/Prevent Communist takeover .15 Quote from Simón Bolivar .11 Truth difficult to establish .03 Repeats paragraph 22 .00 U.S. hopes for free, decent government − .12 Consultations of Ambassador Bunker − .19 A difficult decision − .38 Received cable of urgent danger − .41 OAS team in D.R. − .44 Description of early events − .54 Situation in D.R. out of control − .59 No return to oppression/No delay

Table 4.2 (Continued)

	− .81 No more Cubas
	− .84 Crisis emerges
	− .88 Dominican people to choose own government
	− .90 American troops ordered to D.R./Evacuation of civilians in progress
	− .93 Dominicans an oppressed people
Low stress −1.05 to −1.63	−1.13 Time of national ordeal
	−1.52 U.S. condemned Trujillo government
Slight stress −1.64 to −1.95	−1.72 Issue to OAS
	−1.80 Hemisphere interested in no more Cubas
Minimal stress <−1.96	−2.00 Stakes in the D.R.
	−3.37 Report of situation
	−3.37 Some elements are clear
	−3.70 Closing words

	May 3
Extreme stress 1.96 and above	3.25 U.S. will protect its citizens
	2.28 Country team unanimous in requesting troops
	2.08 No civilians have died
Heavy stress 1.95 to 1.64	1.67 U.S. civilians evacuated successfully
	1.65 Possible epidemic and threat to American lives
Moderate stress 1.63 to 1.04	1.39 Report of troop landings
Average stress 1.03 to −1.04	.58 Measures for stability under way
	.34 No time for indecision
	− .14 U.S. efforts appreciated by other nations
	− .50 Cable told of danger to U.S. lives
	− .80 Vietnam a great problem
Low stress −1.05 to −1.63	
Slight stress −1.64 to −1.95	−2.01 Assessment of situation made
	−2.17 D.R. government overthrown
	−2.78 Bennett reported on D.R.
	−5.68 Reflections on Congress
Minimal stress <−1.96	

	May 4
Extreme stress 1.96 and above	5.30 Needs in D.R. important
	3.33 Bullets entered ambassador's office
	3.07 Military plans consummated
	2.78 Many Communists involved

Table 4.2   (Continued)

	2.73 U.S. troops evacuating civilians
	2.72 Recounting of alert
Heavy stress 1.95 to 1.64	1.93 Revolutionary leaders have Communist history
Moderate stress 1.63 to 1.04	1.31 Appreciative of gathering 1.24 Urgent request for troops received 1.15 Sufficient U.S. troops are present
Average stress 1.03 to −1.04	.87 Rush and McNamara will answer questions .78 Security of others at stake .75 Recounting early moments of crisis .65 U.S. anticipated difficulty in D.R. .56 Congress informed of troop landing .52 Health problem exists .04 U.S. not aggressor in D.R. − .04 Press asked to leave − .15 Desire to review thoughts of committee − .28 Seriousness of events forced action − .85 Not routine appropriations − .88 Hope OAS plan for interim government − .95 Snipering endangers lives
Low stress −1.05 to −1.63	−1.32 Six congressional committees to discuss security −1.36 U.S. informed others of action −1.51 U.S. anticipates OAS action −1.62 U.S. awaits OAS recommendation
Slight stress −1.64 to −1.95	
Minimal stress < −1.96	−2.04 More appropriations needed −2.07 Turmoil exists in D.R. −2.33 Increased appropriations necessary −6.01 U.S. disappointed in OAS delay

	May 28
Extreme stress 1.96 and above	3.80 Dominicans want constitutional government 3.30 Food has been distributed
Heavy stress 1.95 to 1.64	1.90 Political solutions under way 1.74 Communists thwarted
Moderate stress 1.63 to 1.04	1.17 U.S. and OAS have reacted 1.12 Dominicans to shape own future 1.10 What are the next moves?
Average stress 1.03 to −1.04	.85 Hemisphere's people share Dominican hopes .73 Revolutionary explosion in D.R. .68 More unity in hemisphere needed .64 Hemisphere's nations have common aims

Table 4.2 (Continued)

	.16 U.S. met its responsibilities
	.00 Dominicans must make decisions
	− .02 Peacekeeping force a great achievement
	− .13 U.S. a part of inter-American force
	− .29 Peaceful social atmosphere sought
	− .51 First OAS international peacekeeping force
	− .65 Military task force in place
	− .65 Zone of refuge established
	− .68 No extremists to be in government
	− .69 End to violence sought
Low stress −1.05 to −1.63	−1.15 Some U.S. troops to be withdrawn −1.27 A solution is emerging
Slight stress −1.64 to −1.95	
Minimal stress < −1.96	−2.45 Major evacuation took place −3.56 Cease-fire achieved

	June 1
Extreme stress 1.96 and above	6.41 Situation allows U.S. troop withdrawal
Heavy stress 1.95 to 1.64	1.88 One battalion ordered withdrawn
Moderate stress 1.63 to 1.04	1.30 Communists participate in revolution 1.15 U.S. will contribute to peace
Average stress 1.03 to −1.04	.89 Hopeful of an OAS solution .81 Hope for a broad-based government in D.R. − .02 Moderates seem to be gaining − .34 Situation remains serious − .68 U.S. intervention necessary
Low stress −1.05 to −1.63	−1.50 No desire to impose U.S. solutions
Slight stress −1.64 to −1.95	
Minimal stress < −1.96	−2.17 Pleased with inter-American force

	July 9
Extreme stress 1.96 and above	
Heavy stress 1.95 to 1.64	1.72 Situation in D.R. beginning to stabilize
Moderate stress 1.63 to 1.04	

Table 4.2 (Continued)

Average stress
1.03 to −1.04

Low stress
−1.05 to −1.63

Slight stress
−1.64 to −1.95

Minimal stress   −2.91 OAS doing a creditable job
<−1.96

	July 13

Extreme stress
1.96 and above

Heavy stress
1.95 to 1.64

Moderate stress
1.63 to 1.04

Average stress   .48 Compromise between groups possible
1.03 to −1.04   − .84 Need for urgent peaceful solution in D.R.

Low stress
−1.05 to −1.63

Slight stress
−1.64 to −1.95

Minimal stress
<−1.96

	August 29

Extreme stress
1.96 and above

Heavy stress
1.95 to 1.64

Moderate stress
1.63 to 1.04

Average stress   .82 OAS committee recommendation
1.03 to −1.04   .33 Report on OAS committee
                      .32 All encouraged to support decision
                  − .45 Meeting with secretary of state

Low stress   −1.07 U.S. to support OAS committee recommendation
−1.05 to −1.63

Slight stress
−1.64 to −1.95

Minimal stress
<−1.96

ing up to the key speech of May 2. Likewise, during the aftermath period in which a diplomatic solution was sought, no high stress scores are in evidence.

In examining the themes, we again collapsed the substantive issues into large composite themes in the manner described in the previous chapter. In doing so, we looked for multiple representations among our themes. Ten clusters were easily identified:

Concern for U.S. civilians
Concern over Communist takeover
Military maneuvers and concerns
Dominican Republic politics
U.S. concerns/decision making
Hemispheric concerns
Solution/agreement
Organization of American States (OAS)
Description of events
Congress/appropriations

These ten composite themes were developed from lists of possible composite themes suggested by the project staff. These ten are the most distinct and encompass 94 percent of the total paragraph themes. Less than 10 percent of the themes were cross-compositional; e.g., "Hemispheric interest in no more Cubas" was placed in both the "Concern over Communist takeover" and the "Hemispheric concerns" composite theme.

We feel comfortable in stating on the basis of our physiological data that the two issues—the extension of Communist influence in the Caribbean beyond Cuba and the protection of American citizens abroad—were of greatest concern to the president. These two themes represent a posture that can be labelled "U.S. national interest." Thus, the extreme stress stratum for the Dominican crisis can best be described as one in which two very basic national interest issues resulted in the evidence of substantial stress in the president's voice.

If we sum all the Z-scores across all strata by composite theme, it is possible to develop a hierarchy of concerns as perceived by President Johnson during the Dominican crisis. This hierarchy appears in table 4.3. Keep in mind that all ten of these composite themes are separate topics for the president. An analyst might have expected that a description of the gravity of the situation which we have included in "U.S. concerns/decision making" would have been at the top of the hierarchy. However, not finding this is consistent with previous research (Wiegele, 1978b), which established that

Table 4.3   Composite hierarchy of concerns across stress strata, Lyndon B. Johnson, 1965.

Theme designation	Summed Z-Scores	N	$\bar{X}$	Z-Scores for composite themes
Concern for U.S. civilians	12.40	8	1.55	2.18
Concern over Communist takeover	12.94	11	1.18	1.59
Military maneuvers and concerns	15.77	15	1.05	1.38
Dominican Republic politics	10.94	13	.84	1.05
U.S. concerns/decision making	15.63	34	.46	.44
Hemispheric concerns	.55	7	.08	− .16
Solution/agreement	− 5.71	15	− .38	− .89
OAS	−10.93	18	− .61	−1.26
Description of events	−25.38	25	−1.02	−1.91
Congress/appropriations	−11.80	9	−1.31	−2.37

precipitating acts, conditions, or stimuli which force decisional choice are perceived by leaders as "givens" once they occur. These "givens" are less stressing than the subsequent political and military ambiguities that flow from a specific decisional context. Again, the number of cases in each composite theme did not influence the ranking of stress values.

Note also in table 4.3 that the single most stressing theme for the president relates to the protection of U.S. citizens abroad. Several interpretations could be adduced to explain this, but perhaps the most convincing has to do with an appraisal of Lyndon Johnson as a leader whose major political interests were in the domestic realm. Failure to protect U.S. citizens in the Dominican Republic might have been perceived by Johnson as leading to strident domestic criticism which he was unwilling to risk, even at the expense of conducting an intervention which was bound to produce international criticism.

Partial corroboration for this judgment can be obtained from a report by the Center for Strategic Studies. It states that, "There was a serious threat to the lives of foreign nationals from April 27 on. That threat justified the first stage landings on April 28 which had as their purpose the evacuation of Americans and other foreigners" (Center for Strategic Studies, 1966: viii).

Coupled with the protection of U.S. citizens theme in terms of high Z-score values is the extension of Communist influence theme. Johnson frequently used the phraseology of "no more Cubas" in his public statements on the Dominican situation, recalling past U.S. difficulties in the Caribbean. After the Cuban revolution, the Bay of Pigs, and the Cuban missile crisis, Johnson must have sensed the strong potential for the Dominican situation, if not successfully addressed by the United States, to become a damaging domestic political issue. Again, this perception probably contributed to elevated stress levels on this topic.

As one reads down the hierarchy of composite themes, one is struck by the shift from conflictful behavior to more normal, ongoing behaviors. As in the Berlin crisis, military and other action-oriented themes cause more stress than themes relating to diplomatic negotiations or domestic political bargaining.

For example, the themes with the lowest stress levels are the issues dealing with the maintenance of ongoing, "routine" foreign policy. In 1965, Johnson had little reason to be stressful about asking for appropriations from Congress or about submitting his actions to congressional review. He had excellent relations with Congress; and foreign policy was seen as the president's constitutional domain. Congress was simply expected to support a president in his pursuit of U.S. policy interests.

OAS and hemispheric concerns were probably seen as peripheral to the U.S. action. They were necessary to keep in mind, but again only to maintain proper diplomatic relationships. As such, they fit only tangentially into the hard calculations of decision making and are not stressful to the president.

Even the solution, which, like the descriptions, one would expect to be stressful, can be analyzed as the return to maintenance of normal relations. The crisis is over; the actions are taken. In this crisis, the solution and the agreements were not uncertainties; the United States had put down the disturbance and now was biding its time for calm to be imposed and transferred to the Dominican nationals.

The next two composite themes straddle the two dimensions. U.S. and Dominican concerns are both central to the reasons for and result from the crisis, thus fitting into a conflict-reactive dimension. But they also reflect the concern for maintaining the status quo.

Finally, the three most stressful composite themes all are conflict-reactive centered. The first two are U.S. national security related, as already discussed, and the third deals with the military action itself. Being the least normal of actions, it is consistent that this latter type should be the most stressful. As opposed to the ongoing relationship with OAS (Z-score$=1.26$), the unique threats and actions are more fraught with danger and uncertainty and thus produce higher stress levels ($Z=2.18, 1.59, 1.38$).

Word-Level Analysis

Our data set for the word-level analysis of Lyndon Johnson consists of 6,076 words spoken in eleven speeches during the course of the Dominican crisis. Table 4.4 presents the means and standard deviations for stress and derived word length in the aggregate. A breakdown for stress by date and for all the psycholinguistic variables is summarized in table 4.5. It should be noted that word length is recoded for table 4.5 as it was for Kennedy.

Table 4.5 shows that Johnson reaches a maximum mean stress level of 75.52 on May 3, 1965, while his minimum is 56.01 on July 9, 1965. The mean stress value for Johnson's prepared speeches is much higher than that for his unprepared speeches. Johnson exhibits the highest level of stress on long words and the lowest level on short words. We find also that Johnson tends to be more highly stressed on the major parts of speech than on the minor parts of speech, with verbs and adjectives being the most highly stressed of all words. We will return to this information in more detail when we present our comparative analyses in chapter 6.

General Analyses of President Johnson

Thematic analysis. As we did in the Berlin crisis, we might ask whether an analyst could have identified tactical directions by engaging in voice stress analyses of Lyndon Johnson's vocalizations during the Dominican situation. Again, perhaps the best way to answer this question is to examine table 4.2, which displays Z-scores for each speech. At the top of the table is the date for the speech; if the observer reads down from the date, the "extreme" and "heavy" stress themes are easily noted by date. Let us again call these two categories combined "severe" stress.

The statements of April 27, 28, and 30 contained no severe stress. Surprisingly, in the key speech of May 2 there is little in the severe stress range that might alert an analyst to Johnson's internal concerns. However, on May 3 Johnson provides a major tipoff: of the five severe stress themes,

Table 4.4   Stress and word length, mean and standard deviation: Lyndon B. Johnson.

	Mean	SD	N
Stress	71.201	15.703	6,076
Length	21.434	10.724	6,076

Table 4.5 Stress breakdown for Johnson.

| Stress by | Grand mean = 71.20 | |
	Mean	N of words
Speech		
1. (4-27-65)	61.11	115
2. (4-28-65)	70.17	155
3. (4-30-65)	70.60	332
4. (5-02-65)	75.31	2,035
5. (5-03-65)	75.52	624
6. (5-04-65)	70.64	1,508
7. (5-28-65)	69.23	452
8. (6-01-65)	59.67	566
9. (7-09-65)	56.01	78
10. (7-13-65)	62.50	72
11. (8-29-65)	75.01	139
Prepared		
Prepared	72.70	5,222
Extemporaneous	62.04	853
Length		
Short	69.59	2,444
Medium	71.15	2,193
Long	74.01	1,438
Part of speech		
Noun	70.61	2,161
Verb	72.73	1,245
Adjective	72.38	1,047
Adverb	71.71	426
Filled pause	69.96	95
Preposition	69.84	492
Article	70.34	268
Conjunction	68.06	341

four refer to concern for U.S. civilians. The knowledge that this issue resulted in severe stress for the president might have suggested to an analyst that the United States was especially sensitive to the question of civilians in the Dominican Republic. Such sensitivity appears to have been uncovered by voice stress analysis.

Two of the severe stress themes enunciated on May 4 involved references to Communist involvement in the Dominican Republic. Though this is by no means as strong a cue as the four themes dealing with civilians on

May 3, it is, nevertheless, a hint that Johnson viewed Communist activity as highly threatening. Thus, in allowing voice stress–generated inferences to guide the construction of an analytic framework, a researcher could construct an operational milieu by piercing a logic system which might possibly be undecipherable by other means.

Psycholinguistic analysis. As a summary of our psycholinguistic findings in this chapter, we present below in outline form a profile of Lyndon B. Johnson as a language processor during the Dominican crisis.

(1) Johnson's prepared statements and speeches were more highly stressed than his extemporaneous pronouncements.

(2) Across all crisis verbalizations, Johnson exhibited the highest stress on verbs.
  (a) In prepared statements and speeches Johnson exhibited the highest stress on verbs.
  (b) In extemporaneous vocalizations Johnson exhibited the highest stress on adjectives.

(3) Across all crisis verbalizations the three highest stressed parts of speech for Johnson were verbs, adjectives, and adverbs.

(4) Across all crisis verbalizations the three least stressed parts of speech for Johnson were filled pauses, prepositions, and conjunctions.

(5) Johnson's electronically derived long words were consistently the most highly stressed, followed by medium, and then short words.
  (a) A clear difference in the range of stress scores in derived word lengths existed between Johnson's prepared and extemporaneous vocalizations.

(6) Derived medium length words (36.1 percent) were the most frequently used by Johnson, followed by long words (34.3 percent), then short words (29.6 percent).
  (a) Johnson's medium words had a more consistent, narrower range of stress values than his short or long words.
  (b) Johnson increased his use of derived short words toward the end of the crisis.
  (c) In the middle of the crisis, the most frequent word lengths were also the most highly stressed for Johnson.

(7) Johnson displayed no trends that relate mean stress scores to the position of his words in a paragraph.

Summary

Much of what we found in our study of Kennedy was replicated in the examination of Johnson. Johnson's stress levels fluctuated according to the substantive topics of his speech. Moreover, Johnson's prepared speeches were more highly stressed than were his extemporaneous speeches. Part of speech and word length also had an effect on his levels of stress. The issue which concerned Johnson the most, in contrast to Kennedy, was not the possibility of large-scale military involvement, but the safety of American civilians in the Dominican Republic.

The crisis in the Dominican Republic was a discrete situation not linked to a larger international context. The patterning of Johnson's stress levels through the crisis distinguished him from Kennedy, in that there was a clearly discernable pattern in Johnson's configuration across time which was consistent with the political evolution of the crisis itself.

5. Richard M. Nixon
and the Cambodian Crisis

As with the other crises which we have discussed, we will apply a conceptually expanded definition of crisis to the Cambodian incursion. While this situation is perhaps further from "classical" definitions of crisis than either the Berlin or Dominican Republic cases, we feel comfortable in treating the Cambodian incursion as a crisis.

Whether events meet academic definitions of crisis, however, is not always a true measure of their severity or necessarily of their crisis nature. If one's focus is at the individual level of analysis, the critical questions relate to an individual's perceptions of whether he or she is confronted by or involved in a crisis. Even a casual reader of Nixon's memoirs will be struck by the former president's description of Cambodian events in the rhetoric of crisis (Nixon, 1978:445–469). Indeed, he employs the label "Cambodian crisis" to refer to that cluster of occurrences during 1970 (Nixon, 1978:466). For example, speaking of the period prior to the incursion Nixon (1978:447) wrote, "The whole situation over Cambodia and Vietnam was becoming so tense that I felt I had to make a very painful personal decision." Or, "I never had any illusions about the shattering effect a decision to go into Cambodia would have on public opinion at home. I knew that opinions among my major foreign policy advisors were deeply divided over the issue of widening the war, and I recognized that it could mean personal and political catastrophe for me and my administration" (Nixon, 1978:449–450). Nixon (1978:454) describes the period of reaction after the decision as one of "great tension." Indeed "those few days after Kent State were among the darkest of my presidency" (Nixon, 1978:457). Thus, Nixon perceived himself to be in a crisis not only caused by the accelerated pace of events taking place in Cambodia which could have jeopardized the administration's strategy in Vietnam, but also intensified by the outburst of public demonstration coupled with staff disaffection. It would be difficult to find a more compelling example of individually perceived stress and crisis.

As we have done previously, we will provide an overview of the president's vocalizations during the Cambodian incursion. We will then offer data and analysis of the stressed themes, followed by a psycholinguistic analysis. Our conclusions, again, will explore analytic influences combined with a psycholinguistic profile.

Overview of President Nixon's Verbal Statements during the Cambodian Crisis

Table 5.1 presents the now familiar graphic schema in which we display a chronology of events juxtaposed beside a chronology of the president's vocalizations. We have seven measurement points for Nixon, which comprise a large number of words for voice stress analysis.

President Richard M. Nixon addressed the American public concerning the progress toward achieving peace in Vietnam on April 20, 1970. In a nationally televised speech, he announced that the Vietnamization process, until then something of an experiment, had been successful and that an additional 150,000 U.S. troops would be withdrawn over the next year.

Nixon also warned the North Vietnamese government that it would be taking "grave risks" should it use the occasion to jeopardize the security of the remaining American troops. He realized the import of this admonition in view of the fact that, although the number of Americans killed in action had declined to the lowest in five years, the North Vietnamese were increasing their troop strength in Laos and Cambodia. He concluded by thanking the American people for their perseverance and sacrifice. Figure 5.1 indicates that this opening document of the crisis was a very low stress speech.

Ten days later, on April 30, Nixon announced the incursion into Cambodia. In providing a brief political history of relations among Cambodia, North Vietnam, and the United States, he emphasized the questionable ability of Cambodia to defend itself against North Vietnamese aggression. The president spelled out three options that were available to decision makers: (1) do nothing, (2) send massive military aid, or (3) send a joint U.S.–South Vietnamese force to clear North Vietnamese troops from the sanctuaries.

He announced his choice of the third option and defended it on the grounds that if the North Vietnamese were allowed to remain in the sanctuaries, the continued withdrawal of American troops from Indochina would

Table 5.1   Chronology of the Cambodian Crisis and Richard M. Nixon's public pronouncements.

Date	Chronology	Nixon's pronouncements
(1969)		
March 17	Beginning of Cambodian bombing	
(1970)		
March 18	Prince Sihanouk ousted	
April 20	Nixon announces withdrawal of 150,000 troops	Address to the nation
April 22	One-fourth of Cambodia occupied by enemy troops	
April 26	Incursion decision consummated	
April 30	Beginning of Cambodian incursion	Address to the nation
May 1	Elimination of all sanctuaries authorized	
May 5	Students killed at Kent State University	
May 8		News conference
May 26	End of Cambodian bombing	
May 30	End of Cambodian incursion	
June 3		Address to the nation on Cambodian sanctuary
Second week of June	Withdrawal of American troops begins	
June 30	Last American troops withdrawn	
July 1		Conversation with the president
July 30		News conference
October 7		Address to the nation

be halted, thereby delaying the achievement of a final peace. Nixon then recounted the peace initiatives begun by the U.S. government in an attempt to bring an end to the war; and he underscored the intransigence of the North Vietnamese at the negotiating table. He closed by asking the American people not to support the president, but rather the American troops in Vietnam. Henry Kissinger (1979: 504) recalls:

> Adding rhetoric out of proportion to the subject though not to the stresses of the weeks preceding it, the President emphasized that America would not be "humiliated"; we would not succumb to "anarchy"; we

would not act like a "pitiful, helpless giant." Nor would he take "the easy political path" of blaming it all on the previous administrations. It was vintage Nixon.

This critical speech, which announced a major American foreign policy decision, produced the highest level of stress in Nixon during the period of the Cambodian crisis.

One week later, on May 8, after the tragedy at Kent State University, the president held a press conference to respond to questions concerning student protest demonstrations against American involvement in Southeast Asia. Stating that he was not surprised at the intensity of the protests, the president expressed his desire to achieve the same ends that the protestors sought: peace, an end to bloodshed, the elimination of the draft, and withdrawal from Vietnam. In response to a direct question concerning National Guard actions at Kent State University, Nixon refused to be specific until, he felt, all the facts had been accumulated. He vowed to find ways to deal with violent crowds without endangering the lives of innocent people. Moreover, he expressed a desire, if the situation allowed, to meet personally with demonstrators.

As for Vietnamization, the president reiterated his belief that the South Vietnamese army was improving as a fighting force. He emphasized that the Cambodian incursion allowed six to eight months' time for Vietnamization to take hold. With regard to Cambodia's future, Nixon admitted that little progress had been made in the effort to support and maintain Cambodia's neutrality, but that negotiations were underway toward that end. In response to an inquiry regarding the decision to order American troops to Cambodia, Nixon accepted full responsibility. Finally, the president indicated that he viewed the incursion as a limited operation and the American troops would be withdrawn by the end of June.

Given the tense domestic situation flowing from the Kent State shootings, an analyst might have expected the overall levels of stress in Nixon to have been extremely high. On the contrary, we found the mean stress value for this press conference to be quite low, indeed the second lowest measurement point for the entire crisis (see figure 5.1). We will address the reasons for this apparent anomaly in the next section, when we discuss composite themes.

President Nixon delivered a major speech on the Cambodian crisis on June 3, 1970. On national television, he declared the Cambodian incursion the most successful operation of the war. Nixon told the American people that the amount of enemy supplies and equipment captured was higher

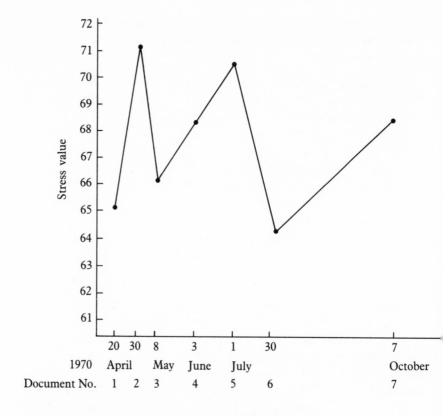

Figure 5.1   Stress levels by speech in Richard M. Nixon
during the 1970 crisis in Cambodia.

than anticipated, that U.S. casualties were lower than expected, and that over one-half of the American troops involved in the incursion had already been withdrawn. The president went on to describe the long-range impact of the operation. By eliminating an immediate and direct danger to American troops in South Vietnam, it afforded precious time to train South Vietnamese soldiers. In doing so, it insured the continuance and success of the administration's troop withdrawal program.

Turning his focus to the North Vietnamese government, Nixon indicated that the door to negotiations remained wide open. He expressed appreciation for the support he had received from the American people; and he assured the nation that if he had not acted in a forceful manner, the credibility of the United States would have been questioned. Nixon closed the speech with a vow to bring peace to Southeast Asia.

Refer again to figure 5.1. While the stress level for June 3 is elevated compared to that of May 8 (the immediate aftermath of the Kent State episode), it must be described as moderate relative to the crisis as a whole.

Almost a month later, on July 1, Nixon again addressed the nation to announce that no American ground troops remained in Cambodia and that they would not be sent there again. However, he pointed out that South Vietnamese troops had not yet withdrawn, remaining instead to complete the elimination of the sanctuaries.

President Nixon reiterated the U.S. commitment to maintain the neutrality of Cambodia. When asked what the U.S. reaction would be if the Lon Nol government fell to the Communists, the president replied that American troops would continue to fight and that ultimately the North Vietnamese would be defeated in the South. In reply to a question concerning the possibility of reescalation in the event of increased enemy activity, Nixon stated his willingness to dispatch U.S. air power to defend American troops. He added, however, that the current status of the conflict did not indicate the need for future reescalation. The president defended his decision not to seek the approval of Congress for the incursion based upon Congress' tendency toward slow deliberation and, more important, upon the need for a surprise attack. Had he gone to Congress, he stated, an attack would have been impossible; instead of losing 330 men, the United States might have suffered three or four thousand casualties.

The July 1 appearance on television, a "Conversation with the President" format, was extremely stressful for Nixon (see figure 5.1). These vocalizations were only slightly less stressing than the April 30 speech which announced the incursion. A possible explanation for this is that by July 1 only a month had passed since the incursion had begun and the Kent State shootings had taken place. During this time period the mood of the national news media had become extremely critical and reporters' questions were sharply hostile. It appears that on July 1, Nixon may have felt threatened by what seemed to be a general lack of approval for the incursion and public dismay at the Kent State events.

In a news conference televised from California on July 30, the president expressed his belief that because of the Cambodian incursion, the North Vietnamese government was in a weaker negotiating position in Paris. When asked to comment on the lack of communication between the administration and college students, Nixon replied that as president he was willing to accept the responsibility for ending the war. But, he continued, college administrators and faculty must take the responsibility for making school curricula richer and more worthwhile. The president felt that some of the protestors' anger, which was directed at the government, was due to an emptiness in the lives of college students. He urged university officials to accept the responsibility for making college studies more rewarding. These were all relatively innocuous issues which had little significant political import. Thus the stress level on July 30 was the lowest of the entire crisis period.

On October 7, Nixon again addressed the American public on national television to outline a new peace proposal approved by the governments of South Vietnam, Laos, and Cambodia. He attributed the existence of this proposal to the success of the Vietnamization process over the past eighteen months. The following steps were suggested: first, a cease-fire in-place in all of Indochina; second, the formation of an international Indochina Peace Conference, which would exist as a separate entity from the Paris peace talks currently under way; and third, negotiation of a timetable for the complete withdrawal of all American troops. He challenged Hanoi to accept the proposal. Stress levels in this statement were moderate and similar to those of June 3.

Stress Themes within the Crisis Documents

Consistent with our analysis of Berlin and the Dominican Republic, we disaggregated the speeches dealing with Cambodia (see table 5.3) into paragraphs and reaggregated the paragraphs into substantive, composite themes. Fifteen composite themes were uncovered. Table 5.2 lists these themes in hierarchical order by the mean Z-score theme stress value.

Generally, the analyses of these themes and the inferences drawn from them follow closely the results of the Berlin and Dominican analyses. Conflict-reactive, uncertain, and future-oriented types of composite themes fall at the high levels of the stress stratification, with maintenance issues and descriptive themes at the lower level.

There are four themes that are very stressful to President Nixon: the U.S. relationship with Cambodia, the South Vietnamese role in the incursion, the outcome of the incursion, and the North Vietnamese aggression/fighting. All four deal with the variables over which the president apparently could exercise little control: South Vietnam, North Vietnam, Cambodia, and the future. Nixon, as with most decision makers, exhibited stress on issues which contained major elements of uncertainty and therefore uncontrollability.

Kissinger (1979:240) explained the administration's thinking on Cambodian neutrality:

Table 5.2 Composite hierarchy of concerns across stress strata, Richard M. Nixon, 1970.

Theme designation	Summed Z-Scores	N	X̄	Z-Scores for composite themes
U.S. relationship to Cambodia	13.83	15	.92	2.67
South Vietnamese role	8.17	9	.91	2.64
Outcome of incursion	9.52	16	.60	1.69
North Vietnamese aggression/fighting	7.23	15	.48	1.32
Withdrawal from Cambodia/Southeast Asia	1.07	14	.08	.10
Diplomatic considerations	.86	13	.07	.06
U.S. determination	.39	15	.03	− .06
The sanctuaries	− .09	10	−.01	− .18
Justification of incursion	−1.07	9	−.12	− .52
No U.S. return to Cambodia	−3.77	6	−.13	− .55
Domestic turmoil	−4.72	22	−.21	− .79
Congress	−1.61	4	−.40	−1.38
The role of the president	−6.76	11	−.61	−2.02
Statements about peace	−8.57	13	−.66	−2.17
Decision context	−9.68	14	−.69	−2.27

Revisionists have sometimes focused on the Nixon Administration's alleged assault on the "neutral" status of a "peaceful" country. These charges overlook that the issue concerned territory which was no longer Cambodian in any practical sense. For four years as many as four North Vietnamese divisions had been operating on Cambodian soil from a string of base areas along the South Vietnamese border. . . . From these territories North Vietnamese forces would launch attacks into South Vietnam, inflict casualties, disrupt government, and then withdraw to the protection of a formally neutral country. It requires calculated advocacy, not judgment, to argue that the United States was violating the neutrality of a peaceful country when with Cambodian encouragement we, in self-defense, sporadically bombed territories in which for years no Cambodian writ had run, which were either minimally populated or totally unpopulated by civilians, and which were occupied in violation of Cambodian neutrality by an enemy killing hundreds of Americans and South Vietnamese a week from these sanctuaries.

Though we have no doubt that Nixon believed in the correctness of his policy, the simple fact that the United States allowed the recognized war

Table 5.3   Stress stratification of paragraph themes, Richard M. Nixon, Cambodian Crisis, 1970.

Z-Scores	April 20
Extreme stress 1.96 and above	
Heavy stress 1.95 to 1.64	1.70 Threat: don't escalate level of conflict
Moderate stress 1.63 to 1.04	
Average stress 1.03 to −1.04	.84 Escalation in Laos and Cambodia .30 North Vietnamese troops moving into Laos − .06 North Vietnamese moving men and supplies South −1.04 North Vietnamese troops moving against Cambodia
Low stress −1.05 to −1.63	−1.21 Overall decline in North Vietnamese forces −1.23 North Vietnam guilty of aggression in Indochina
Slight stress −1.64 to −1.95	
Minimal stress <−1.96	

	April 30
Extreme stress 1.96 and above	5.85 North Vietnam has not respected Cambodian neutrality 3.15 Option 1: U.S. could do nothing about Cambodia 2.95 In one area, U.S.–South Vietnam joint action necessary 2.53 Time for action has come 2.08 U.S. cannot appear helpless
Heavy stress 1.95 to 1.64	1.68 South Vietnam a major actor in Cambodia
Moderate stress 1.63 to 1.04	1.63 North Vietnamese aggression has increased 1.59 Americans are coming home from Vietnam 1.56 Political considerations unimportant 1.31 North Vietnam might outflank South Vietnam 1.20 Possible threat to South Vietnam from Cambodia 1.08 North Vietnam has kept military sanctuaries in Cambodia
Average stress 1.03 to −1.04	1.00 Key attack under way tonight .94 Sanctuaries contain base camps, etc. .91 Anarchy rampant in world .85 U.S. has made many concessions .75 U.S. will not merely protest diplomatically .73 U.S. will not be defeated .71 U.S. & South Vietnam to attack sanctuaries .60 Nixon threatens North Vietnam .55 U.S. has no desire to violate neutrality

Table 5.3   Nixon (Continued)

.47 Cambodia has requested help
.42 Great decisions have been made in Oval Office
.42 U.S. has reached a decision
.36 U.S. cannot tolerate rejection of conciliation
.31 Option 3: Clear out sanctuaries
.23 Decision will have political effects
.21 Previous decision to withdraw troops
.19 U.S. has respected Cambodian neutrality
.04 U.S. to end war
− .03 U.S. cannot fail to meet challenge
− .07 U.S. to avoid wider war
− .31 Cambodia a small country
− .37 Recent enemy action an unacceptable risk
− .37 Intense activities by North Vietnam in sanctuaries
− .44 To describe U.S. actions
− .45 Americans want us withdrawn from Vietnam
− .46 Support U.S. fighting men
− .52 Possible threat to American lives
− .54 U.S. to withdraw from sanctuaries
− .66 One-term presidency possible
− .73 Larger considerations at stake
− .86 North Vietnam has been intransigent
− .87 U.S. has three options
− .99 U.S. aim is to end war in Vietnam

Low stress   −1.17 Option 2: U.S. provides military assistance to Cambodia
−1.05 to −1.63   −1.17 Opinion leaders counsel doubt
                    −1.19 U.S. not threatening any nation's security
                    −1.20 Incursion will minimize casualties
                    −1.25 U.S. ready to negotiate
                    −1.33 Sanctuaries being used to attack Cambodia
                    −1.62 Different opinions in U.S.

Slight stress   −1.66 Can U.S. meet a direct challenge?
−1.64 to −1.95   −1.81 Americans want war ended

Minimal stress   −2.09 Political considerations rejected
<−1.96   −2.50 U.S. to achieve just peace
                    −3.29 Decisions based on following reasons

---

                    May 8
Extreme stress   3.34 Full report on Cambodia at end of June
1.96 and above   2.56 Those who dissent are not "bums"

Heavy stress   1.76 U.S. needs to deal more effectively with violence
1.95 to 1.64

Moderate stress
1.63 to 1.04

Table 5.3   Nixon (Continued)

Average stress 1.03 to −1.04	.98 U.S. will negotiate while in Cambodia
	.87 South Vietnamese troops a majority in Cambodia
	.85 Sanctuary decision will end war
	.70 Cambodia's future subject to Nixon Doctrine
	.67 Decision to intervene will help end war
	.62 All facts not known about Kent State
	.58 U.S. has moved decisively in Cambodia
	.57 Incursion bought time and saved lives
	.50 Diplomatic discussions about neutrality under way
	.26 National Guard could emulate federal troops
	− .06 Not surprised by intensity of protests
	− .08 U.S. to be out of Cambodia by end of June
	− .10 Increased enemy activity led to incursion
	− .15 Troop withdrawals continue
	− .57 South Vietnamese to withdraw with U.S.
	− .72 Understanding of presidency needed
	− .73 President is responsible for sanctuary decision
	− .78 Lyndon Johnson wanted peace
	− .78 President will talk to demonstrators
	− .82 Critics of administration not repressed
	−1.01 Washington demonstration handled well
Low stress −1.05 to −1.63	−1.22 U.S. not headed for revolution
	−1.30 Administration agrees with student aims
Slight stress −1.64 to −1.95	−1.73 Administration desires dialogue with college students
Minimal stress <−1.96	−2.89 Vietnamization proceeding well

	June 3
Extreme stress 1.96 and above	4.20 Incursion has won time
	3.12 Effect of incursion was to limit casualties
	2.29 Differences exist over means to achieve peace
Heavy stress 1.95 to 1.64	1.82 Troop withdrawal program preserved
	1.80 Introduction: long-range impact
Moderate stress 1.63 to 1.04	1.62 Immediate danger to Americans in Vietnam reduced
	1.44 Only U.S. air missions to remain after July 1
	1.30 Many weapons captured
Average stress 1.03 to −1.04	1.00 Timetable for troop withdrawals kept
	.98 Captured rice to feed refugees
	.77 Asian initiatives on Cambodia supported
	.67 South Vietnamese do not covet Cambodia
	.66 Captured ammunition prevented casualties
	.62 Nine months ammunition captured

Table 5.3   Nixon (Continued)

	.52 U.S. deadline for withdrawal will be met
	.45 Review of decision context
	.31 All military objectives achieved
	.24 President cannot avoid threat to troops
	.25 Rebuilding of sanctuaries will take months
	− .06 Thank you for your support
	− .14 Decision announced one month ago
	− .18 Review of decision context
	− .29 Threat was emerging in Cambodia
	− .31 Review of decision context
	− .42 U.S. diplomatic offers to North still open
	− .63 Effectiveness of South Vietnamese in Cambodia high
	− .64 Review of decision context needed
	− .74 Promise to end war will be kept
	− .88 Progress report to president last weekend
	− .97 15,000 rifles and machine guns captured
	− .99 Earlier sanctuary effort might have saved lives
Low stress	−1.07 We all want peace
−1.05 to −1.63	−1.18 Review of decision context
	−1.50 Administration plans need support
	−1.57 Renewed intensity of conflict will be met by force
Slight stress	−1.68 Attention called to film of operation
−1.64 to −1.95	−1.76 Pledge to withdraw troops kept
Minimal stress	−2.14 Most successful operation of war
<−1.96	−2.75 Pledge to withdraw from Cambodia kept

	July 1
Extreme stress	2.03 Extent of destruction was effective
1.96 and above	1.97 Cambodia decisive in several ways
Heavy stress	1.88 U.S. not committed to defend Cambodia
1.95 to 1.64	1.82 South Vietnamese completing sanctuary operation
	1.74 Congress moves too slowly
Moderate stress	1.14 U.S. relationship to Cambodia
1.63 to 1.04	1.14 President has no plans to send back troops
	1.04 Situation in Cambodia remains difficult
Average stress	1.03 No U.S. military defense of Cambodia
1.03 to −1.04	.98 U.S. air power to interdict supplies
	.84 U.S. to respect Cambodian neutrality
	.57 Future Vietnams need congressional approval
	.48 Cambodian incursion will be seen as decisive
	.47 Many reasons for improved chances of survival
	.44 President must defend U.S. lives
	.26 Hypothetical question on Cambodia

Table 5.3   Nixon (Continued)

	.20	All Americans out of Cambodia
	.11	Loss of surprise would have been costly
	.08	American people support president
	.06	South Vietnamese to prevent North Vietnamese return
	.04	No U.S. advisors with South Vietnamese
	− .05	No plans to return to Cambodia
	− .10	U.S. had to move against sanctuaries
	− .32	History will judge decisiveness of Cambodia
	− .44	President must defend U.S. troops
	− .50	Reescalation not a possibility
	− .70	Cambodia's chances of survival improved
	−1.03	Description of air situation
Low stress	−1.10	Unnecessary to return to Cambodia
−1.05 to −1.63	−1.13	President must make difficult choices
	−1.25	History declares some events decisive
	−1.27	Not necessary for U.S. troops to return to Cambodia
	−1.33	Surprise important
	−1.52	U.S. reconnaissance planes under attack
Slight stress	−1.87	Congressional approval for incursion not sought
−1.64 to −1.95		
Minimal stress	−1.96	Threat: Possible U.S. air attacks
<−1.96	−1.99	No plans to send back troops
	−2.05	Consultations with Congress held
	−2.13	President has a role in defense
	−2.14	Given dissent, was incursion worth it?
	−2.45	Degree of decisiveness in doubt

July 30

Extreme stress 1.96 and above		
Heavy stress 1.95 to 1.64		
Moderate stress	1.37	Will consider recommendations on students
1.63 to 1.04	1.25	Problems of communication
	1.24	Violence on campus a university problem
Average stress	.92	Faculty share blame
1.03 to −1.04	.64	Enemy should negotiate
	− .20	Government and students share blame
	− .40	We are ending war
	− .54	Government is responsible for university problems
Low stress	−1.46	Enemy set back
−1.05 to −1.63	−1.49	Government responsive to people
	−1.59	Enemy weaker after Cambodia

Table 5.3 Nixon (Continued)

Slight stress
−1.64 to −1.95

Minimal stress
<−1.96

	October 7
Extreme stress 1.96 and above	
Heavy stress 1.95 to 1.64	
Moderate stress 1.63 to 1.04	1.48 Casualties decreased since Cambodia
	1.33 Troop levels reduced in Vietnam
Average stress 1.03 to −1.04	.53 Conference must be broad-based
	.25 Complete U.S. withdrawal possible
	− .33 Negotiations in Paris to continue
	− .36 New diplomatic initiative
	− .43 Indochina peace conference proposal
	− .98 All Indochina in cease-fire proposal
Low stress −1.05 to −1.63	−1.29 Geneva accords of 1954 and 1958 valid
Slight stress −1.64 to −1.95	
Minimal stress <−1.96	

zone to be broadened, and thus that a general escalation was an alternative outcome, must have been one of the causes of his high stress regarding the U.S. relationship to Cambodia.

After the highest stress themes, there are four rather neutral composite themes: withdrawal from Cambodia/Southeast Asia, diplomatic concerns, U.S. determination, and the question of the sanctuaries. All four deal with U.S. behaviors and their causes. The first two are future oriented: the U.S. timetable for future withdrawals and the U.S. desire for a negotiated settlement. The latter two deal with U.S. posture, positive action, and an anticipated successful outcome. The president used the determination theme to describe U.S. actions; and thus this theme is somewhat similar to Kennedy's and Johnson's "description of events" themes. It is consistent that these themes do not appear in the high stress category.

Of the seven remaining stress themes, the four least stressful (at the bottom of the list in table 5.2) are all maintenance oriented: Congress, the role of the president, statements about peace, and the decision context. Nixon describes Congress and pressures on the president with virtually no stress. These are descriptive paragraphs which explain ongoing behaviors. His statements on peace appear to be routine. The expectations for their realization or even the conviction behind them is probably low; but not to enunciate reflections regarding peace would have been inconsistent with the now established rhetoric of conflict statements. Finally, the decision context theme is Nixon's phrase for introducing background and historical information into his statements. As in the previous cases, we find that descriptive and non-crisis-centered statements are less stressful than active, crisis-oriented themes.

Moving up from the least stressful themes, the remaining three low stress themes are of mixed character: justification for the incursion, no U.S. return to Cambodia, and domestic turmoil. The first two are essentially descriptive themes. The justification theme is presented in the past tense and is essentially a statement of situational factors up to that point; and the "no return" theme is again, like the peace theme, a routine diplomatic addition which apparently was of little concern to Nixon.

The low stress level of the composite theme dealing with domestic turmoil was a surprise to us. We had expected that a highly emotional and conflict-ridden internal crisis would loom near the top among the stressed themes. But when we tried to explain this apparent anomaly, we discovered that hindsight is not always a useful tool. The Cambodian incursion was a major catalyst for the beginning of the national antiwar movement. Prior to 1970, this movement was not particularly strong. The Kent State incident, which occurred in the aftermath of the Cambodian incursion, became a springboard for future protests. What we have in our data, therefore, are Nixon's reactions to the early protests which took place, for the most part, on university campuses—i.e., outside what the president in all likelihood perceived to be the more salient political arena. Nixon took no blame for the protests; rather, he placed blame on what he referred to as misguided college administrators and professors. Indeed, the president probably anticipated that the protests would at best be a temporary phenomenon. Moreover, at this point there was little public support for antiwar protests.

Given what we now know about the flow of events following the Cambodian incursion, it appears logical to assume that questions of domestic turmoil would produce high stress in the president. Such an appraisal might form a typical element in most current social science analyses of this event;

but this would indeed represent an imposition of the analyst's logic on the reality of the situational context as seen by the president himself.

Word-Level Analysis

Our data set for the word-level analysis of Richard Nixon consists of 5,251 words spoken during his vocalizations concerning the Cambodian incursion, encompassing seven speeches. Table 5.4 presents the means and standard deviations for stress and derived word length for the aggregate of Nixon's pronouncements. Table 5.5, in which word length has again been recoded, presents a breakdown on stress for Nixon.

Nixon's mean stress level of 68.67 places him between Kennedy and Johnson. It is clear, however, that Nixon's stress level fluctuates greatly, as demonstrated by the fact that his standard deviation is larger than that of either of the other two speakers. Moreover, this variation is only weakly related to such variables as speech, part of speech, the prepared/extemporaneous dichotomy, and word length, although word length seems to be the most important factor affecting Nixon's level of stress.

Nixon's mean word length of 16.61 is also shorter than that of either Kennedy or Johnson and has a standard deviation of only 6.52. This, of course, indicates that Nixon favors short words and uses longer words rarely.

Turning to table 5.5, we note that Nixon's minimum mean stress level is 65.37 on April 20, 1970, while his maximum is 71.16 on April 30, 1970. Thus, there seems to be little variation in Nixon's stress or level of arousal across speeches. Nixon's prepared speeches are more highly stressed than his unprepared speeches. This is as we expected, though the range between the two types of pronouncements is rather narrow. Long words are the most highly stressed in Nixon's vocabulary, followed by medium and then short words. Again, as in our previous cases, the major parts of speech are more highly stressed for Nixon than are the minor parts of speech. As we stated in chapter 4, we will return to this information in more detail when we present our comparative analyses.

Table 5.4 Stress and word length, mean and standard deviation: Richard M. Nixon.

	Mean	SD	N
Stress	68.673	21.198	5,251
Length	16.609	6.515	5,251

Table 5.5   Stress breakdown for Nixon.

Stress by	Grand mean = 68.67	
	Mean	N of words
Speech		
1. (4-20-70)	65.37	145
2. (4-30-70)	71.16	1,534
3. (5-08-70)	65.72	987
4. (6-03-70)	68.67	984
5. (7-01-70)	69.55	1,070
6. (7-30-70)	64.27	307
7. (10-07-70)	68.49	223
Prepared		
Prepared	69.80	2,886
Extemporaneous	67.24	2,361
Length		
Short	66.42	2,115
Medium	68.65	1,810
Long	72.21	1,322
Part of speech		
Noun	67.61	1,910
Verb	69.35	1,116
Adjective	70.21	1,132
Adverb	71.20	449
Filled pause	61.85	80
Preposition	67.29	294
Article	66.76	94
Conjunction	65.22	172

General Analyses of President Nixon

Thematic analysis. Consistent with the questions and procedures followed in drawing the analytical inferences from the Berlin and Dominican data, we will confront similar questions using the now familiar procedures with regard to Cambodia. Again, keep in mind that voice stress data would unfold to an analyst in a chronological fashion, as is displayed in table 5.2.

On April 20, before the incursion began, the president spoke about his concern for the increased flow of North Vietnamese troops into Cambodia. Only one paragraph in his presentation reached the severe stress range: a threat to the North Vietnamese not to escalate the level of conflict in Indochina. It would have been risky to draw strong conclusions from this single severely stressed paragraph, yet its appearance should have been a clue to the seriousness with which the Nixon administration viewed the pace of events in Cambodia.

Ten days later, the president announced that an attack on Communist sanctuaries was underway in Cambodia. In this major address Nixon enunciated several themes which reached the severe stress level. Among those themes a determination cluster can be identified: "Option 1: U.S. could do nothing about Cambodia," "Time for action has come," and "U.S. cannot appear helpless." An analyst might comfortably have interpreted these three themes as reinforcing each other with respect to the U.S. determination to eliminate the sanctuary problem in Cambodia. Again, that determination themes exceed the mean for the speech is consistent with all previous findings; that is, in such an instance the speaker is viewing the situation as serious and critical.

An interpretation that an investigator could have placed on this information might have been that the president was willing to pay very high costs to drive the North Vietnamese out of the sanctuary areas. Indeed, corresponding costs to be incurred by the North Vietnamese in order to maintain their positions in the sanctuaries might have reached prohibitively high levels.

While no leakage of information appears to have taken place on May 8, Nixon's vocalizations of June 3 reveal severe stress on a cluster of paragraph themes which relate to the administration's justification for the operation: "Incursion has won time," "Effect of incursion was to limit casualties," and "Troop withdrawal program presented." An analyst might have interpreted this as a display of psychological discomfort regarding the publicly announced arguments justifying the incursion. If this is an accurate inference, the president may have been vulnerable to diplomatic or propagandistic pressure regarding these justifications.

Precisely the same conclusions could be drawn from the president's July 1 vocalizations. Again, themes which spelled out the justification for the incursion caused severe stress in Nixon. On July 30 and October 7, none of the president's vocalizations reached the severe stress level, indicating, conceivably, that Nixon's psychological sensitivity to events in Cambodia had dissipated.

Psycholinguistic analysis. As we have done in the two preceding chapters, we present below an outline summary of Richard M. Nixon's psycholinguistic characteristics.

(1) Nixon's prepared statements and speeches were more highly stressed than his extemporaneous pronouncements.

(2) Across all crisis verbalizations, adverbs were the most highly stressed part of speech for Nixon.

    (a) In prepared statements and speeches, Nixon exhibited the highest stress on filled pauses.

    (b) In extemporaneous vocalizations Nixon exhibited the highest stress on adverbs.

(3) Across all crisis verbalizations, the three highest stressed parts of speech for Nixon were adverbs, adjectives, and verbs.

(4) Across all crisis verbalizations, the three lowest stressed parts of speech for Nixon were articles, conjunctions, and filled pauses.

(5) Nixon's electronically derived long words were consistently the most highly stressed, followed by medium, and then short words. There were no exceptions to this hierarchy.

    (a) Nixon's range of stress scores for derived word lengths was greater in prepared vocalizations than in extemporaneous remarks.

(6) Derived short length words (47.8 percent) were the most frequently used by Nixon, followed by medium words (36.6 percent), then long words (15.5 percent).

    (a) Nixon's derived medium words exhibited a narrower range of mean stress values than either short or long words.

    (b) Nixon's short and long words had a constant, inverse relationship in terms of frequency of usage.

    (c) With the sole exception of Nixon's first document in the crisis, a perfect inverse relationship existed between high stress and high frequency derived word lengths.

(7) Nixon's words at the beginnings of paragraphs (or themes) tended to be more highly stressed than words in the middle or at the end.

Summary

Nixon's stress levels, like those of the previous speakers, varied with the themes of his presentations. He was most concerned about the American political relationship with Cambodia and the role of South Vietnam in the crisis. Moreover, as has become the pattern across these crisis cases, his prepared speeches were more highly stressed than his extemporaneous speeches, with part of speech and word length also affecting his stress level.

What was most striking about Nixon was that the differences he exhibited on part of speech, word length, and the prepared/extemporaneous distinction were not as large as those for Johnson and Kennedy. Nixon appeared to be more even tempered or more psychophysiologically balanced than the other speakers in that there was less range in his stress levels across speeches and across the other variables.

6. Comparative Analyses

In this chapter we will examine in a comparative manner the results of our study of the three speakers. In doing this, we will present comparisons across several familiar categories. Beyond these, however, we will subject our data to a number of new tests. Knowledge from these comparisons will then be used to establish the characteristics of normal language behavior of U.S. presidents during international crises.

Fluctuating Levels of Stress

In figure 6.1, we reproduce the time/stress level tables found in each individual crisis analysis. Each displays the changes in the mean stress values for the speeches within the crisis. As can be seen, these stress levels vary from the simple curve of the Dominican crisis to the complex zigzag of the Berlin crisis. We believe that the complexity embodied in a single line indicates information about a crisis vis-à-vis its relationship to noncrisis foreign policy behavior. The Dominican crisis is a discrete event for President Johnson. It deals with a relatively minor nation; and the situation was not directly threatening to U.S. security. The other two crises, as previously discussed, are "embedded" crises, i.e., crises that occur within the context of a broader situational field. The expanded situational context in these cases included larger conflict arenas. Berlin is a crisis manifestation of a U.S.-Soviet contest which was direct and intense in the late 1950s and early 1960s; and the Cambodian incursion was an element in the larger Vietnamese conflict.

In our discussion of Berlin (see chapter 3), we spelled out the embedded crisis conceptualization. Rather than reacting solely to the crisis, Kennedy fluctuates between belligerent stances (high stress) and compromising positions (low stress). This is apparently *not* due to particular actions within the crisis itself, but is, presumably, a regular pattern attributable to the opposing needs of appearing strong and determined while at the same time inhibiting the Cold War from escalating to a direct military confrontation. Likewise, the Cambodian incursion, although distinct from the Vietnam war, was undeniably linked to it.

These alternating high and low stress levels are similar to the findings of Snyder and Diesing (1977) and Leng and Wheeler (1979) regarding bargaining strategies of contestants during international crises. The findings of these two studies are compared and carefully examined in Leng and Walker (1982).

Markov Chain Analysis and Transition Probabilities

One way to illustrate the effect of an embedded crisis is through a first order Markov chain analysis. A Markov chain assumes that a condition at time e_t is determined by a condition at time e_{t-1} and that alone. For example, one could try to determine tomorrow's weather entirely upon today's weather. Suppose we only allow for warm and cold weather. We might generate the following matrix.

	Yesterday's weather	
	Warm	Cold
Warm	6	1
Cold	1	8

Today's weather

This matrix would tell us that we had six days when warm followed warm and eight days when cold followed cold. We also had one day when cold followed warm and one day when warm followed cold. Now, in carrying out a X^2 (chi-square) test on this matrix we can easily determine whether there is an association between yesterday's and today's weather. This, then, is an example of a Markov matrix.

We developed Markov matrices (see table 6.1) from the time lines in figure 6.1. Thus, the analysis involves mean speech stress level.

In all these matrices there is significant association between stress levels on consecutive days. It would therefore seem that there are predictable patterns of stress behaviors throughout international crises.

Nevertheless, although these predictable patterns may be observed within each crisis, it may very well be the case that the patterns differ among different crises.

To test for differences observed in the patterning of the time lines in the

Markov matrices, a Hilton test of significance can be used (see Hilton, 1971 for explication). We tested the three possible pairs of patterns (see table 6.2).

As can be observed from the table, results are as expected: the Kennedy and Nixon patterns are clearly indistinguishable since they are both embedded crises. However, the Johnson pattern is significantly different from the other two; and this provides a face validity test of our hypothesis regarding embedded crises.

Returning our attention to the transition probabilities, we asked questions about changes in the psychological arousal level of a speaker from one time period to another. Given that a speaker is at a certain level of stress, high or low, what is the probability that he will be at the same level in the next time period? And, conversely, what is the probability that his level will change from one period to the next? These probabilities are shown in figure 6.2.

As can be seen from figure 6.2, the probability that either Kennedy or Nixon's level of arousal would be different at e_t than at e_{t-1} is high, demonstrating an oscillation between high and low arousal in successive periods. For Johnson, the probability of leaving one state and entering another is low, indicating a more stable arousal pattern. This is what we would expect from looking at the timelines in figure 6.1.

To facilitate an understanding of figure 6.2, a brief summary of the findings is in order. The results show that, for Kennedy, given that his stress level is low, there is only a .20 probability that it will be low in his next pronouncement and a .80 probability that it will be high. If his current stress level is high, there is a .12 probability that it will remain high and a .88 probability that it will be low in his next vocalization, an erratic but still predictable behavior.

However, when Johnson's stress level is low, there is a .67 probability

Table 6.1 Markov boxes for stress time lines.

		Kennedy e_{t-1}			Johnson e_{t-1}			Nixon e_{t-1}		
		High	Low		High	Low		High	Low	
e_t	High	1	8	9	3	2	5	1	3	4
	Low	8	2	10	1	4	5	2	0	2
		9	10	19	4	6	10	3	3	6
		$\chi^2 = 9.02$			$\chi^2 = 4$			$\chi^2 = 4$		
		$p < .005$			$p < .025$			$p < .025$		

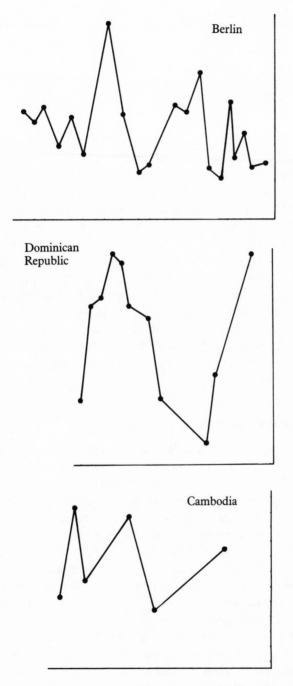

Figure 6.1   Stress levels over time for Kennedy, Johnson, and Nixon.

Table 6.2 Hilton tests on pairs of Markov boxes.

		df	
Kennedy/Johnson	$\chi^2 = 8.8$	2	$p < .02$
Kennedy/Nixon	$\chi^2 = 1.0$	2	
Johnson/Nixon	$\chi^2 = 5.7$	2	$p < .10$

that it will be low the next time and a .33 probability that it will be high. If his stress is high, there is a .75 probability that it will remain high and a .25 probability that it will be low, perhaps a more balanced response.

In Nixon's case, if his stress level is low it will be high the next time, i.e., the probability of Nixon moving from low to high is 1.0. Therefore, if his stress level is low, there is no chance that it will remain low. On the other hand, if Nixon's stress level is high, it will remain high with a probability of .33 and move to low with a probability of .67, as with Kennedy, both displaying an erratic form of response.

These observations are confirmed by our analysis of variance on psycholinguistic stress which tests the effects of the aggregate speech variable, the variable most closely associated with the temporal evolution of the crises. We found that the speech variable had the greatest effect on Johnson ($F=73.00$), followed by Kennedy ($F=45.58$), and exerted very little effect on Nixon ($F=9.94$).

Prepared vs. Extemporaneous Documents

Table 6.3 displays aggregate data for the prepared/extemporaneous variable across the three presidents. One of the clearest findings of this study is that for all three speakers, prepared statements and speeches were more highly stressed than extemporaneous vocalizations. In mixed or hybrid vocalizations, which occurred in Kennedy's pronouncements, the prepared portions were more highly stressed than the extemporaneous, thereby maintaining the basic bifurcation of type of vocalization which we have just noted. Johnson's range of mean stress values from prepared to extemporaneous was the greatest, with Nixon the least and Kennedy in the middle. If we are indeed tapping a psychological state associated with discomfort or anxiety, then Nixon appears to be the most stable, balanced, controlled, or perhaps even-tempered of the speakers. Furthermore, the different ranges of stress scores between prepared and extemporaneous vocalizations for the three speakers is, in all likelihood, attributable to the individual speaker's perception of the gravity and the uncertainty of the situation.

Nixon's range is narrower because, since he was in control of the military events, he apparently did not perceive himself to be in a serious confrontation. The broader the range, therefore, the more concerned or perhaps even anxious the speaker is regarding the crisis.

In terms of the rhetoric of international crisis, prepared documents tend to be delivered during the early stages of a crisis. Johnson and Kennedy followed this pattern closely, while Nixon delivered prepared statements and speeches throughout the Cambodian episode. This clustering of prepared statements early in the crisis no doubt occurs because the gravity of events demands clearly considered ideas and careful articulation. Further, the first stages of a crisis involve careful signalling by contestants regarding interests, perceptions, and likely actions. These communications, espe-

Figure 6.2   Comparison of transition probabilities.

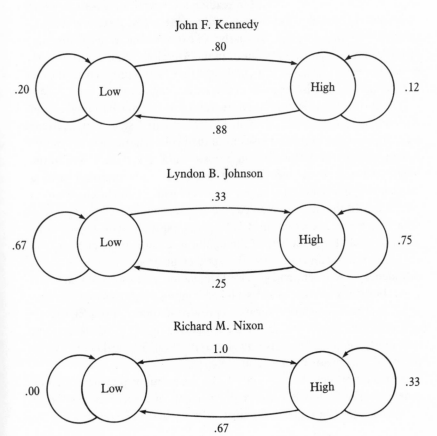

Table 6.3   Mean stress values for prepared and extemporaneous documents.

Speaker	Mean stress value of prepared documents	Mean stress value of extemporaneous documents	Range, prepared to extemporaneous
Johnson	72.70	62.04	10.66
Kennedy	70.87	64.03	6.84
Nixon	69.82	67.14	2.68

cially when they are delivered publicly, need to be expressed with the precision and measured comprehensiveness that only a prepared statement can provide.

As discussed in earlier chapters, our initial supposition regarding the distribution of stress levels between prepared and extemporaneous vocalizations was precisely the opposite of our finding: we reasoned that speakers would be less stressed in reading a prepared statement in which all words and thoughts had been carefully preselected, thereby leaving no room for the unanticipated. Similarly, we expected that press conferences would produce high stress because, in the American context at least, they are spontaneous, often brutally frank, and they force a presidential speaker to respond to major issues more or less extemporaneously.

It is worthwhile to summarize the several reasons why our initial reasoning was incorrect. First, when making a prepared statement, speakers were apparently extremely conscious of their role as heads of state; and the weight of such a realization during a crisis could contribute to a condition of high personal stress. Second, as we stated previously, prepared vocalizations during international crises by their very nature contain important information. In the cases we studied, the speakers announced major foreign policy decisions and/or outlined U.S. policy positions with regard to the crisis at hand. Third, in light of the significance of the message being conveyed, it was incumbent upon the speaker to project an impression of confidence, resolution, and precise formulation of information and positions. Fourth, a speaker in a crisis is confronting a serious subject directly in a prepared document; whereas in a press conference, a president has the option of avoiding an uncomfortable or delicate topic. All of these reasons apparently combined to drive up the stress levels in speakers delivering prepared documents during crisis situations.

A final point should be mentioned with regard to the prepared/extemporaneous variable. Nixon's prepared statements and speeches may not be clustered at the beginning of the crisis, as were those of Kennedy and Johnson, because of the different nature of the Cambodian situation. Johnson and Kennedy were responding to crises which were provoked by forces outside of the U.S. government, while Nixon initiated the crisis with which he was dealing. Nixon therefore was in a position to exercise a greater degree of control over the flow of events than were either Johnson or Kennedy, who were reacting to other nations' initiatives. Thus, in a rhetorical sense Nixon's prepared documents are distributed over the entire time period of the crisis because these vocalizations are reports in the finite time space which Nixon consciously perceived, delineated, and controlled. Such control was not available to either Johnson or Kennedy.

Part of Speech

Several interesting comparative tendencies are discernible with respect to various parts of speech. In terms of frequency of occurrence, content words (nouns, verbs, adjectives, adverbs) are consistently and more frequently used than function words (filled pauses, prepositions, articles, conjunctions). Table 6.4 shows the breakdown on this variable for all three speakers. The occurrence of a greater proportion of content words is consistent with Miller's work (1951) on the frequency distributions of parts of speech. In addition, these types of data may be used, in combination with other factors, to determine the relative degree of a speaker's psychological discomfort. Brown (1973) has found that function words in high stress situations may be indicative of psychological discomfort. The relatively higher proportion of function words in Johnson's and Kennedy's vocalizations may indicate that they were experiencing a greater degree of anxiety during their crises than Nixon was during the Cambodian incursion. This is plausible in light of our conclusion in the previous section that Nixon exhibited fewer signs of anxiety because he exercised more control over the situation in Cambodia than the other two presidents did during their respective crises.

Not only were content words found to be more frequent than function

Table 6.4 Frequency distributions: content words vs. function words.

	Johnson (%)	Kennedy (%)	Nixon (%)
Content words	80.3	84.8	87.6
Function words	19.7	15.2	12.4
Total	100.0	100.0	100.0

Table 6.5   Hierarchy of stress scores for parts of speech.

Johnson		Kennedy		Nixon	
verb	$\bar{X} = 72.73$	adjective	$\bar{X} = 68.81$	adverb	$\bar{X} = 71.14$
adjective	72.38	adverb	68.75	adjective	70.13
adverb	71.71	verb	67.88	verb	69.31
noun	70.62	noun	67.44	noun	67.55
article	70.34	preposition	64.24	preposition	66.92
filled pause	69.96	conjunction	63.83	article	66.76
preposition	69.84	article	61.97	conjunction	65.31
conjunction	68.06	filled pause	58.38	filled pause	61.85
aggregate	71.20	aggregate	67.11	aggregate	69.60

words, but they were also consistently more highly stressed. Overall, content words tended to raise the mean stress levels for speakers, while the function words tended to lower them. As is clearly illustrated in table 6.5, this is especially evident for adjectives, adverbs, and, to a lesser extent, verbs. The high stress levels for adjectives and adverbs may be indicative of the manner in which the speaker chooses to convey his message. Generally, in describing events or announcing policies, the speaker may consider nouns and verbs to be the "givens" in a situation, i.e., "things" and "gross actions" may be reasonably well established by the time a president makes a public presentation. On the other hand, precision and nuance in his vocabulary may be reflected through his choice of modifiers (adjectives and adverbs).

Another "part of speech" which merits some attention is the filled pause. We found that when filled pauses are a normal part of a person's speech, as they were for John F. Kennedy, they tend to lower the mean stress level for a document. However, when filled pauses do *not* occur regularly in a person's speech and they are present in situations where the speaker is under stress, as was the case for both Lyndon B. Johnson and Richard M. Nixon, they occur immediately before the discussion of important topics and tend to display relatively high mean stress scores.

The general tendencies discussed above for our data apply to prepared statements and speeches as well, with one exception. In prepared documents, verbs and adverbs are the most highly stressed parts of speech overall, while in the aggregate, adjectives and adverbs are the most highly stressed. Table 6.6 shows the stress hierarchies for parts of speech for Johnson, Kennedy, and Nixon in prepared, extemporaneous, and aggre-

Table 6.6 Hierarchy of parts of speech, from highest to lowest mean stress scores, in aggregate, prepared, and extemporaneous pronouncements.

	All speeches	Prepared	Extemporaneous
Johnson	verb	verb	adjective
	adjective	adjective	verb
	adverb	adverb	adverb
	noun	noun	noun
	article	article	article
	filled pause	filled pause	preposition
	preposition	preposition	filled pause
	conjunction	conjunction	conjunction
Kennedy	adjective	verb	adverb
	adverb	adverb	adjective
	verb	noun	verb
	noun	adjective	noun
	preposition	conjunction	preposition
	conjunction	preposition	conjunction
	article	article	article
	filled pause	filled pause	filled pause
Nixon	adverb	filled pause	adverb
	adjective	adverb	verb
	verb	adjective	noun
	noun	verb	article
	preposition	noun	preposition
	article	conjunction	adjective
	conjunction	preposition	conjunction
	filled pause	article	filled pause

gate vocalizations. We see here that for Johnson and Kennedy, verbs and adverbs, respectively, are the most highly stressed parts of speech for prepared statements. But for Nixon, in prepared statements, filled pauses are the most highly stressed "part of speech." These filled pauses accounted for only 0.1 percent of the words in his speech, and therefore played a rather insignificant role in determining the mean stress value here. For comparative purposes, then, adverbs, the next most highly stressed part of speech after the filled pause, may be considered to be highest stressed. These higher stress levels for adverbs and verbs may be due to the nature of prepared vocalizations, in which the speaker is likely to be describing *action* taken or to be taken or the prevailing *condition* of a crisis situation.

In extemporaneous pronouncements, the tendencies are the same as those of parts of speech in the aggregate.

Derived Word Length

Regarding derived word length, we found that for all three speakers long words consistently had the highest mean stress values, while short words consistently had the lowest. This finding accords with research on the physiology of language (Miller, 1951; Cherry, 1978).

This tendency was equally strong in both prepared and extemporaneous statements. An interesting datum was found, however, with respect to the range between the highest and lowest mean stress levels for derived word lengths in prepared and extemporaneous vocalizations. Table 6.7 displays the relevant data for Presidents Johnson, Kennedy, and Nixon.

In this table we see that Johnson and Nixon exhibit a similar pattern. The ranges for prepared statements and speeches of Johnson and Nixon are larger than either the aggregate ranges or the extemporaneous ranges. In addition, the ranges between highest and lowest mean stress scores of derived word lengths in extemporaneous documents are smaller than either the aggregate ranges or the prepared ranges. The greater range in prepared documents may indicate that under more stressful conditions, i.e., those inherent in the delivery of prepared statements and speeches, psychological discomfort may be detected through the relatively large difference between the means of the most and least stressed word lengths. Similarly, in extemporaneous speech, the relatively lower stress of the speaker may be indicated by the smaller range between the highest and lowest mean stress scores for word lengths. That these tendencies are not present in Kennedy's pronouncements may be simply an idiosyncracy of Kennedy's psychological makeup. Obviously, further comparative work is needed here.

Table 6.7   Ranges of mean stress scores for derived word lengths in prepared and extemporaneous pronouncements.

	All vocalizations	Prepared	Extemporaneous
Johnson	3.89	5.08	1.21
Kennedy	5.09	3.55	4.17
Nixon	6.16	7.10	3.61

Table 6.8   Relative frequency of derived word lengths.

Word length	Johnson (%)	Kennedy (%)	Nixon (%)
Short	29.6	32.0	47.8
Medium	36.1	34.7	36.6
Long	34.3	33.3	15.5
Total	100.0	100.0	100.0

Frequencies of Word Length

Table 6.8 displays the relative frequency of derived word lengths for all three speakers. The data show that both Johnson and Kennedy tended to use more medium and long words, while Nixon used more short and medium words. Again, Miller (1951) and Zipf (1949) show that normal speech is characterized by the presence of far more short than long words. Given this pattern in human language, Nixon's vocalizations may be considered here to be normal and Kennedy's and Johnson's to be abnormal in terms of frequency of occurrence of derived word lengths. Nixon's normal distribution of derived word lengths may indicate that he was not overly anxious or fearful about the substance of his messages during the Cambodian crisis. As mentioned earlier in this chapter, Nixon probably felt in control of the situation in Cambodia, and therefore he did not perceive it as a great threat to national security. In contrast, the anxiety that Kennedy and Johnson felt during their crises, perhaps produced by their sense of lack of control over the international situation, may have been subconsciously expressed through the use of more long words, which in turn elevated their stress levels as measured by voice stress analysis.

Table 6.8 also illustrates quite clearly the steady influence which medium length words exert on each speaker's psycholinguistic profile in terms of frequency of occurrence. The medium length words account for an average of just over 35 percent of all words for each speaker. The stability of medium length words indicates that long and short words are more likely to influence the psycholinguistic profile of a speaker.

For Johnson and Kennedy, the most highly stressed derived word length (usually with respect to long words) was also the most frequently used in certain documents. This relationship is seen specifically in instances where the speaker perceives situations as being particularly threatening. For Nixon, however, with one exception, there is no correspondence between high stress and high frequency of derived word length. Short words are the most frequent and the least stressed, a pattern which is found in normal speech (Miller, 1951; Zipf, 1949). This again corroborates the apparent lack of high stress in Nixon's verbalizations during the Cambodian crisis.

Position within Paragraph

This final variable does not seem to be very significant as an indicator of a speaker's psychological state. Not only are there no discernible tendencies among the three speakers studied here; but even within the data for each speaker, any trends toward higher or lower stress for a particular position within a paragraph are so slight (less than two points difference in mean stress level) as to be inconsequential.

Comparison of Influence of Key Variables

Based on our earlier analysis of variance, we can delineate the differences among the three speakers with regard to the relative influence on stress of three key variables: the prepared/extemporaneous dichotomy, part of speech, and derived word length. The main effects, in order of influence for each of the these variables for the three speakers, are shown in table 6.9 below.

Kennedy and Johnson follow the same pattern of influences. The most important influence for these two speakers is whether or not the speech was prepared. This is followed by word length and part of speech. The prepared/extemporaneous dichotomy and word length exert a greater influence on Johnson than on the other speakers, while part of speech exerts greater influence on Kennedy. The variable which exerts the greatest influence on Nixon is word length, although none of the variables provides a very strong influence.

Table 6.9   Relative influence of three key variables for each speaker.

	Kennedy F		Johnson F		Nixon F
Prepared/ Extemporaneous	338.58	Prepared/ Extemporaneous	391.30	Word length	26.05
Word length	32.31	Word length	43.91	Prepared/ Extemporaneous	9.61
Part of speech	16.18	Part of speech	4.92	Part of speech	3.78

Estimation Models for Psychophysiological Stress

The model. Previous studies (Wiegele 1976a, 1980a) have sought to enhance our understanding of stress as it is manifested by presidents during international crises. These studies, however, did not attempt to develop an estimation model for stress. In this section we will attempt to develop and test a model of stress for each of our three speakers using paragraph-level data. Each paragraph, therefore, forms a unit of observation. The statistical model used is the standard multivariate regression model. This model contains one dependent variable, or effect, which in this case is stress, and several independent or causal variables.

The models tested here are based on the assumption that for each speaker certain parts of speech are associated either positively or negatively with stress. These associations may differ from one speaker to the next. Thus, these parts of speech act as markers indicating a speaker's state of psychological arousal. Our model also includes a binary variable indicating whether or not a speech was prepared, since previous work (Center for Biopolitical Research, 1980) has demonstrated that this variable is highly associated with stress. Moreover, this assertion is well documented by the present study.

Our first task, then, is to develop the model for estimating stress. This model is shown in (*i*) below and will be tested for each speaker.

$$(i) \quad Y = B_0 + B_1X_1 + B_2X_2 + B_3X_3 + B_4X_4 + B_5X_5 + B_6X_6 + e$$

where, Y = stress,

B_0 = a constant,

B_1 to B_6 are ordinary least squares (OLS) regression slopes,

X_1 = prepared (1 = prepared, 0 = not prepared),

X_2 = percentage of nouns in the paragraph,

X_3 = percentage of verbs in the paragraph,

X_4 = percentage of adjectives in the paragraph,

X_5 = percentage of adverbs in the paragraph,

X_6 = percentage of filled pauses in the paragraph

and e = the error term.

Each of these explanatory variables was chosen for a specific reason. Our prepared variable was included because we hypothesize that, when under stress, i.e., in a situation where the exactness of language is critical, a president will prepare a speech or participate in the preparation and revision of a speech. Nouns and verbs are indicative of normal speech and appear in virtually all sentences. Nouns, however, can be considered a pas-

Table 6.10
OLS regression results: John F. Kennedy.

	B	SE	t	p
Constant	71.61	4.28	16.72	.000
Prepared	4.84	.84	5.78	.000
% Noun	−.14	.06	−2.51	.012
% Verb	−.04	.06	−.77	.442
% Adjective	.04	.05	.78	.432
% Adverb	−.06	.06	−.92	.357
% Filled pause	−.32	.09	−3.37	.001

N =   243
F =   22.30
F probability =   .000
SSR = 3525.55 df =   6
SSE = 6219.21 df = 236
Adjusted R^2 =   .35

OLS regression results: Lyndon B. Johnson.

	B	SE	t	p
Constant	70.70	5.00	14.14	.000
Prepared	9.28	1.24	7.51	.000
% Noun	−.13	.07	−2.01	.046
% Verb	−.04	.07	−.60	.551
% Adjective	−.03	.08	−.43	.670
% Adverb	−.14	.09	−1.62	.107
% Filled pause	−.16	.21	−.74	.459

N =   146
F =   9.99
F probability =   .000
SSR = 1561.69 df =   6
SSE = 3621.66 df = 139
Adjusted R^2 =   .27

Table 6.10   (Continued)
OLS regression results: Richard M. Nixon.

	B	SE	t	p
Constant	78.07	8.57	9.11	.000
Prepared	1.67	1.52	1.10	.274
% Noun	−.26	.10	−2.57	.011
% Verb	−.09	.11	−.82	.415
% Adjective	.03	.11	.28	.782
% Adverb	.04	.12	.37	.711
% Filled pause	−.21	.23	−.88	.383

N	= 187
F	= 3.89
F probability	= .001
SSR	= 1692.36
SSE	= 13040.92
Adjusted R^2	= .09

$df = 6$
$df = 180$

sive part of speech, and therefore should drive a speaker's stress level down. Verbs are an active part of speech and should increase the level of stress experienced by a speaker. Adjectives and adverbs, as qualifying words, indicate the need for precision in a speaker's language and are expected to increase the stress level. That is, the more there is a need for precision, the more frequent the use of adjectives and adverbs and the more pressure a speaker will feel to be exact in his language. Filled pauses generally signal a relief from stress and therefore should force the level of stress down. The other three parts of speech, articles, prepositions, and conjunctions, have less connotative meaning and are not included in the model.

The results of our test of this model are shown in table 6.10. The test was run for each speaker individually. Table 6.11 presents the correlation matrices for all variables in the equation.

Looking at table 6.10 we can see that our model has the best results for Kennedy (adjusted R^2=.35), followed by Johnson (adjusted R^2=.27), and last, Nixon (adjusted R^2=.09). Again, Nixon stands apart from the others in his behavior. The models also differ in terms of regression parameters. Percentage nouns is the only slope which is significant at $p \le .05$ or better across all three speakers. Nouns are usually givens in a particular communication and they tend to drive the stress level down. The most significant slope, excluding, of course, the constant, for both Kennedy and Johnson is the binary prepared variable. The prepared variable, however, is again not significant for Nixon. The only other slope which proves significant is per-

Table 6.11
Correlation matrices from OLS
John F. Kennedy.

	Stress	Prepared	Noun %	Verb %	Adjective %	Adverb %	Filled pause %
Stress	—						
Prepared	.54	—					
% Noun	−.04	.15	—				
% Verb	−.05	−.11	−.32	—			
% Adjective	.36	.39	−.12	−.37	—		
% Adverb	−.05	−.12	−.22	−.11	−.14	—	
% Filled pause	−.46	−.56	−.21	−.04	−.40	−.08	—

Correlation matrices from OLS
Lyndon B. Johnson.

	Stress	Prepared	Noun %	Verb %	Adjective %	Adverb %	Filled pause %
Stress	—						
Prepared	.52	—					
% Noun	−.08	.06	—				
% Verb	.01	−.05	−.24	—			
% Adjective	.04	−.04	−.30	−.30	—		
% Adverb	−.03	.05	−.39	−.14	−.06	—	
% Filled pause	−.04	−.02	−.17	−.10	−.25	.16	—

Table 6.11 (Continued)
Correlation matrices from OLS
Richard M. Nixon.

	Stress	Prepared	Noun %	Verb %	Adjective %	Adverb %	Filled pause %
Stress	—						
Prepared	.11	—					
% Noun	−.27	.15	—				
% Verb	−.05	−.12	−.24	—			
% Adjective	.21	.36	−.26	−.49	—		
% Adverb	.11	−.14	−.28	−.08	−.23	—	
% Filled pause	−.10	−.45	−.09	−.12	−.24	−.05	—

centage of filled pauses ($p<.001$) for Kennedy. It does not appear significant for either of the other two speakers. Table 6.12 summarizes the direction and significance of each slope for each speaker.

Table 6.12 demonstrates that both the prepared variable and percentage nouns behave as expected. Filled pauses also function as expected, though they appear to be significant only for Kennedy. Our findings for adjectives and adverbs, the qualifying parts of speech, are mixed. This is apparently attributable to idiosyncratic factors. Verbs, rather than driving the stress level up, actually drive it down. This indicates to us that in all likelihood verbs should be treated as givens along with nouns in any particular vocalization.

We conclude that the variables exhibiting the most influence on the paragraph mean stress level are nouns and whether the speech was prepared.

The correlation matrices (refer to table 6.11) show the associations between all variables in the equation. It is interesting to note that percentage nouns is only weakly associated with stress in Kennedy and Johnson and more strongly in Nixon. The prepared variable shows a strong correlation for both Johnson and Kennedy and a weaker correlation for Nixon. Verbs are only modestly correlated with stress in all speakers. Adjectives show a sizable correlation for both Kennedy and Nixon and little for Johnson, although adjectives do not prove to be a significant predictor of stress. Adverbs show a weak inverse correlation with stress in Kennedy and Johnson and a moderate positive correlation in Nixon. Filled pauses show a moder-

Table 6.12   Summary of regression slopes.

Variable	Expected sign	Kennedy	Actual sign Johnson	Nixon
Prepared	+	+ *	+ *	+
% Noun	−	− *	− *	− *
% Verb	+	−	−	−
% Adjective	+	+	−	+
% Adverb	+	−	−	+
% Filled pause	−	− *	−	−

*Indicates a slope is significant at $p \leq .05$.

ate negative correlation in Nixon, a weak negative correlation in Johnson, and a strong negative correlation in Kennedy.

Methodological Observations on the Estimation Model

The major methodological concern with our model is the possibility of collinearity or multicollinearity among the independent variables. When we consider that the total of all eight parts of speech must add up to 100 percent, it becomes obvious that the larger the percentage for one part of speech, the smaller the percentage of the other parts. Had we constructed a model using all eight parts of speech multicollinearity may have rendered it useless. However, since we used only five parts of speech no percentage for any part was determined. Nonetheless, the possibility for collinearity or multicollinearity exists. The problem of collinearity and multicollinearity is treated by Hilton (1976: 157–159). Following his suggestion, we tested for collinearity among the variables. Very high correlations (i.e., between −.8 and −1.0 or .8 and 1.0) between two variables are indicative of collinearity to the extent that the effects of one variable cannot be separated from the other. By studying the correlation matrices in table 6.12, we would be able to detect collinearity among the variables. After examining the matrices, therefore, we are confident that we have no problem with collinearity.

Since all of the independent variables may be related, we felt it appropriate to check for multicollinearity as well. Hilton (1976: 168) also offers a test for this problem. If a regression line as a whole is significant at $p \leq .05$ while none of the individual slopes is significant at $p \leq .05$, then multicollinearity exists and we cannot separate the effects of the various independent variables upon the dependent variable. An examination of table

6.10 illustrates that we do not have this problem. Thus, we conclude that neither collinearity nor multicollinearity poses a problem in our model.

Differences among the Speakers

In order to test for differences among our three speakers with regard to our estimating equations we used the added observations test (Hilton 1976:175).

The first procedure is to run an OLS regression on one speaker with n observations as shown in (ii) below.

(ii) $y = b_0 + b_1 x_1 + \ldots b_{k-1} x_{k-1}$ $(i=1, 2, 3, \ldots n)$

Second, an OLS regression is produced for the second speaker with m observations as shown in (iii) below.

(iii) $y = a + a_1 x_1 + \ldots a_{k-1} x_{k-1}$ $(i=n+1, n+2, n+3, \ldots n+m)$

Next, an OLS regression is run for the two speakers combined with $n+m$ observations as shown below in (iv).

(iv) $y = B_0 + B_1 x_1 + \ldots B_{k-1} X_{k-1}$ $(i=1, 2, 3, \ldots n+m)$

An F-statistic is then used to test the effects of adding the second speaker's observations to the first. The F formula is shown in (v) below.

(v) $F = \dfrac{(SSE_c - SSE_1 - SSE_2)/K}{(SSE_1 + SSE_2)/(n+m-2k)}$

Where, SSE_1=sum of squares unexplained by the regression
for speaker one,
SSE_2=sum of squares unexplained by the regression
for speaker two,
SSE_c=sum of squares unexplained by the combined
regression,
n=the number of observations for speaker one,
m=the number of observations of speaker two,
and k=the number of variables in the regression equation.

This test will tell us whether or not the results for the speakers are the same. We are testing the following null hypothesis:

H_0: $b_0 = a_0$, $b_1 = a_1$, $\ldots b_{k-1} = a_{k-1}$

The regression results for each speaker were given in table 6.10. Table 6.13 presents the results for the three combined regressions required for

Table 6.13
Combined OLS regression results: John F. Kennedy—Lyndon B. Johnson.

	B	SE	t	p
Constant	71.86	3.09	23.57	.000
Prepared	6.59	.65	10.14	.000
% Noun	−.15	.04	−3.59	.000
% Verb	−.06	.04	−1.36	.175
% Adjective	−.01	.04	−.37	.710
% Adverb	−.09	.05	−1.76	.080
% Filled pause	−.29	.08	−3.68	.000

N = 389
F = 40.66
F probability = .000
SSR = 6515.36 df = 6
SSE = 10203.02 df = 382
Adjusted R^2 = .38

Combined OLS regression results: John F. Kennedy—Richard M. Nixon.

	B	SE	t	p
Constant	76.94	4.30	17.90	.000
Prepared	3.26	.82	3.99	.000
% Noun	−.23	.05	−4.25	.000
% Verb	−.09	.05	−1.60	.111
% Adjective	.02	.05	.31	.756
% Adverb	−.02	.06	−.36	.718
% Filled pause	−.36	.10	−3.66	.000

N = 430
F = 17.10
F probability = .000
SSR = 4823.60 df = 6
SSE = 19892.27 df = 423
Adjusted R^2 = .18

Table 6.13 (Continued)

Combined OLS regression results: Lyndon B. Johnson—Richard M. Nixon.

	B	SE	t	p
Constant	80.71	4.78	16.89	.000
Prepared	4.59	.97	4.73	.000
% Noun	−.26	.06	−4.29	.000
% Verb	−.12	.06	−1.96	.051
% Adjective	−.07	.06	−1.14	.256
% Adverb	−.06	.07	−.85	.395
% Filled pause	−.19	.16	−1.16	.247

N = 333
F = 8.34
F probability = .000
SSR = 2742.77 df = 6
SSE = 17877.86 df = 326
Adjusted R^2 = .12

the procedure; Kennedy and Johnson, Kennedy and Nixon, and Johnson and Nixon.

Using the data from tables 6.10 and 6.13, we are able to test whether or not these regression results do differ. This is done in table 6.14.

As can be seen from table 6.14, the only difference which proves to be significant at $p \leq .05$ is that between Johnson and Nixon. Kennedy does not differ from either of the other two. However, since the critical value of F at .05 for this test is 2.01, we feel that the differences between the pairs Kennedy and Johnson and Kennedy and Nixon are, in fact, of some substantive importance. We conclude that the three speakers do differ from one another with regard to predictive models of stress and we reject the null hypotheses.

The only variable which proves significant in the regression model is percentage of nouns. Even the prepared variable is not uniformly significant. Kennedy exhibits a significant slope for filled pauses, while the others do not. Furthermore, given that our best adjusted R^2 for any single speaker is .35, we also conclude that contextual effects, which differ for each speaker, exert a significant effect on stress. Thus, a model of psychophysiological stress for one speaker will differ from that for others. It is a combination of linguistic variables and contextual effects which produces an idiosyncratic pattern of psychophysiological stress in a given speaker. This work will not attempt to account for those idiosyncratic contextual effects, but clearly a considerable amount of further in-depth, longitudinal

Table 6.14   Added observations test for OLS results.

John F. Kennedy—Lyndon B. Johnson

$$F = \frac{(10203.02 - 6219.21 - 3621.66) / 7}{(6219.21 + 3621.66) / (243 + 146 - 14)} = 1.97** \; df = 7,375$$

John F. Kennedy—Richard M. Nixon

$$F = \frac{(19892.27 - 6219.21 - 13040.92) / 7}{(6219.21 + 13040.92) / (243 + 187 - 14)} = 1.95** \; df = 7,416$$

Lyndon B. Johnson—Richard M. Nixon

$$F = \frac{(17877.86 - 3621.66 - 13040.92) / 7}{(3621.66 + 13040.92) / (146 + 187 - 14)} = 3.32* \;\; df = 7,319$$

*Indicates F is significant at $p \le .05$.
**Indicates F is significant at $p \le .10$.

research is required. Studies might be designed, for example, to conduct voice stress analyses of presidents across their entire terms of office. Alternatively, all international crises of a single president might be studied, though it would be unusual for such a person to have experienced a large enough number of crises in his/her term of office to provide a meaningful comparative data base.

Thematic Analysis

It is now possible to offer several comparative observations regarding the uses which an analyst might have made of voice stress analysis data during the crises examined. These observations may also prove to be relevant for future crisis studies.

In two of the crises, Berlin and Cambodia, we found that determination themes were high stress topics for Presidents Kennedy and Nixon. As we indicated previously, when the mean for the determination theme exceeded the overall mean for the crisis speech, we felt comfortable in inferring that the speaker viewed the situation as critical, dangerous, and possibly leading to war. Not only does this accord with past voice stress research, but we have every reason to believe, on the basis of the historical facts of the Berlin and Cambodian crises, that this was indeed the case.

A second comparative dimension involves what might be referred to as a clue or analytic "tip-off" in the voice data that might not have been easily anticipated in a routine monitoring of the situation or an examination of a documentary record. We found two "tip-offs" in the three cases. In the Dominican crisis President Johnson's extreme concern for the fate of U.S.

civilians on Dominican soil was a clue to a situational factor which was placed high in all likelihood on the administration's list of priorities, but which probably could not have been discovered from a "normal" deductive analysis. The high stress exhibited by Nixon during the Cambodian crisis when he warned North Vietnam not to escalate the conflict in Indochina—a threat made shortly before the incursion was launched—was a clue that the administration was predisposed to make a serious response. Furthermore, as the Cambodian crisis developed, the president exhibited high stress on his verbal justifications for the incursion. As we mentioned earlier, this latter datum certainly was a clue to a possible psychological weakness in President Nixon regarding the appropriateness of the incursion itself.

Unequivocal "tip-offs" do not appear to be an easily derived aspect of voice stress analysis. Indeed, we found no "tip-offs" in the Berlin data. The high-stress threat statement by President Nixon was a single item early in the crisis which historical events later verified, but which probably would not have been recognized as a clue at the time of its utterance. Nevertheless, Nixon's leakage of stress on the "justification themes" does appear to be a reasonably strong clue. Only in the Dominican crisis can the "tip-off" be described as a clearly powerful finding capable of influencing subsequent decisional behavior. More work with crisis data should provide clearer information to an analyst of how, when, and where to look for clues to issues which are causing stress and discomfort in heads of state or other leaders who provide public verbal data.

Psycholinguistic Analysis

This study has attempted to explore the internal psychological states of leaders during international crisis situations. It has utilized a research design which employed remote electronic mapping procedures in a psycholinguistic context. We believe that we have advanced our capabilities considerably in terms of producing remote psychological assessments of policy makers in one type of decisional situation. This exploratory work has been done in the American milieu because that is the one in which we feel most comfortable both intellectually and culturally. Furthermore, because our work has proceeded in this context, the quality of our inferences is probably more accurate and precise. However, it is imperative that remote electronic mapping, both thematically and psycholinguistically, be performed on elite speakers in other cultures.

The Psycholinguistic Profiles

We have developed psycholinguistic profiles for three U.S. presidents during international crises. These profiles have revealed both individual idiosyncracies as well as common components of psycholinguistic behavior. Let us briefly review these profiles.

Lyndon B. Johnson:
highest stress in prepared vocalizations
highest stress on verbs in prepared statements
highest stress on adjectives in extemporaneous statements
lowest stress on filled pauses, prepositions, and conjunctions
highest stress on long words
medium length words most frequently used
use of short words increases toward end of crisis
exhibits a broad range in stress values between prepared and extemporaneous vocalizations

John F. Kennedy:
highest stress in prepared vocalizations
highest stress on verbs in prepared statements
highest stress on adverbs in extemporaneous statements
lowest stress on conjunctions, articles, and filled pauses
highest stress on long words
medium length words most frequently used
exhibits a medium range in stress values between prepared and extemporaneous vocalizations

Richard M. Nixon:
highest stress in prepared vocalizations
highest stress on filled pauses in prepared statements
highest stress on adverbs in extemporaneous statements
lowest stress on articles, conjunctions, and filled pauses
highest stress on long words
short words most frequently used
exhibits a narrow range in stress values between prepared extemporaneous vocalizations

The following are characteristics common to all three speakers in international crisis situations:

highest stress in prepared vocalizations

highest stress on modifiers in extemporaneous vocalizations
lowest stress on function words (articles, conjunctions, filled pauses, prepositions) overall.
highest stress on long words

The following are characteristics common to two of the three speakers
in international crisis situations:

highest stress on verbs in prepared statements
medium length words most frequently used

Normal language behavior. What can be said about these characteristics?
In general, they delineate what can be considered to be the normal, electronically derived language behavior of U.S. presidents in crisis situations.
Thus, during crises we should expect speakers to show more stress in their
prepared than in their extemporaneous statements; their modifying parts
of speech should be highly stressed, with their function words exhibiting
low stress; and their long words again producing high stress. In addition,
we should find that presidents have a tendency to use more medium length
words than any other length, and that in prepared statements verbs will
tend to be highly stressed. If analysts find deviations from one or more of
these characteristics, they should be alerted to the possibility that some
type of psychological dysfunction has probably taken or is taking place. It
is conceivable that the more violations of the norm that are noted, the more
destabilizing the dysfunction has become.

Knowledge from the electronic mapping process that a change in psycholinguistic behavior has taken place could be of use in analytic assessments of the timing of policy initiatives. For example, leaders might un-
knowingly reveal themselves to be psychologically vulnerable by a sudden
shift from a normal psycholinguistic posture or by the exhibition of high
stress on unexpected or illogical themes. Such shifts conceivably might be
viewed as the leakage of a signal that a leader had entered a period of personal vulnerability. From a different point of view and in a different situation, a sharp change in psycholinguistic behavior might indicate especially
critical decision periods. In either case, dramatic shifts from the norm can
be viewed as a psychological disengagement from a previous posture by an
individual leader.

Idiosyncratic characteristics. We have looked at characteristics common to
our three speakers all and most of the time. Let us now examine the psycholinguistic idiosyncracies for these same individuals. We can delineate
the following for each:

Lyndon B. Johnson:
use of short words increases toward the end of the crisis
exhibits a broad range in stress values between prepared and extemporaneous vocalizations

John F. Kennedy:
exhibits a medium range in stress values between prepared and extemporaneous vocalizations

Richard M. Nixon:
short words most frequently used
exhibits a narrow range in stress values between prepared and extemporaneous vocalizations

It is somewhat risky to describe the characteristics above as idiosyncratic, because by adding additional crisis data to each president a new pattern might emerge. Nevertheless, a *principle* for understanding these presumed idiosyncracies can be advanced. We might refer to these characteristics which each speaker possesses but which are *not* shared with any other speaker as *psycholinguistic markers*. Once identified, these idiosyncratic markers might provide the most salient leakage for the analyst to track in examining a crisis.

Of those few markers which we have found, the range in stress values between prepared and extemporaneous vocalizations is particularly interesting. This range can be easily determined by calculating the mean stress values for prepared and extemporaneous vocalizations. Establishing the difference between the two provides the range. Because in our cases the range appears so person-specific, a careful monitoring of it might provide the strongest *single* indicator of psycholinguistic behavior. For example, if the range marker changes significantly during a crisis, an analyst might be alerted to a sudden change in psychological orientation in the speaker. It if should prove impossible to perform the full toolbox of psycholinguistic analyses in real time, future research might demonstrate that tracking the range marker alone could prove a suitable surrogate.

The additional marker for Johnson ("use of short words increases toward the end of the crisis"), and that for Nixon ("short words most frequently used"), deserve some explanation. Readers should recall that word length in this study was based upon electronic determination, not the conventional counting of letters. Nevertheless, "shortness" is a useful conceptualization for both voice stress analysis and psycholinguistics. Moreover, electronic shortness is often similar to syllabic shortness. As indicated previously, short words are the most frequently used words in all languages. Indeed, they form the basis for routine speech. It is possible that a marker for shortness can track for "normalcy." As the Dominican crisis came to an end, Johnson's use of derived short words increased. It is true that all of Johnson's extemporaneous vocalizations took place at the end of the crisis; and it is also correct that extemporaneous speech has a tendency to have more routine, short words in it than prepared speech. However, the latter is not necessarily the case. It is, therefore, possible to infer that short words marked the return of Johnson to a normal arousal state at the end of the crisis.

Likewise, the fact that Richard Nixon used more short words all through the Cambodian crisis appears to indicate his lowered stress levels, which could be a function of his perception of his own control of the situation. Table 5.1, furthermore, provides evidence that the stress value range for Nixon is lower than that for either Johnson or Kennedy. As we said earlier, Nixon's psycholinguistic profile appears the most normal of the presidents that we studied.

General Conclusions

Recipients vs. provokers. We noted that Johnson and Kennedy had to deal with crises that were the result of the activities of others, while Nixon launched the Cambodian incursion on his own initiative. The fact that, overall, Nixon's stress levels were lower than Kennedy's or Johnson's may be explained in either of two ways. First, Nixon might be a more relaxed person by nature, and this would account for his generally lowered stress level.[1] Second, and perhaps more important, a leader's perception of his control over a crisis situation might strongly influence his internal psychological environment and therefore his voice patterns. The latter is consistent with the findings of M. G. Hermann (1977) and Kobasa (1982).

Anxiety/Discomfort. As a result of this study, we feel much more confident in being able to assess and understand the kinds of issues and situations which cause leaders to experience psychological stress. This is—it should be evident—a complex topic and process, but one which we have

---

[1] A recent volume by Eliot and Breo (1984) discusses the concept of hot and cold reactors to stressing stimuli. Experimental research has established that regardless of their exterior behaviors, individuals have modal patterns of physiological arousal which appear to be person-specific. Hot reactors, for example, always exhibit significantly greater arousal than the norm in experimental situations. Conversely, cold reactors are always significantly under-aroused.

been able to approach from a very nontraditional but useful perspective. In general, decision makers exhibit negative affect when they must act conflictfully in the name of the state. They also display discomfort on certain highly salient selected issues which normally cannot be uncovered through standard analyses of printed texts. Routine decisional behavior for a head of state does not induce significant negative affect as revealed by voice stress analysis.

The fit with other literatures. In the course of our research, we found it useful to consult works in the information sciences and psycholinguistics. It is not an overstatement to remark that we were astonished that our findings were strongly consistent with the literature in both of these fields. Electronic voice stress analysis appears to be, in crisis situations at least, a reliable and valid instrument of remote psychological assessment. We are confident that future work will make this case even more strongly.

Language. A research orientation focusing on the many aspects of language analysis should be vigorously pursued in the study of international crises. Such an orientation has yet to be energetically exploited. Indeed, one wonders why the discipline of political science, which deals routinely with communicative acts, has yet to develop a meaningful subfield of political communication or political linguistics.

Voice stress analysis and political behavior. Our analysis of substantive themes in crisis communications has resulted in a model of a decision maker's internal affect states (in terms of a hierarchy of stress values) as they relate to perceived political reality. We uncovered, through the examination of leaked signals, an individual's pattern of affect organization. What we have, therefore, is a mental template which is used by an individual to process political stimuli in the environment. The question confronting us is: what is the usefulness of this information to the study of political behavior?

Knowing how individuals organize their internal affect states gives us a foundation or benchmark from which to assess behavior. Is behavior meaningful and/or consistent with the focal person's affective posture? This question is significantly different from asking whether the behavior of a political decision maker is meaningful and/or consistent with a definition of a situation *as constructed by political researchers themselves.* Thus, a decision maker's internal affect posture and the idiosyncratic rationality that accompanies it is a more realistic measure to apply to subsequent behavioral analysis than a presumed reality as perceived by a researcher. Therefore, linking voice stress analyses, i.e., the direct measurement of individuals themselves, to elite behavioral outputs should provide more accurate appraisals of political decision making, because such appraisals intimately link actors with their acts rather than hunches or presumed rationality with acts.

Thus, as we stated in chapter 1, verbal documents become coded environments which researchers can penetrate with voice stress analyses. We may have reached the point envisioned by Snyder, Bruck, and Sapin (1962:65) in which those early scholars of the foreign policy decision-making process called for the "re-creation of the 'world' of the decision makers as *they* view it" (italics in original). Voice stress analysis, by its very nature, is focused at the individual level. As such, it does indeed allow us to examine the affect states of decision makers, and to interpret their behavior on the basis of a distribution of stress values across substantive themes related to the behavior itself. The "world of decision makers as they view it," therefore, can be remotely tapped by an analyst and used to assess decisional behavior, at least in international crisis situations.

To carry this reasoning a step further, conventional analyses of crisis behavior frequently begin with an examination of a documentary record and move to a combing of memoirs of participants (when they exist) in order to establish as far as possible the situational milieu confronting a decision maker. A decision is appraised in the light of a reconstruction that is made from a "paper" record. Voice stress analysis provides an additional record—a psychophysiological one—which can be built into crisis behavior studies. When ultimately integrated, these multiple indices should provide measures correlating with decisional outputs to provide a comprehensive understanding of behavior itself.

We hasten to add, however, that political scientists have not developed a reliable record of predicting elite behavior. Can voice stress analysis contribute to such prediction? It may, but considerably more work must be undertaken. This might be accomplished by repeated voice stress analyses of a single individual in order to uncover affect patterns over long periods of time and in a variety of circumstances. Complex profiles could then be constructed which would be tested for their predictive capacity. Combined with traditional situational analyses, these profiles might provide powerful tools for predicting decisional behavior. We have, therefore, simply scratched the surface of the analysis of elite behavior. More reflections on these possibilities will be offered in chapter 7.

Summary

In this chapter we compared the three speakers in our study on several dimensions. All three speakers exhibited a higher mean stress for prepared statements than for extemporaneous statements. Johnson's range between the two is the broadest, followed by Kennedy; Nixon's range is small in comparison. The other variables, including word length and part of speech, also exert less influence on Nixon than on the other two speakers.

We also developed a Markov process for determining the transition probabilities for each speaker as he moves from high to low stress or vice versa. The probabilities for Kennedy and Nixon are similar. This was expected since they both exhibited a zigzag pattern of stress from one speech to the next. Johnson, on the other hand, tends to stay in a single state longer. This we suspect is because both Berlin and Cambodia were embedded crises, while the Dominican crisis was not. A good deal of further work is needed on a larger number of cases before this can be accepted as a confirmed hypothesis.

We also developed an estimation model for psychophysiological stress. The model performed best for Kennedy and least for Nixon. The added observations test showed that the three speakers differ from one another with regard to the estimation models.

The percentage of nouns in a vocalization proves to be most consistently related to the psychophysiological arousal level of a speaker, i.e., there is a strong negative relationship. For both Kennedy and Johnson, a strong positive relationship exists between stress level and prepared speeches. Filled pauses are significant only for Kennedy in that there is a negative relationship with stress.

We outlined some markers or "tip-offs" in the Cambodian and Dominican crises which gave clues to the psychological discomfort caused by certain issues for a speaker. For example, Johnson was extremely concerned about the fate of U.S. civilians, while Nixon exhibited high stress during pronouncements regarding justifications for the incursion. Determination themes were found to have resulted in high stress for both Kennedy and Nixon.

7. Conclusions and Afterthoughts

This study has made a number of contributions to the areas of crisis research methodology, communications, and biopolitics. As might be expected, with these contributions come several corresponding difficulties. These topics are the subjects of the present brief chapter which will conclude with some suggestions for future research.

Crisis Research Methodology

We are confident in asserting that voice stress analysis is a useful analytic tool for making remote psychophysiological assessments of political elites during international crises. Perhaps most important is that it allows the researcher to engage in meaningful, individual-level analyses. This is especially significant because one of the consistent findings of previous crisis decision-making studies, both political and nonpolitical, is that during crises the behavior of single human beings becomes highly salient. We discussed the theoretical foundations for this observation more fully in chapter 1.

In designing the various components of this study, it quickly became clear that little text-oriented work had been done with voice stress analysis. Prior to our inquiry, most voice stress analysis studies had been based on the single-word responses of a subject in some type of experimental or interrogation situation. This work provided a minimal foundation for the far more complex analyses of the large blocks of spoken texts that we have used in our examination of leaders in real, stressing, decisional environments. The present study demonstrates that it is indeed possible and fruitful to subject extended texts to voice stress analysis. The value of such large-scale studies is that they provide comprehensive profiles of negative affect and psycholinguistic behavior for an individual person. This fact, of course, opens the door to a broad range of political research designs, some of which we will discuss shortly.

Despite these advances, much work remains to be done in the development of the voice stress analysis method. The clearest and most important need is for more basic, experimental research on the physiology of the voice under conditions of psychological stress coupled with careful experimental work on the voice stress analysis instrumentation itself. Quite simply, we need to know considerably more about what is taking place in the vocal cords during periods of psychological stress. Unfortunately, although political scientists stand to profit substantially from a fully developed voice stress methodology, they are not appropriately trained to undertake the type of experimental psychophysiological and electronic research suggested here. Such research is more appropriately done by psychophysiologists, specialists in communicative physiology, and electrical engineers. Until this work is completed, voice stress analysis will remain only a modestly tested methodology with a somewhat circumscribed applicability limited to known stressful situations.

More specifically, a high priority ought to be attached to developing fully automated scoring equipment. Scoring electronic traces manually, as we have done, is not only time-consuming, it is costly. The development of automated equipment would greatly enhance the usefulness of the methodology because it would make it possible to efficiently perform real-time analyses of elites during international crises. We are aware that there are several challenging electronic problems associated with the development of an automated scoring system, but a concerted engineering effort could probably overcome them.

Communications and Rhetoric

Both communications and rhetorical analyses are related to the voice stress approach. Communications, of course, includes both verbal and nonverbal components. We reiterate the suggestion made previously that political scientists ought to become more centrally involved in the study of communications. Beyond the acquisition of theoretical knowledge about general communications, however, political scientists could profitably design multi-indicator studies of both verbal and nonverbal behavior. Voice stress analysis could prove complementary to each in powerful research designs of individual-level behavior. Druckman et al. (1982) have carefully examined paralanguage, facial expressions, kinesics, and visual behavior within a communications context. Their work is quite amenable to blending with voice stress analysis.

The area of abnormal language behavior ought to be energetically entered by political scientists. We have suggested what we consider to be normal language behavior of U.S. presidents during international crises, and we stated that deviations from this might constitute abnormal behavior. Asserting this, however, simply spotlights how little we really know about a set of behavioral indicators which might be very useful in studying political elites. Considerable energy ought to be devoted to incorporating into political communications studies the large bodies of literature on the psychological and psychiatric aspects of language, especially psychotic language.

An important area related to communications is rhetoric. Our voice stress work has added an electronic dimension to traditional rhetorical analysis. In identifying certain types of themes and several factors in language usage, voice stress analysis can comfortably provide important and complementary information for empirical rhetorical studies. We have demonstrated that there are identifiable rhetorical patterns in crisis verbalizations. Further, our work reveals how little we know about the rhetoric of international crisis communications. Given the fact that much political behavior during international crises is communications behavior, a combination of intensified rhetorical analysis plus voice stress analysis should yield information that is far more powerful than that which might be gained from only one of these methods.

Biopolitics

This study fits comfortably into a biopolitical orientation to the analysis of political phenomena, based as it is on the physiology of the voice. We feel that we have presented a strong case for the inclusion of biological indicators in the analysis of political elites. Such indicators or markers have long been used in making psychiatric assessments of individuals (Usdin and Hanin, 1982). It is time now to incorporate them into standard analyses of political elites. This will not be easy, because political scientists are generally uncomfortable working with knowledge from the life sciences. However, if our appraisals of individual level behavior are going to be accurate and comprehensive, we would do well to build biological information into them.

What is needed here is a package of several physiological indicators which can be utilized simultaneously and remotely to assess the internal arousal states of individual decision makers. Voice stress is one such indicator, pupil dilation and micro-affect displays in the face are others. Hess (1965) has shown that pupil size correlates with attitudes and anxiety. It may be possible to generate data remotely on breathing patterns by measuring movement in the chest, since rapid breathing often indicates increased anxiety.

From a somewhat different orientation, but certainly as a component of a life science approach, if we know that a leader suffers from a physical malady, we can determine the behavioral correlates of that particular illness. Because leaders have a tendency to be advanced in years, the probability of illness increases. Although not all illnesses have behavioral correlates, many do. For example, coronary artery disease, a frequent condition of males over fifty years of age, has a corresponding set of behavioral characteristics that have been firmly established by over two decades of medical research (Price, 1982, and Wiegele, 1984). These characteristics, referred to as the Type A behavior pattern, establish a clear personality type that is impatient, competitive, and hostile. Such characteristics, which encompass not only political life and operational codes but also the more basic life-style, ought to be of major interest to researchers analyzing decisional behavior during international crises.

Beyond the study of physiological indicators and illness is a body of knowledge involving the human brain which holds the promise of providing insights into and fresh pathways toward elite assessments. Peterson (1982), Schubert (1981), and White (1982) have explored developments in brain research for political scientists. Bessinger and Suojanen (1983), working in the context of organizational behavior, demonstrate the importance of brain research for an understanding of decisional processes. Without question, this is a frontier area, and its prospects for making a major contribution to our understanding of political leaders is great.

One other area in which biology and political science converge and which is relevant to the study of international crises has to do with cognitive processes. Raphael (1982), working with cognitive complexity theory and a sensitivity to psychological stress, examined the U.S.-Soviet relationship in Berlin during the period 1946 to 1962. He found that changing levels of individual cognitive complexity are related to variations in perceptions of threat. The neurophysiological foundations of cognitive processes, as Thatcher and John (1977) point out, cannot be ignored in assessing those processes. Without question, the blending of neurophysiological knowledge from the life sciences together with the reasonably well-established cognitive process approach in international relations could provide imaginative hypotheses and new knowledge. Voice stress analysis appears to lie at the intersection of neurophysiology and cognitive processing.

Future Research in Political Science

Although we have pointed to the need for more basic research on the voice stress instrumentation, we feel, nevertheless, that it might be useful to sketch out several research designs which would be relevant in studying elite behavior during international crises. In doing so, we fully recognize that voice stress analysis could be used in numerous research projects not related to international studies.

Our work has been done in the American context, i.e., with U.S. presidents as the subjects of our investigations. A next step, especially since we are concerned with the crisis management process, would be to study leaders in other nations during international crises. This, of course, raises the question of voice analyses in languages other than English. We do not have a good data base on non-English studies, but we suspect that, when they are done, such studies will be consistent with the findings in English. However, suspicions are not a substitute for actually performing the studies. Finding appropriate cases for this work might be difficult because other societies are frequently not as open to scholars as is that of the United States.

Another potential study would track a single speaker over an extended period of time and across all contexts. For example, an American president's words might be analyzed beginning with his inaugural address and continuing on to every public pronouncement, including press conferences, political speeches, bill signings, greetings to foreign visitors, major crisis addresses, etc. All of these verbalizations—dealing with both domestic and international issues—would be carefully analyzed in a manner similar to that of the present study. This would result in an enormous body of data which would increase further our confidence in analytic judgments. Moreover, it would provide insights into verbalized presidential characteristics in a broad range of situational contexts. Such a longitudinal study could be done with virtually any head of state for whom it would be possible to obtain audio tapes.

Our justification for focusing on U.S. presidents was that as role-responsible administrators, they embodied all the many dimensions of the decisional process. In a research design which could more comprehensively tap the breadth and depth of affect during a crisis, a researcher might subject to voice stress analysis (in addition to the president) all administrative elites that are associated with the crisis. Such individuals might include the secretaries of state and defense, the national security advisor, the presidential press secretary, and the U.S. ambassador to the United Nations. Because these individuals would be dealing with the same international crisis as the president, themes on which they exhibit stress can be compared with similar themes for the presidents. Differing configurations of high stress themes among individuals might reveal conflicting positions within a decisional group or among bureaucratic units. Correspondence of stress levels on critical themes could provide evidence for a strong consensus. Though this type of analysis would be most complex, it would provide group psychophysiological profiles which would yield a fresh dimension to decision-making analyses. Indeed, to even approach the possibility of conducting remote analyses of decision-making *groups* would be an Orwellian development.

A Final Thought

As we said at the outset, we are aware that our work is nontraditional. We have utilized a physiologically based method of content analysis to study changes of affect in U.S. presidents. Although this work is related to cognitive and communications approaches, psychological analyses, bargaining strategies, and decision-making case studies, it is not a substitute for them, but rather an important complement to them. Further, as we mentioned in chapter 1, it is also a complement to standard case studies of international crises.

Moreover, intensive exploitation of each single line of intellectual connectedness should proceed with determination. For example, a major effort to blend voice stress analysis into the broad area of political communication can be undertaken. Although we have mentioned many relevant areas, concentration on one area might be more productive. Such a strategy might be preferable to trying to develop multiple points of relevance that are only superficially informing.

We believe we have made a case for the usefulness of voice stress analysis in political research. Further work will be limited only by the creative abilities of the researchers themselves.

Appendix 1
Equipment, Scoring, and Coding

Description of Equipment

The tape recorder used, a Uher 4000 Report-1C, is relatively compact and can perform various functions. The machine has the normal controls of a tape recorder. This recorder allows different tape speeds to be set—an important capability because male and female voices require different input speeds. Since it is constructed to use five-inch reels, the more common seven-inch-reel tapes must be transferred, often an awkward procedure. However, its relatively large reel size is an advantage because it is easier for an operator to control. The tape recorder is connected to a voice stress analyzer by a patch cord plugged into the socket on the right side of the recorder.

We used what is generally recognized as the best voice stress analysis equipment available today, the PSE-101, manufactured by Dektor CIS, Inc. of Savannah, Georgia. This instrument, marketed under the trade name "Psychological Stress Evaluator" or PSE, is very compact and portable, being built into a normal-sized attaché case. Its manual controls consist of a vertical arrangement of three knobs on the right and a series of six switches in the lower area of its surface. Toward the left center of the surface is the carriage, elevated an inch and a half, containing the stylus and the heat sensitive chart paper for the production of voice traces. (See photo.)

The three knobs perform the following functions. The top knob is the heat modulator, which regulates the amount of heat emitted by the stylus which rests on the heat-sensitive paper. Heat levels range from zero to ten. The middle knob, designated as the "zero knob," regulates the position of the baseline on the heat-sensitive paper. The baseline is a straight line produced by the machine when there are no recorded sounds being transferred through the PSE. The third knob is the earphone gain, which we had no need to use.

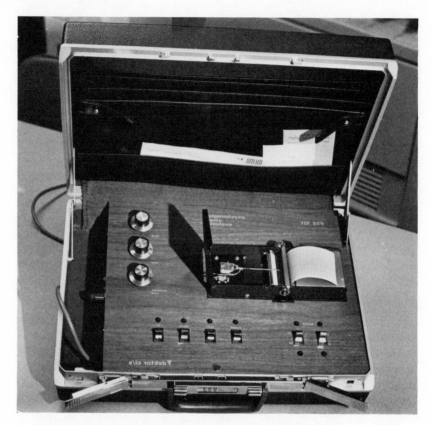

Figure A1.1 PSE-101 without tape recorder.

The six switches are divided into two groups. Two switches on the left can be moved up or down to engage one of four modes available for use. Each mode produces traces with varying combinations of amplitude and wave form. Mode III produces the most easily codable traces, and it is the mode on the basis of which the majority of the research literature has developed. We used Mode III exclusively in this project.

Four switches on the right perform the following operations. From left to right, the first is the power switch for the entire instrument. The second directs heat to the stylus. (As stated above, the heat temperature is regulated by a separate knob.) The third switch engages the motor, which in turn releases the chart paper from the carriage. The fourth switch performs the same task but at twice the speed. Doubling the speed of the chart paper drive makes the traces more elongated and to some extent easier to assess visually. However, this doubles the amount of chart paper utilized, thereby increasing research costs. All switches have red pilot lights to indicate when their specific tasks are being performed.

On the right-hand side of the instrument are two sockets: one for the power supply, and another which transfers the voice data from the tape recorder to the voice stress analyzer.

The heat-sensitive chart paper is similar to electrocardiogram paper. It is 2⅜ inches wide, the only width the loading mechanism will hold. In width the paper is divided into ten large squares, which in turn are subdivided into five smaller squares. These squares are important for establishing scoring rules.

Operation of the Equipment

To operate the voice stress analyzer, the power and heat switches must be on. The heat modulator knob is normally set above five. This must be done at least one minute before operation to allow warm-up time. The zero knob is manipulated to give a baseline at the height of two small squares from the bottom of the chart paper.

A tape is threaded into the tape recorder. Though the normal recording speed of the recorded tape is 7½ inches per second, for analytic purposes the speed is slowed to 1⅞ inches per second to produce a more readable and therefore codable voice trace.

To produce a graphic voice trace, the motor is activated by pushing the "drive" switch forward, and the tape recorder is started by depressing the "play" lever. When the pattern has been produced, the process is halted by pressing the pause lever on the tape recorder and by returning the "drive" switch to the "off" position. All of this is done manually by a human operator. It is an awkward process and requires a good deal of physical coordination and skill.

A written text of the speech must be available at all times because speakers have a tendency to mispronounce or to run words together. Without a text, the operator may commit data-gathering errors. The text is also used to delineate the beginning and ending of paragraphs. The importance of this function will be discussed below.

The isolation of words is tedious and time-consuming. Once the operator identifies a word to isolate, he or she must locate the point in the tape where the word begins and ends. Since the operator extracts only the single word, great skill is required to be certain that only one word at a time is processed through the instrument. To facilitate the exact isolation of the word, we used a word locator, a disc cut from cardboard which rests on top of the left reel on the tape recorder. Its diameter is equal to that of the reel, and it has a line drawn the length of its radius. Although the word locator assists the operator in determining the beginning and ending of a word, he or she will need to run the tape back and forth until the word is isolated precisely. No automated system has yet been devised to perform this function, and this represents a major impediment to efficient, real-time analyses.

For methodological reasons the word trace must be displayed within certain ceiling and floor boundaries on the heat-sensitive chart paper. On the basis of an experiment performed early in this project and an extensive search of the literature, we determined that stress level can be measured only if at least one pulse in a trace reaches above the sixth large square on the chart paper. It was also determined that having more than two pulses above the ninth large square distorts the stress level by implying a higher level than that which exists.

The chances of an instrument operator physically fitting a word pattern into these parameters on the first run are slim. Thus, the operator must rewind the tape and adjust the volume arbitrarily in order to fit the word trace into the paper width. If the pattern is too high, the volume must be decreased; if too low, it must be increased. After adjusting for volume, the operator runs the word through the instrument again. After the first adjustment the probabilities of meeting the requirements are increased, but the operator must be prepared to go through the process a third or even a fourth time. These volume adjustments must be made because speakers raise and lower their voices as they speak.

After producing an acceptable trace, the operator writes the word on the chart paper above its voice pattern. It is necessary thus to indicate to the coder which pattern to score because the discarded test traces are also included in the running tape.[1] Other labelling on the chart paper includes an indication of the beginning of the paragraph, a paragraph sequence number, and, at the beginning of the chart paper, the name of the speaker and the date of the speech. The rolls of chart paper are numbered sequentially. Designating each paragraph beginning simplifies the coding process somewhat because it eliminates the necessity of constantly referring to the printed text. Labelling the rolls organizes the chart paper for storage and retrieval of the data if desired.

Thus far, attempts to automate the process have been less than com-

---

[1] In an initial effort we cut the final trace from the tape and discarded the test traces. This, however, proved to be much too time-consuming and was therefore abandoned.

pletely successful. Apparently, a computer or other device has not been manufactured to discern words from other vocalizations or to determine word beginnings and endings. Generating the data requires a human being with good hearing and knowledge of the language to isolate the words, since speakers frequently run words together, especially in rapid-paced speech. Another problem lies in the inability of a voice stress analyzer to compensate automatically for changes in the volume (amplitude) of the speaker's voice. Automatic gain control devices have been shown to electronically distort the configuration of traces. A change in pitch or tone often requires an adjustment of volume, which is necessary to insure that each word trace lies within the floor and ceiling boundaries. Until a sufficiently sensitive instrument is devised to handle these problems, we must depend on a human operator. The Human Factors Research Group at the Patuxent River, Maryland, Naval Air Test Center has developed a semiautomated, computerized, *scoring* procedure. More will be said about this in the following section on scoring procedures.

Of course, there are problems involved with human operators. Our workday consisted of two or three four-hour shifts, with rest periods approximately every thirty minutes. Because of the length of this study, we used six separate operators. The training of each was laborious and time-consuming. It usually took several weeks for an operator to become reasonably adept in the use of the instrument. During the first two or three weeks, traces were produced very slowly and sometimes improperly. Experienced staff had to monitor continuously. The tedium of the operator's task often took a physical and psychological toll, and boredom was common. A completely automated system would solve many of the problems associated with operator fatigue.

Scoring Procedures for Voice Stress Traces

Critics of voice stress analysis point to the subjectivity of the coding and the resulting low intercoder agreements as indicators of the "softness" of such data. Some analysts have used a five-point scale, others a two-point, stress–no stress scale (Wiegele, 1978b). With a five-point scale, coders have great difficulty in visually differentiating stress values. Reliability is high in a two-point scale, but a major amount of information is disregarded. Horvath has reported an intercoder agreement score of .38, and Worth and Lewis, a score of .56. Normally, a score of .80 is considered necessary for minimal reliability.

Since such low scores are unacceptable, we have devised an objective coding scheme to increase the coefficient. Building from some assumptions we made about the physiology of the voice as related below, we developed manual coding procedures which can give a numerical (interval scale) score for any word.

Smith (1977) and Dektor (1972) have attempted to deal with the problem of reliability, but with rather limited success. Smith designed a voice pattern rating procedure that eliminates experimenter bias in small data samples and provides precise assessment. A trace for a particular word is scored by measuring the height of the response and then delineating its midpoint. Coders measured "the time (x) for which the response is above this mid-point, as well as the total time of the response (y)." A percentage score is calculated by computing x/y. We found this method not only tedious, but open to great error because it required the measuring and adding together of very small distances when only one or two pulses in a trace went over the midpoint at a time.

In its discussion of traces, Dektor uses the concept of center of mass to show the dampening of the FM signal within the trace. It appeared to us that if we could in some way quantify this line, we might break through the morass of subjective coding. Two avenues of analysis seemed fruitful— one dealing with the degree of the slope(s) of this line, one dealing with slope direction changes.

Although we believe that some aggregation of slopes within a trace is viable, the mechanical difficulties in this type of analysis are enormous. One must measure the angles for all slope changes and average out. Questions of whether to start at the bottom (thus having large first angles) or whether to start at the third point, second quarter, etc., had to be answered—and all subjectively.

At this point we realized that using center of mass, i.e., measuring each excursion of the pen for a center point and then connecting these points, is also unnecessarily tedious. We also realized that it would be more efficient to use the top points of the excursions (pulses) for our analysis.

The latter judgment is based on the assumption that the fluctuations of the pulses in a trace should dampen as stress increases. Using this assumption, we hypothesized that the number of changes in slope direction (controlling for the length of the trace) should indicate the frequency modulation, or lack of it. As a blocked pattern (straight across, 0 slope) is highest in stress, zero slope between pulses can also be analyzed and scored. We developed explicit rules for coding (see appendix 2) and then tested for the validity of this objective coding scheme.

To develop these coding conventions, five trained coders were asked to individually rank 300 pairs of traces (25 words in all combinations) as to which one of the pair was more stressful. Thus for each coder, we could rank the 25 words on a continuum, test for within-coder agreement, and compare intercoder ranking scales. Even though all of the coders had been trained together, substantial differences came through.

Within-coder agreements were derived by applying a Guttman scale to the paired rank decisions. A perfectly internally consistent coder would receive a coefficient of reproducibility (Cr) of 1.00. The Cr's for our coders ranged from .83 to .93. Although this is high, it shows enough within-coder inconsistency to create concern for the analyst. Intercoder reliabilities were derived from Pearson correlations of Guttman scores for each coder. These correlations ranged from .69 to .88 (all significant at .001), substantially better than reported intercoder reliability scores, as should be expected from the method of paired ranking employed. These correlations represent high intercoder agreement scores; and they question whether consistently reliable visual scoring of large amounts of data is possible.

Objective scores were calculated for each word and correlated with the coders' Guttman scores. These correlations ranged from .59 to .74 (all significant at .002). Though these are lower than the intercoder reliability scores, an examination and discussion of the traces and the differences in the scoring satisfied us that the objective coding scheme was valid and that personal biases in the subjective coding accounted for a large percentage of the unexplained variance. The intercoder agreement score for the objective coding ranged around .95, and we felt that this afforded a more consistent basis for analysis.

Five aspects of the objective coding process deserve amplification.

(1) *Short traces.* We found that a trace with fewer than ten pulses was inconsistently coded subjectively and, therefore, unsuitable for objective coding. Because the number of pulses in each trace becomes the denominator in computing stress values, fewer than ten pulses makes each pulse too important a determinant of the final result. Consequently, we coded only words with ten or more pulses. About one-fourth of all words in our vocalizations are thus too short to code.

(2) *Number of syllables evident in the trace.* Some polysyllabic words produce traces that appear as monosyllabic and vice versa. We had to decide whether to use only the major portion or the totality of the trace. Our decision was to ignore the break and treat all of the trace as one word.

(3) *Tight configuration.* A tight trace configuration occurs when the sub-

ject is shouting, and thus it is very difficult to code accurately. We decided
to code it nonetheless but to mark it for future analysis.

(4) *Run together.* Occasionally, there was no graphic separation between
words and we had to divide them arbitrarily. We made this division at the
lowest point in the trace configuration. Moreover, we found that this occurred most often with prepositional groups (*to/a*, *as/to*, etc.) and frequently resulted in two words with less than ten pulses.

(5) *Cluttered bottom.* Due to the restricted range of voice stress analysis
equipment, and in order not to stretch the stylus to its upper excursion
limits, we tended to depress fluctuations in the lower part of the trace
when we positioned the trace on the strip paper. This became especially
important at the beginning and at the end of words. Because the restricted
range at the bottom and the cluttering that this causes inflated the stress
score, we decided, after a good deal of analysis, that the first pulse to be
counted would be the first one over the first bold line on the strip chart
paper. The last counted would be the last pulse above this same line.

This coding scheme still needs some refinement, but we are satisfied
with its basic logic and its ability to quantify the stress levels in the traces.
Although the theoretical range for the scores is -1 (total stress) to $+1$
(total lack of stress), the normal working range we have found is $-.15$ to
.60, with a mean around .30.

Our data have been derived from presidential speeches on crisis matters,
and therefore they represent a subset of the totality of human speech.
They further represent a limited phenomenon within the range of all political behavior. This scoring technique gives a reliable interval scale score
and thus allows for finer analysis of baseline and deviation scores.

Working conditions

From the foregoing discussion it is obvious that counting traces and
slope changes for each word necessarily makes coding a time-consuming
process. The concentration required to detect slope changes in tight configurations causes physical and mental strain. The coding area must be
well lit to minimize eyestrain. In addition, it is sometimes helpful to use a
magnifying glass when coding words with particularly tight configurations
or long traces. Coders usually found it necessary to take a rest break after
thirty to forty-five minutes of work.

Training coders and verification

Training the coders is perhaps the most important factor in the coding
process. To assure maximum precision and minimum distortion of data, a

new coder must constantly be supervised by an experienced coder for at least the first week of training. During this period, the new coders are encouraged to ask questions whenever they are in doubt about how to score particular traces. Above all, coders must be consistent in their work. After two to three weeks of practice, the need for supervision diminishes, but a senior coder must verify regularly the work of all coders, even the most experienced, to assure continued accuracy. This we regularly did. A sample of the coding form can be found in appendix 2.

The coding operation used several coders, each of whom was trained by the project director. Coders were under constant supervision for the first thirty to forty hours of work, and afterwards the project director was on hand to answer questions.

Although some coders who were very familiar with English grammatical structure reached rates of 180 to 190 words coded per hour, the average rate after one week of experience ranged from 100 to 150 words per hour. The most difficult part of the coding was identifying the various parts of speech. For this reason, it was absolutely essential that coders be familiar with English grammar and/or one or more foreign languages and their grammatical structures.

Another desirable attribute for coders was attention to detail. Because coding for the most part involved copying words and numbers, it quickly became tedious work. Coders needed to take regular breaks.

All coding was verified within a week. Verification consisted of checking for proper identification at the top of the coding sheets, for proper numbering and transfer of data, and for correct paragraph divisions. Careful attention was paid to consistency in the identification of parts of speech. The list of "difficult combinations," as explained later, grew out of this desire for accurate and consistent coding of various word combinations. Once this list had been compiled, all of the data were checked for consistent coding in known problem areas.

Coding procedures: paragraph-level data

To code an oral document, coders filled out the top of the form, figure A1.2, with the crisis name, president's initials, and date of speech. The PARAGRAPH # indicates which paragraph of the speech is coded on the sheet. The paragraphs should have already been numbered successively both in the written text and on the traces themselves. At the start of each paragraph, a new coding sheet is begun. The PAGE __ OF __ line refers to the number of pages-of-coding sheets for the paragraph. In the past, we copied all of the words in a paragraph onto the coding sheets from the writ-

Fig. AI.2   Paragraph Data Coding Form.

1. CRISIS _____   2. PRESIDENT _____ | 6. Σ par = _____ | CODER __
3. SPEECH DATE ___   4. PARAGRAPH # __ | 7. N WORDS = ___ | DATE_____
5. THEME _____   PAGE ___OF ___ | 8. N WORDS = ___ | VERIFY __
                                                | 9. $NW - NW$ _____ | DATE_____
                  11. $\bar{X}$par = _____ . (6/9) | 10. SD = _____ |

WORD	A. SLOPE CHANGES	B. # OF PULSES	RATIO A/B	SCALE SCORE	COMMENTS

ten texts before beginning to actually code them so that we could fill out this entry before doing the coding itself. We found, however, that the actual speeches and their traces do not exactly correspond to the written texts since speakers often add words by beginning a sentence, then changing their minds and beginning it again, by repeating words, or by adding filled pauses (uh, ahh, er). All of these deviations from the printed text, which do result in voice stress traces, affect the word total of a paragraph. Because coders do not know from the printed text when they may encounter such variations, it has proved to be much more efficient for coders to write down each word as they come upon it in the voice traces so that these variations may be more easily incorporated into the scoring process. The coder completes the top of the coding sheet by initialling it and dating it in the upper right-hand corner. Coders should leave the VERIFY and second DATE areas blank as well as numbers 6 to 11, which are used for calculations. Coders fill out the top of each coding sheet for each paragraph with the above-mentioned information.

When beginning to code a document, coders start with the first roll of traces, which should already be labelled with the speaker's initials, the date of the speech, and the roll number. Throughout the speech, the machine operator should already have indicated the beginning of each paragraph on the chart paper. It is good practice, however, to have a written text at hand while coding. If the machine operator has neglected to indicate the beginning of the text, the coder can avoid mixing the data from one paragraph and the next. Traces with no words written above them are wasted traces that the operator has discarded. In most instances, this word will be the first word of the first paragraph, but it can also be a pause filler. This word is written at the top of the column on the left side of the coding sheet. To determine whether the trace is long enough to allow objective coding, we first count the number of pulses in the trace, beginning and ending with the first and last peaks above the first large square from the bottom of the chart paper. Pulses at the beginning and the end of a word are not counted if their peaks are below this line since they would arbitrarily influence the stress score. If there are fewer than ten pulses, the trace is too short to code objectively. In this case, the coder simply puts a dash in both the "slope changes" (A) and the number of "pulses" (B) columns next to the written word and proceeds to the next word.

If the number of pulses above the first large square is ten or more, the trace is codable. In this case, the coder enters the number of pulses in the "B" column on the coding sheet next to the written word. Then, beginning with the first peak of the first pulse on the left, the coder counts the number of times that the slope direction of the pulses changes, scoring 1 point for each time the slope direction changes by at least one small box on the chart paper. If the difference between two peaks is less than one small box, the coder scores −1 point for each time there is such a lack of change between two pulses. The coder adds the number of slope changes with the number of negative slope changes, and records this number in the "A" column next to the written word. The coder then notes in the area labelled "COMMENTS" whether the trace contains a different number of syllables (discernible by a return of the stylus to the base line for a distance between pulses in the same word) than the word itself, whether the trace has a cluttered bottom, peaks that are low and difficult to count within a word, whether the trace exhibits a tight configuration, whether the trace consists of two words run together which makes it difficult to discern where one ends and the next begins, or whether the trace falls into our parameter of having at least one peak above the sixth large box and no more than two above the ninth large box. Comments are noted only if such conditions are present in the trace of the word, but if a trace does not meet these parameters, it is noted in the "COMMENTS" that it is distorted.

This done, the coder moves on to the next trace with a word written above it and goes through the same procedure for it and each successive word trace in the paragraph. When all the words in the paragraph have been coded and the sheets have been properly numbered, the sheets are stapled together in successive order, and coding is begun on the next paragraph.

Preliminary calculations

After a paragraph has been coded, preliminary calculations must be performed. These calculations are simply the ratio of column A (slope changes) to column B (number of pulses) for each word in the paragraph. A calculator is essential here for both speed and accuracy. The result is entered in the column RATIO A/B for each word. It is not necessary to include the decimal point, as all scores are between −1.00 and +1.00. Our ratios were taken only to two places and rounded according to normal rules. It is necessary to be alert for negative numbers and zeros in column A, which result in negative ratios and scores of zero for ratios, respectively. For words that were not coded and thus had dashes in their columns, a dash was put in the RATIO A/B column also.

When finished with the ratios, the person doing the calculations must fill out numbers 6 to 9 in the box at the top of the coding sheet. On the coding sheets "6.Σ par" is the sum of all the ratios in the paragraph; "7.*N* WORDS" is the total number of words written in the column on the left-hand side of the coding sheets for the entire paragraph; "8.*N* WORDS" is the total number of words that were uncodable in the paragraph, signified

Fig. AI.3 Word Data Coding Form.

1. CRISIS _____ 2. SPEECH # _____

3. PREPARED ? _____ 4. PARAGRAPH _____

5. DATE OF SPEECH _____

6. *N* WORDS _____

7. PAGE _____ OF _____

CODER _____

DATE_____

VERIFY _____

DATE_____

ENTER _____

DATE_____

	A	B	C	D	E	F	G
WORD	WORD #	# OF PULSES	STRESS	PART OF SPEECH	PLACE IN PARAGRAPH	POSITION RATIO	PARAGRAPH DIVISION

Table A1.1 Percentage distribution of randomly sampled word lengths.

Number of pulses	%
10–14	34
15–19	24
20–24	16
25–29	9
30–34	8
35–39	4
40–44	2
45–79	3
	100

by dashes in the columns next to the words; "9.Nw $-$ Nw" is the difference between items 7 and 8 above.

Coding procedures: word-level data

This section will describe briefly each of the categories on the coding form. As stated previously, only words with ten or more pulses were coded in this project.

In order to keep track of the amount of data in each paragraph, words were numbered consecutively and entered in "WORD #."

One of the relationships we wished to study was that between stress and individual word length. Several ways of determining length were discussed, including the number of letters in a word, the number of syllables in a word, and the number of pulses obtained for a word through voice stress analysis. In this context, the number of letters in a word is not a meaningful measure of word length because many letters in English words have no effect on the pronunciation of the word itself, i.e., they are silent and are included only to satisfy historically based spelling rules. A different but related problem arose with using the number of syllables as a measure of word length. The essential difficulty was deciding by what criteria to measure the number of syllables. Regional and personal speech patterns are manifested frequently by the addition or deletion of syllables from some words. Often the pronunciation of certain words by a speaker differs from that found in a dictionary. Given these discrepancies, it would have been necessary to go back to the audio recordings used to generate the voice stress data in order to determine whether the number of syllables pronounced was the same as the number in a dictionary. Once any discrepancies had been noted, it would have been necessary to decide how to analyze them. In light of the great amount of time needed just to locate such words, to say nothing of the scoring problems that would have been encountered, we abandoned this method of determining word length. In its place, we decided to use the number of pulses generated by each word on the voice stress analyzer to determine word length. From a random sample of words taken from all three speakers (Kennedy, Johnson, and Nixon) table A1.2 presents the distribution of word lengths in a range from 10 to 80 pulses. The percentage distribution is displayed in table A1.1.

In order to divide this distribution into easily identifiable categories to be labelled "short," "medium," and "long," with approximately one-third of the total in each category, it was necessary to reexamine the 20–24 pulse group and divide it so that it was possible to assign the limits to each category. These can be found in table A1.2. Stress scores were taken directly from the data in our initial paragraph coding effort. Again, stress scores could fall within a range of −1.00 to +1.00, but in general the working range was −.15 to +.60. Decimals have been omitted. From a random sample of words taken from all three speakers, stress scores were distributed as presented in figures A1.4 and A1.5. For greater precision in determining possible effect of stress levels on other variables, stress scores were divided into five levels as shown in table A1.3. In addition to the eight normal PARTS OF SPEECH, filled pauses (er, uh, ahh, etc.) were included. Although they were not in the written texts of speeches, filled pauses were on the audio tapes, and they produced codable voice traces even though they are not true words. Including filled pauses in the analysis allowed us to explore differences in their frequency across all three speakers, especially in extemporaneous speeches. Indeed, the mere presence of filled pauses may indicate stress or uncertainty in a speaker. We wished to examine our findings relative to those on filled pauses in the literature on communication.

Parts of speech were numbered according to their frequency distribution in random samples of data taken from all three speakers as shown in table A1.4.

Table A1.2 Frequency distribution of word lengths.

Length	Pulses	%
Short	10–14	34
Medium	15–22	33
Long	23+	33

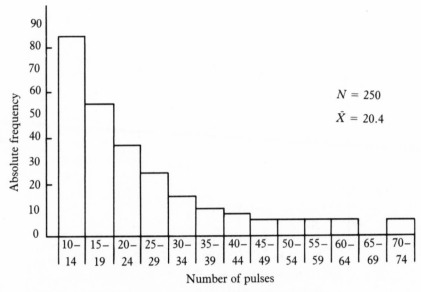

Figure A1.4   Poisson frequency distribution of number of pulses in a random sample of words from three presidential speakers.

$$P(r) = \frac{\lambda r^{-\lambda}}{r!}$$

In addition to the nine categories listed in table A1.4, we had to decide how to deal with contractions, which, like filled pauses, were not present in written texts but which did occur in the actual speeches. There are two types of contractions in English, pronoun-verb and verb-adverb. The verbs that are used in contractions are most often auxiliary verbs such as *to do, to have,* and *to be*; and modal verbs such as *can/could, shall/should, will/would, must/might.* After much analysis, we decided to code noun-verb contractions as nouns and verb-adverb contractions as verbs. Because a noun-verb contraction in spoken English emphasizes the noun (*we've, I'll, he's*) through voice inflection, it was coded as a noun. A verb-adverb contraction, however, which almost always includes the adverb "not," emphasizes the verb; therefore it was coded as a verb (e.g., *couldn't, don't,* etc.).

In developing the coding instructions, considerable time and effort were devoted to identifying parts of speech because of the complexity of language structure and usage. As coding proceeded, we accumulated a list of difficult word combinations, usually involving adverbs, prepositions, and conjunctions, and added them to the coding instructions to assure inter-

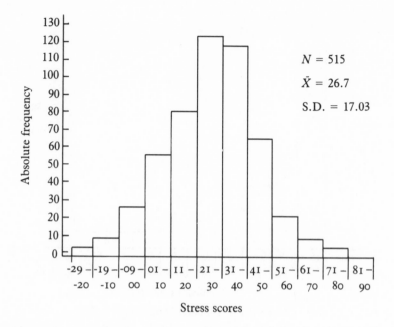

Figure A1.5   Bar graph of stress score frequencies.

coder consistency. We also checked and verified these particular combinations after they were coded. The variable PLACE IN PARAGRAPH, when compared with the N-WORDS entry, shows the position of a word in a paragraph in relation to the total of words in the paragraph. It was not used in our analysis. Under POSITION RATIO, paragraphs were divided into three segments primarily because a speaker himself is aware of the beginning, middle, and end of his speech, whereas he might not be able to determine whether a certain idea was in the thirtieth or fortieth portion of the discourse. The three categories were also easier to deal with than five or ten. Paragraphs, moreover, represented essentially complete substantive themes. PARAGRAPH DIVISION is simply a visual indication of the beginning (first third), middle (second third), and end (last third) segments of the paragraph. "E," "F," "G" (on the coding form) were used to determine boundaries for sections of the paragraph, which were needed to establish whether a word's place in a paragraph is in any way correlated with its stress level. We were looking for specific patterns between the beginning (or middle or end) segments of paragraphs throughout a speech and throughout the course of an international crisis.

Table A1.3   Stress level categories.

Extreme stress	−100 to 00
Heavy stress	01 to 20
Average stress	21 to 40
Low stress	41 to 60
Minimal stress	61 to 100

Coding procedures for psycholinguistic analysis

This section describes the variables used for our psycholinguistic analysis, the reasons for their inclusion, and a brief overview of the coding procedures used to make data manageable.

Data preparation

To employ the data we gathered, it was necessary to devise a coding scheme which allowed for the development and manipulation of several variables (STRESS, WORD LENGTH, PART OF SPEECH, PLACE IN PARAGRAPH, PREPARED VS. EXTEMPORANEOUS PARAGRAPHS) at different levels of analysis (word, paragraph, speech, crisis). The sheer size of the data base—21,040 words comprising 627 paragraphs and 38 speeches spread across three different speakers in international crisis situations—made it imperative that the data be put into machine readable format for easy manipulation and retrieval. The psycholinguistic data were compiled from information on the "Word Data Coding Form" (fig. A1.3).

Our thematic analysis employed the paragraph as the basic unit of observation, but our psycholinguistic analysis employed the word. As described above, specific data for each word were collected, in addition to the already collected, paragraph-level data. The development of our coding scheme made it possible to group the data in a number of ways, e.g., by speaker, by speech, by paragraph, etc., which allowed for the analysis of several specific characteristics for each word. In appendix 3 we reproduce the coding scheme for the paragraph-level and word-level data sets. Each of the variables in the data sets was included for a specific reason.

In the paragraph-level data set we included a variable called SPEAKER in order to separate the vocalizations of the three speakers since we were concerned with developing profiles for each speaker and drawing comparisons across speakers. SPEECH NUMBER simply identifies each speech in chronological order since part of the study was concerned with comparing each

Table A1.4   Percentage distribution of parts of speech.

Code	Part of speech	% of total words
1	Noun	30
2	Verb	25
3	Adjective	16
4	Adverb	12
5	Filled pause	6
6	Preposition	5
7	Article	3
8	Conjunction	3
9	Interjection	0

speaker's vocalizations across time. The PARAGRAPH variable identifies each paragraph within each speech and was used to separate and group the vocalizations by theme for our thematic analysis. As will be evident from the study, we had reason to expect that prepared and unprepared vocalizations by the presidents would differ in several ways. Therefore, a PREPARED variable was included to indicate whether or not a particular speech was prepared.

The variables $\bar{X}$ NOUN, $\bar{X}$ VERB, $\bar{X}$ ADJECTIVE, $\bar{X}$ ADVERB, $\bar{X}$ PAUSE, $\bar{X}$ PREPOSITION, $\bar{X}$ ARTICLE, and $\bar{X}$ CONJUNCTION are paragraph mean stress scores for each of the eight parts of speech. These were included because they have characteristics that we believe cause their stress levels to differ. The variable called $\bar{X}$ STRESS is the overall mean paragraph stress score. Using this variable we were able to determine which paragraphs had the highest stress levels and thereby which themes were producing the highest level of stress in a speaker.

The rest of the variables in our paragraph-level data set consist of percentages of each paragraph made up of each of the eight parts of speech. These were included because we believed that the more critical the situation, and therefore the greater the need for precision, the more qualifying words (adverbs and adjectives) a president would use.

Our word-level data set included fifteen variables. WORD 1 to WORD 5 contain the actual words spoken by the presidents. The word forms five variables rather than one because SPSS, our primary data retrieval system for this project, allows alphanumeric variables of only four characters or less. The CRISIS variable identified the crisis and thereby the speaker. It also allowed us to separate the data, develop profiles of each speaker, and then make comparisons across speakers. Since we were again interested in making longitudinal comparisons, we included a SPEECH variable to identify each speech chronologically.

For the same reasons, we included a variable called PREPARED to distinguish prepared from extemporaneous vocalizations. The PARAGRAPH variable identifies the paragraph within the speech in which the word appeared. This facilitated comparisons from paragraph-to-paragraph to supplement our speech-to-speech comparisons. WORD NUMBER is simply a sequencing variable which has no analytic meaning. WORD LENGTH is an electronically derived measure which we included because we believed that the length of a word affected the stress level of the speaker.

STRESS is a raw vocal stress score for each word included because a major part of this study was concerned with determining the covariates of stress in presidents during international crises. PART OF SPEECH was believed to influence stress, and therefore each word was identified as one of the eight parts of speech. A ninth category, interjections, turned out to be empty and therefore does not appear in our study. PLACE I and PLACE II identify the location within the speech and paragraph for each word. Each speech and paragraph was divided into thirds for the construction of this variable. The place variables were included in order to determine whether our speakers exhibited a pattern of stress as they progressed from the beginning to the end of a speech or discussion of a given theme (paragraph).

Appendix 2

Instructions to Coders
for Completing
"Paragraph Data Coding Form"

1. 1, 2, and 3 are self-evident.
2. 4, "PARAGRAPH #," is the successive enumeration of the paragraphs of the speech. You should number all of the paragraphs in each speech when you start coding it, so that others who may finish it can easily find where you stopped. The coding is done by paragraph, each paragraph being a self-contained item within the speech. You should start a new coding sheet at the start of each paragraph. The "PAGE __ OF __" line refers to the pages of coding sheets within the paragraph. Each page has 25 words, so that a paragraph with 80 words will have 4 sheets. The first will read "PAGE _1_ OF _4_," etc.
3. Leave 5–11 blank.
4. Sign your initials and the date in the upper right-hand box, leave VERIFY and the second DATE empty.
5. Copy all of the words in each paragraph down the word columns before you start coding the paragraph; this will aid in the "PAGE" line in #4.

Coding Rules—PSE Change of Slope Direction

6. Start at the peak of the first spike (a), end at the last peak (z).
7. Score 1 point for each positive or negative direction slope segment (B, C, D, E, G, I).
8. Score −1 point for each 0 slope segment (F, H). If the difference between two peaks is less than one small box on the tape, consider the slope to be 0. This gets scored each time there is a lack of change between two spikes, even if there are four such spikes in a row. Thus this pattern would be −3. This is different from the +1 score where we are looking for the change in slope direction and do not separately count the direction of the changes between each spike and its following one.

If you are not sure whether the difference is 1 small box (i.e., it is very close to 1 box), err on the positive side and assume that there *is* change. This holds especially at the lower levels.

9. Add 7 and 8. This is the "SLOPE CHANGES" (A) column on the coding sheet.

A

10. Count spike peaks. This is the "# OF SPIKES" column on the coding sheet (B).

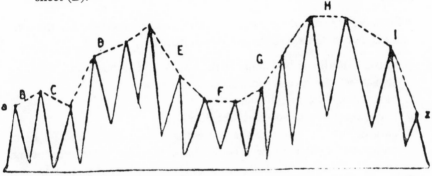

B

Common Comments

11. "x" S—# of syllables *evident in the trace*.
12. CB—cluttered bottom, the trace has parts that are low and difficult to count. Do not count cluttered bottom spikes in either the changes or the # of spikes if they *clutter* within the first box (large).
13. T—tight design.
14. RT—run together.

Appendix 3
Protocols for Word Data
Coding Form

Part I

All numbers are coded for computer entry, so it is important that the correct number of digits be entered for each item.

1. CRISIS: Berlin=1   Dominican Republic=2   Cambodia=3
2. SPEECH #   see speech codes sheet
3. PREPARED?   see speech codes sheet
4. PARAGRAPH #   see speech codes sheet

   PAGE ___ OF ___: refers to the number of coding sheets used for each paragraph. A paragraph with 60 codable words will require three coding sheets (25 words per sheet), the first of which will be Page 1 of 3.
5. DATE OF SPEECH   Enter for I.D. purposes
6. N WORDS: Copy from previous coding sheets (#7)
7. Enter initials and "DATE." Leave "VERIFY" and second "DATE" and "ENTER" and third "DATE" empty.

Part II

Copy codable words from previous coding sheets
A. WORD #—number words successively with four digits
   0001
   0002
   0003
   00 etc.
B. # OF SPIKES—copy from previous coding sheets—column B.
C. STRESS—two-digit number = Ratio A/B from previous coding sheets (omit decimal points)

D. PART OF SPEECH (see supplementary instructions for determining parts of speech)

Noun = 1, verb = 2, adjective = 3, adverb = 4, pause filler = 5, preposition = 6, article = 7, conjunction = 8, interjection = 9.

E. PLACE IN PARAGRAPH—find word on previous coding sheet. Count all words (codable and uncodable) from the beginning of the paragraph to determine the word number. Record it as a three-digit number. Example #35 = code 035.

F. POSITION RATIO—to be calculated only when all other coding is completed for the entire paragraph. Use a calculator and standard rounding procedures.

position ratio = place in paragraph/N words paragraph

Record a three-digit number:

Example PR = 13/26 = .50 = code 050

Standard rounding procedures: If the third digit to the right of the decimal point is 0–4, record only the first and second digits. If the third digit is 5–9, add one to the second digit.

Example .565 = .57, .623 = .62, .398 = .40, .266 = .27

G. PARAGRAPH DIVISION—is marked in order to more easily identify the beginning, middle, and end sections of a paragraph.

beginning—position ratio   001–033
middle—   034–067
end—   068–100

Locate in the position ratio column (F) the division between the beginning and middle sections of the paragraph, and draw a horizontal line on the dividing line. Do the same for the division between the middle and end of the paragraph. Write the words "beginning," "middle," and "end" in their appropriate places.

Speech Codes

	Crisis #1 Berlin		Crisis #2 Dominican Republic		Crisis #3 Cambodia	
I.						
2, 5.	Date of speech	Code	Date of speech	Code	Date of speech	Code
	6-28-61	01	4-27-65	01	4-20-70	01
	7-19-61	02	4-28-65	02	4-30-70	02
	7-25-61	03	4-30-65	03	5- 8-70	03
	8-10-61	04	5- 2-65	04	6- 3-70	04

8-21-61	05	5- 3-65	05	7- 1-70	05
8-30-61	06	5- 4-65	06	7-30-70	06
9-25-61	07	5-28-65	07	10- 7-70	07
10-11-61	08	6- 1-65	08		
11- 8-61	09	7- 9-65	09		
11-29-61	10	7-13-65	10		
1-15-62	11	8-29-65	11		
1-31-62	12				
2-14-62	13				
2-21-62	14				
3-14-62	15				
3-21-62	16				
3-29-62	17				
4-11-62	18				
4-18-62	19				
5- 9-62	20				

3. Is the speech prepared?
   A prepared paragraph is one which the speaker reads to an audience, including statements, addresses, reports, and remarks. A nonprepared or extemporaneous paragraph is generally the response to a question at a news conference. Yes = code 0, no = code 1

4. Paragraph #? (from previous coding sheets) 1 = code 01, 3 = code 03, 14 = code 14,

Identification of Parts of Speech

A word is considered to be a particular part of speech (noun, preposition, etc.) according to its usage in a sentence. In most cases, it is relatively easy to determine the function (or usage) of a word if one has a general understanding of the rules of usage. For specific problems with certain word uses, see the attached sheets. If the use of a word is still uncertain, consult a dictionary.

1. NOUN:	A. a person, place, or thing, including abstract concepts such as love, liberty, justice, etc.
	B. includes *pronouns*, which refer to nouns without actually naming them.
2. VERB:	expresses action, condition, or being.
3. ADJECTIVE:	modifies a noun or pronoun by description, limitation, or comparison.

4. ADVERB: modifies a verb, adjective, or another adverb by a limitation, or comparison.
5. FILLED PAUSE: a sound that is not a complete word.
6. PREPOSITION: shows the relationship between a noun and some other word in the sentence.
7. ARTICLE: indicates the specificity or generality of a noun.
8. CONJUNCTION: joins words, phrases, clauses, and sentences.
9. INTERJECTION: an exclamatory word or phrase.

Specific Examples of Parts of Speech

Words marked with an asterisk (*) require special attention when coding, as they may be used as more than one part of speech.

1. NOUN   A. a person, place, or thing, including abstract concepts such as love, liberty, fear, etc.
                 B. includes pronouns, which refer to nouns without actually naming them.

Some common pronouns

all*	itself	that*
another*	many*	theirs
any*	me	them
anybody	mine	themselves
anyone	myself	these*
anything	neither*	they
both*	nobody	this*
each*	none	those*
either*	no one	us
everybody	nothing	we
everyone	one*	what*
everything	oneself	whatever
few*	other*	which*
he	others	whichever
her*	ours	who*
hers	ourselves	whoever
herself	several*	whom
him	she	whomever
himself	some*	whose
his*	somebody	you

I	someone	yours
it	something	yourself
its*	such*	yourselves

2. VERB: expresses an action, condition, or being, and includes auxiliary verbs:

to do   to be   to have
and modals:

can	may	shall	will	must
could	might	should	would	

3. ADJECTIVE: modifies a noun or pronoun by description, limitation, or comparison; and numbers: one, two, three; first, second, third (ly)

can include present and past participles:
a whimpering child   a stolen book

also includes possessives:

my	his*	our	this*	these*
your	her*	their	that*	those*

4. ADVERB: modifies a verb, an adjective, or another adverb by telling how, when, where, or how much

how	*when*	*where*	*how much*
neatly	afterwards	above*	almost
clumsily	beforehand	down*	completely
fluently	first	forward	entirely
well	last	north	extremely
	later	there	less
	next	up*	much
	now	upstairs	nearly
			quite
			surely
			very

Other common adverbs

accordingly	moreover	where*
as*	nevertheless	not
besides	nonetheless	also
consequently	why*	else
finally	otherwise	too
furthermore	so	sometimes
how*	still	no

however	then	yes
indeed	therefore	
in fact	when*	

5. FILLED PAUSE: a sound or series of sounds that is not a complete word.
   Example: ahh, eer, uh, um

6. PREPOSITION: shows the relationship between a noun and some other
   word in the sentence

   Example

above*	by	out of
across	despite	past*
against	down*	since*
around	except	through
at	for*	throughout*
because of	from	to
before*	in	under*
behind	in spite of	until*
below*	of	with
between	on	without

7. ARTICLE: indicates the specificity or generality of a noun:
   a, an, the

8. CONJUNCTION: joins words, phrases, clauses, and sentences

   Common conjunctions

after	only
although	or
and	since*
as*	so*
as if	so that
as long as	that*
because	through
before*	till
both*	unless
but	what*
either*	when*
for*	where*
how*	which*
if	while
in order that	who*
nor	why*

9. INTERJECTION: an exclamatory word or phrase

    Example: oh, ouch, darn, (expletives included)

Problem words

above—adv., prep.	*one—adj., n.
after—adv., conj.	other—adj., n.
all—adj., n.	past—adv., prep.
another—adj., n.	several—adj., n.
any—adj., n.	since—conj., prep.
as—adv., conj.	some—adj., n.
before—conj., prep.	such—adj., n.
below—adv., prep.	these—adj., n.
both—adj., n., conj.	this—adj., n.
down—adv., prep.	those—adj., n.
each—adj., n.	under—adv., prep.
either—adj., n., conj.	until—conj., prep.
few—adj., n.	up—adv., prep.
for—conj., prep.	what—conj., n.
her—adj., n.	when—adv., conj.
his—adj., n.	where—adv., conj.
how—conj., adv.	which—conj., n.
its—adj., n.	who—conj., n.
many—adj., n.	why—adv., conj.
neither—adj., n.	
no—adj., adv.	*All numbers are adjectives.

CONTRACTIONS: There are two types of contractions, those which combine a noun and a verb (I've, she'll, we're), and those that combine a verb and an adverb (can't, doesn't, shouldn't, won't). A noun-verb contraction is coded as a noun, while a verb-adverb contraction is coded as a verb.

Example

we'll	code	1
he's		1
I'm		1
couldn't		2
won't		2
don't		2

Difficult combinations

Word	Code			
aide-memoire		1	1	
another million dollars	3	3	1	
as far as	6	4	6	
as well as	8	4	8	
both x and y	8	1	8	1
either . . . or	8	. . .	8	
first, second, third (ly)	3			
one, two, three	3			
in 1948	6	1		
in addition	6	4		
in order to	6	8	6	
of course	6	1		
quote . . . unquote	2	. . .	2	
there is (are, was, were)	1	2		
to do, to be, to see	6	2		
World War Two	3	1	3	
yesterday afternoon	3	1		
33,000 (thirty-three thousand)	3	3	3	
Soviet Union, United States, Domini-can Republic, South Vietnam, East Germany	3	1		

Appendix 4
Historical Descriptions
of the Crises

The present study is analytical rather than historical, but a brief history of the crises may help the reader to understand the substance of each case. These descriptions are at best outlines and not complete historical records. Those desiring more detailed coverage are directed to the works cited in the descriptions.

The Berlin Crisis

President John Kennedy inherited various domestic and foreign problems when he took office. By far the worst foreign problem was the generally tense situation with the Soviet Union, already in its second decade. The short-lived Kennedy Administration was tested severely by the Soviets—first in Berlin and later in Cuba.

The events that culminated in the Berlin crisis began long before President Kennedy took office (see Windsor, 1963; Schlesinger, 1965; Sorensen, 1968; Slusser, 1973; and Tanter, 1974). When the United States, Great Britain, and the Soviet Union met on September 12, 1944, they divided Germany into four zones. Berlin, which is located 110 miles east of the demarcation line, was also divided into four parts. Because of its location inside the Soviet sector, Berlin's defense is untenable, and from the beginning, Soviet leaders have used Berlin to apply pressure on the Western powers.

In 1948–1949, Joseph Stalin used the blockade of Berlin as a means of protesting currency reform in the Western zones (Schick, 1971; xiii). The reform was sponsored by the United States, Great Britain, and France as a means of reviving the West German economy.

During the Korean War, the United States expressed an interest in West German rearmament. The Soviet Union reacted by proposing a peace treaty to freeze Germany in a state of permanent disarmament and neutrality (Schick, 1971:1). A crisis was avoided when the plans for rearmament failed.

In 1955, the Soviet Union expressed concern about Bonn and the Western powers signing the Paris protocols in 1954. These agreements allowed West Germany to rearm and Bonn to speak for all German people. The prospect of a strong Germany made the Soviets uneasy, and they began to promote a permanently divided Germany.

From 1955 to 1958, the Soviet Union proposed various agreements to the Western powers in the hopes of making Germany free of armaments. Most of these proposals called for the neutrality of Germany, both East and West. This implied that West Germany would have to leave NATO and Western troops would have to leave West German soil. Such an arrangement was not acceptable to the United States. In 1958 Khrushchev began to threaten the Western powers with the possibility of a separate peace treaty with East Germany. Such an action was in contradiction to the existing protocol. The threat also conveyed to the Western powers that once the treaty was signed, accessibility of Berlin to westerners would be renegotiated. From 1958 onward, the situation in Berlin became increasingly tense.

For the purpose of this brief survey we will begin the chronology of the Berlin Crisis with the delivery of the aide-memoire from Premier Khrushchev to Bonn in February 1961. This document stated Khrushchev's impatience with the entire Berlin issue. He had committed himself to a settlement in Berlin during 1958, and he felt the time had come to resolve the matter. To emphasize his impatience he set a deadline, insisting that a settlement be accomplished by the end of 1961. If no agreement were reached the Soviet Union would carry out its threat of signing a separate treaty with East Germany.

Although the aide-memoire was delivered on February 17, 1961, the Kennedy Administration did not respond publicly until May 19. In its early days, the administration was preoccupied with the Bay of Pigs affair and the conflict in Laos. By late April, the Kennedy Administration was ready to begin work on a Berlin settlement. On May 19, the White House announced that a meeting in Vienna would take place on June 3 and 4 between President Kennedy and Premier Khrushchev.

The Vienna conference did not produce any substantive agreements. Most of President Kennedy's energies were consumed in an attempt to make Khrushchev aware of the position of the United States on the Berlin issue by stressing to the Soviet premier that the United States had a commitment to Berlin and to all the free people of the world. Kennedy emphasized that the United States would not sit idly by if Western accessibility to Berlin were impaired.

When Kennedy left Vienna he felt that Khrushchev would continue the gambit until the United States demonstrated its intentions. At the same time, Kennedy would not close the door on further negotiations. In Washington, Kennedy began to develop a Berlin strategy. He would continue to stress negotiations with the Soviets, clearly favoring this method over a military showdown. Yet Kennedy felt that the commitment to Berlin and the military strength of the United States had to be demonstrated to the Soviet Union.

On July 25, the president went before the American people on national TV to explain the decisions the administration had made on the Berlin issue as a response to Khrushchev's aide-memoire. He spoke on the military and diplomatic decisions taken by the administration. The former attracted more publicity than the latter, but in reality the administration's posture mixed military activity and diplomatic participation equally. Kennedy reiterated the United States' commitment to the free people of the world, stating that "the immediate threat to free men is in West Berlin . . . but there is also a challenge in Southeast Asia . . . in our own hemisphere, and indeed wherever else the freedom of human beings is at stake" (Kennedy, 1961 : 533).

He requested an increase of 125,000 in the Army's force level, with additional increases of 19,000 for the Navy, and 63,000 for the Air Force. He also sought increased draft calls. The president also put 50 percent of the B-52 and B-47 bombers on alert and asked for a special congressional appropriation of more than three billion dollars for the armed forces.

Kennedy spelled out that the choice in Berlin was not between mutual destruction or surrender. "We are willing to consider," said Kennedy (1961 : 538), "any arrangements or treaty in Germany consistent with the maintenance of peace and freedom, and with the legitimate security interests of all nations." He made it clear that the freedom of West Berlin "is not negotiable" (1961 : 537).

Although it appeared as if the July 25 speech was a direct response to Khrushchev's announcement of a military buildup of Soviet forces on July 8, the Kennedy Administration had been planning such an increase since January. The president (1961 : 534) made this point explicitly when he stated, "the new preparations that we shall make to defend peace are part of the long-term buildup in our strength which has been underway since January."

Underlying the rise of tension between the two powers was a problem increasingly embarrassing not only for the Soviet Union but especially for the East Germans. It involved the heavy traffic of defectors from East Berlin into West Berlin. There were several reasons for this exodus. The Ulbricht regime was altering the economy of East Germany under the direction of the Kremlin into a system of cooperative labor and collective farming. Another important reason was the high demand for technicians to work in the rapidly industrializing West Germany. As the months passed the numbers fleeing East Berlin rose. There were 30,000 refugees in July and in the first 12 days of August the traffic reached 20,000. The East German government was becoming increasingly nervous over this drain of labor power.

Surprisingly, the Western powers' concrete response to the flurry of activities and the refugee problem was minimal. President Kennedy never mentioned the issue in his speech of July 25. When the Western leaders met in Paris in early August, they discussed the situation, but no public announcement was delivered.

Then on August 13, in the middle of the night, barbed wire was laid all along the common border of East and West Berlin. A wall was constructed gradually, allowing the Soviets such flexibility as the situation might demand. As the Western powers demonstrated no sign of military opposition because of the deployment of the wall, Moscow continued its construction.

West Berliners were disheartened and concerned about the absence of Western military action. In an attempt to reassure the disillusioned Germans, President Kennedy ordered an Army battle group to proceed to West Berlin on August 19. On August 23 Moscow threatened to interrupt air access. The White House warned the Soviet Union not to disrupt military or civilian access to West Berlin (U.S. Senate, 1961 : 755–757).

The volley of ground activity and diplomatic maneuvers intensified the confrontation. On August 30 Moscow announced its intention to resume the atmospheric testing of nuclear weapons. The United States delayed the resumption of its nuclear weapons testing. This would provide the Soviet Union with a chance to halt the testing if it chose to do so and at the same time allow world opinion to turn against the Soviet Union. However, once Kennedy realized that the Soviet Union would not cease testing, the president gave the nod for American resumption of underground testing. The first American detonation came on September 15. By this time the Soviets had detonated seven explosions, all in the atmosphere.

In September the United States and the U.S.S.R. began exploratory talks in New York. The result was that Foreign Minister Gromyko was able to return to Moscow with the assurance that the United States was prepared to participate in serious negotiations in settling the Berlin issue. On October 17, Khrushchev withdrew his demand that a Berlin settlement be reached by the end of 1961. This diminished the pressure on the Western powers, and the increasing tension over Berlin receded. The antagonism remained, but the chances for military conflict had been diminished.

A second stage of negotiations, between Llewelyn Thompson and Andrei Gromyko, emphasized the issue of accessibility to Berlin by the Western powers. Gromyko found the proposals unacceptable, and on February 7, 1962, Ivan Konev, the commander of the Warsaw Pact forces, began air harassment of Western passenger flights over East Germany. The purpose of the harassment was apparently to test the length to which the United States would go to defend Western accessibility to Berlin. The Kennedy Administration retaliated by flying military planes in air corridors previously reserved for the Soviet Union. These aerial acrobatics continued sporadically from February 9 to March 29.

On March 11 a third stage of negotiations began in Geneva while the Eighteen Nation Disarmament Conference was being held. For the first time, the Soviet Union fully revealed its position on the Berlin issues. The discussions entailed very specific issues including accessibility to West Berlin and regional disarmament.

A fourth stage, starting on April 16, began under ominous conditions. Bonn had been displeased with the proposals the United States had been presenting since the beginning of the negotiation process. The displeasure surfaced on April 13, and without the confidence of Bonn, the Kennedy Administration was forced to stall for time until consensus within the West German government could be reached. A collective opinion could not be attained, and, as a result, the negotiations in the fourth stage never got under way. The Soviet Union's position hardened, and the possibilities of an agreement vanished. The crisis dissipated.

The Dominican Intervention

On April 28, 1965, the United States landed 400 Marines in the Dominican Republic. The succeeding days produced a relatively large-scale intervention of 23,000 troops. There were two officially stated, major reasons for the intervention: (1) American lives and property were believed to be in danger and (2) the U.S. government feared that the Dominican Republic might fall into the hands of Communist elements (Johnson, 1971; Martin, 1966; and Draper, 1968).

The civil war in the Dominican Republic had its origins in the assassination of Generalissimo Trujillo on May 30, 1961. The months and years following Trujillo's death were filled with coups and countercoups.

After the Trujillo assassination, Joaquin Belaguer became the head of the Council of State which governed for approximately eight months until a coup led by General Rafael Echeverria succeeded in the removal of Belaguer. In turn, Echeverria was overthrown two days later by Captain Wessin y Wessin. Wessin retained his post until free elections were held in December 1962. As a result of the election, Juan Bosch was elected by a large margin of votes. However, Bosch became the victim of a bloodless coup in September 1963 and took refuge in Puerto Rico after being exiled from the Dominican Republic.

The government came under the control of a triumvirate led by Foreign Minister Donald Reid Cabral. Reid had a good reputation and was considered a nonpolitical figure (Center for Strategic Studies, 1966:2). During his term the United States named W. Tapley Bennett, Jr., as Ambassador to the Dominican Republic. Almost from the beginning the two officials formed an amiable relationship. Reid had Bennett's total support, and both worked together in formulating a reform policy.

Late in 1964, Reid Cabral proclaimed that national elections would be held in September 1965. At the time Cabral assumed a leadership role, it was believed that he should not and would not run for office. During his tenure he was harsh with the armed forces as well as the Communist faction in that he had several members from each group exiled. Despite his removal of "undesirables," by early 1965 the conditions for civil war began to appear on the surface of the Dominican political system.

The U.S. government had supported Reid Cabral. In viewing him as the most viable leader for the Dominican Republic, Washington felt that the only alternatives to Reid were Joaquin Belaguer or Juan Bosch. Belaguer had been associated with the late dictator Trujillo, and Bosch was perceived as a pro-leftist agitator deficient in administrative skills (Lowenthal, 1972:45). Since Reid had removed a publicly elected official, the ruling triumvirate never enjoyed the full confidence of the Dominican people. As a result, it was expected that not only would the tenure of the triumvirate be limited, but that the leaders would step down in favor of the popularly elected winner of the September elections.

In succeeding weeks, the U.S. government became aware of the deterioration of Reid's position. As rumors spread that he was considering extending his tenure in office, the little support that he had possessed began to dwindle.

By late April, Reid became suspicious of a possible coup. On April 24 he received information which apparently confirmed his suspicion. Reid thereupon ordered the Army's Chief of Staff, General Marcos Rivera Cuesta, to cancel the commissions of Colonels Hernando Ramirez and Alvarez Holquin (Lowenthal, 1972:61). When Rivera confronted the two officers at the 27th of February camp, he was arrested. His arrest precipitated the split in the Dominican Army. Shortly thereafter, a radio broadcast announced the fall of Reid Cabral's regime. However, the government-owned radio station denied any such action. Confusion reigned throughout the country.

The United States embassy was not prepared for the turn of events. Ambassador Bennett was in Georgia visiting his mother who was ill; the chargé d'affaires, William B. Connett, Jr., had less than six months of experience; and other pertinent officials were in Washington, D.C. Almost immediately after hearing the volley of radio announcements, Connett sent a "CRITIC" (high priority) message to Washington. He informed Washington of the rumor of a coup but added that Reid seemed in control.

The early hours of Sunday, April 25, found Reid's position deteriorating further. The Minister of the Interior, a former Army Chief of Staff, threw his support to the rebel movement. Reid asked for assistance from the Air Force and Tank Division. Both groups refused to support Reid. By noontime, Washington had become aware of the quickly deteriorating situation. President Johnson had been briefed, and a Naval Ready Group was ordered to proceed to the troubled area but to remain away from land and out of sight (Lowenthal, 1972:70). On the same day Reid Cabral was arrested, and Radio Santo Domingo proclaimed that Dr. Molina Urena would be sworn in as president. It appeared that Molina would remain in office until Juan Bosch could return from exile in Puerto Rico.

The series of events described above forced the anti-Bosch factions to unify. U.S. representatives initiated negotiations in an attempt to choose a provisional junta. Although no decision was reached, the Dominican Air Force and Navy began strafing the National Palace.

U.S. embassy reports of April 25 displayed a lack of insight into the crisis (Lowenthal, 1972:83). Embassy personnel misperceived the negotiations as a sign of total unity. It was expected that the anti-Bosch forces would be mobilized, and General Wessin had assured the embassy that his tanks would move into Santo Domingo and bring order to the city (Lowenthal, 1972:83). A message to Washington stated the availability of only two choices: accept Bosch's return or form a junta. For reasons stated above, the embassy favored the latter.

During the evening, Commodore Rivera Caminero of the Navy withdrew his support from the anti-Bosch faction. Although he was eventually dissuaded from this action, it gave an indication of the military's weakness. On the morning of April 26, Generals Wessin and de los Santos requested U.S. troops to help restore order. The embassy did not endorse the request, but acting on instructions from Washington, it did begin to negotiate a cease-fire. Although embassy personnel succeeded in stopping the fighting on four separate occasions, the calm was temporary.

By Monday night, April 26, the embassy and Washington realized that the violence, already at a high level, would probably worsen. Procedures for the evacuation of American citizens were initiated. The Defense Department alerted the Caribbean Ready Amphibious Squadron (1,790 men) as well as the 82nd Airborne Division at Fort Bragg (Lowenthal, 1972:88).

On Tuesday, April 27, the anti-Bosch leaders delivered an ultimatum to the Molina regime: negotiate for the formation of a junta and a cease-fire or the city will be attacked. To force compliance they began to strafe sections of Santo Domingo. Thus, as the city approached civil war conditions, the lives of U.S. citizens appeared in jeopardy. Specifically, a group of rebels had entered the Hotel Embajador, the point of evacuation for citizens of the United States, and threatened American lives (Lowenthal, 1972:90).

By the end of the day on April 27, it appeared that the antirebel forces were beginning to win the battle. The rebels found themselves being attacked from both the eastern and the western sectors of the city. Already fatigued from the continuous fighting, the rebels began to retreat. The evacuation of American citizens was underway, and Ambassador Bennett had returned from Washington. A short time later rebel leaders met with the anti-Bosch faction and Ambassador Bennett for negotiations. What transpired at the meeting is unclear. Reports have it that Bennett offended the rebel leaders. Believing that the rebellion had been squelched, he neglected the opportunity for exerting American influence by bringing about a resolution of the crisis (Lowenthal, 1972:94).

By Wednesday, April 28, it became apparent the Dominican armed forces did not have the capability to restore order. In the morning Colonel Pedro Benoit was chosen as leader of a junta. One of his first acts was to inform Ambassador Bennett that the safety of U.S. citizens could not be guaranteed. That afternoon Benoit asked for the landing of 1,200 United States Marines to aid in the restoration of order. Although Bennett did not support this action, he did forward the request to Washington.

By 5:00 P.M., April 28, conditions in the Dominican Republic were deteriorating rapidly. Bennett sent a "CRITIC" message to Washington advising policy makers of the existing conditions. He requested that the U.S.

government proceed with the sending of Marines into the Dominican Republic. President Johnson was informed of the series of events, and with apparently little discussion ordered the landing of Marines (Lowenthal, 1972:100). From the time the intervention was authorized, a primary concern of U.S. officials was how to perceive the intensity of Communist strength in the Dominican Republic. Publicly, the reason for the intervention was the protection of American lives, but the action was justified to congressional leaders as a means of preventing another Cuban-type Communist takeover.

The first wave of Marines consisted of 400 troops. Their area of mobility was confined to the surroundings of the Hotel Embajador. In the early hours of April 29, an additional 2,500 men were landed at the urging of Ambassador Bennett. His request resulted from the fear of a Cuba-type conflict and an exaggerated count of Communist rebels. As the day progressed, the rebels continued to hold the initiative. Ambassadors from other nations asked the U.S. embassy for protection during the crisis. For the first time American Marines protecting the embassy came under attack from snipers. Fire was returned and two rebels were killed.

The Organization of American States had been convened at the request of the United States Ambassador to the OAS, Ellsworth Bunker. After several attempts the Council of the OAS passed a resolution urging a cease-fire and the establishment of an International Security Zone (ISZ). The OAS involvement was welcomed by President Johnson; he had instructed Secretary of State Rusk and Undersecretary Ball to try to involve the OAS in resolving the crisis and to avoid isolating the United States from the member states of the OAS (Lowenthal, 1972:117).

On April 30, U.S. Marines began to spread out from the areas surrounding the Hotel Embajador, intending to occupy approximately nine square miles in the western part of Santo Domingo. This area included most of the foreign embassies that had come under siege. The protected sector was to be considered the International Security Zone (ISZ). Later in the day, a formal cease-fire was signed by representatives from both sides with Ambassador Bennett representing the United States. Although there was partial restoration of order, it was obvious that the cease-fire was not being upheld. Washington responded by landing three more battalions of troops, which were used to form a cordon from the ISZ to the airport. Although this action required direct confrontation with the rebels, the U.S. government viewed the move as the only means of restoring peace. Once the cordon was established the rebels were sealed within the center city area, thereby allowing the easy elimination of rebel strongholds.

On May 1, the effect of the American troops was beginning to show. There was partial restoration of order, but pockets of rebel resistance were still visible. Washington responded by dispatching another Marine battalion and two more battalions of paratroopers. Meanwhile, the OAS, meeting in Washington, selected a peace committee whose purpose was to bring order to the Dominican Republic. The committee consisted of Ambassadors to the OAS from Argentina, Brazil, Colombia, Guatemala, and Panama. The committee was responsible for the passage of the Act of Santo Domingo on May 5. This authorized the OAS to supervise the cease-fire and to bring a constitutional government to the Dominican Republic.

On May 2, having realized that direct confrontation between the U.S. troops and Dominican rebels would be the only way to bring order, President Johnson ordered an additional 6,500 troops. By the end of the first week in May, the total number of American troops in the Dominican Republic reached over 21,000.

On May 7, the Benoit junta resigned and was replaced by a Government of National Reconstruction headed by General Imbert Barreras. Eventually the rebel pockets of resistance were eliminated, but occasionally an individual or small group of Dominicans would ambush an American patrol or attack the house of a prominent official. This sporadic, low-level resistance continued until free elections were held on June 1, 1966.

American troops were withdrawn over a period of fifteen months, with the last military personnel leaving the island on September 20, 1966. By that time the Dominican Republic had achieved order and stability.

The Cambodian Incursion

The U.S. decision to bomb Cambodia in 1969 appeared at the time as the only viable means of combating North Vietnamese sanctuaries and supply lines just inside Cambodian territory. Since 1964, the South Vietnamese army had regularly pursued North Vietnamese soldiers across the South Vietnam–Cambodia border. Over time, the North Vietnamese soldiers began to form sanctuaries just inside the Cambodian boundary in a blatant violation of Cambodian neutrality. Prince Norodom Sihanouk, who from the inception of his reign adroitly managed to maintain a neutral foreign policy, requested an international police force to guard the border (Simon, 1974:18). This plea fell on deaf ears.

As the sanctuaries became more firmly established, the North Vietnamese troops engaged in hit and run tactics against South Vietnam. By 1969, General Creighton Abrams, Commander of the United States Military Assistance Command Vietnam, requested permission to conduct B-52 bombing strikes against North Vietnamese sanctuaries in Cambodia. On March 17, 1969, the president agreed to General Abrams's request. The strikes, code-named Operation Menu, lasted until May 26, 1970. By that time 4,309 B-52 sorties had dropped 120,578 tons of bombs in Cambodia (Committee on the Judiciary, 1974:6).

The sorties, however, were insufficient to destroy the sanctuaries. Throughout the bombing period the operation was kept secret for political reasons. Although the administration had been given permission to bomb by Prince Sihanouk, the Cambodian government desired to maintain a policy of overt neutrality. The prince acquiesced in the bombings provided that Cambodian civilians were not injured and that the United States kept the mission a secret (Nixon, 1978:382).

On March 18, 1970, Prince Sihanouk, while on an extended visit to Moscow and Peking, was overthrown by Lon Nol. The new premier felt threatened by the large number of Vietcong troops in his country. To impede the supply process from North Vietnam to the sanctuaries, Lon Nol closed the port of Sihanoukville. Nonetheless, with the change in government, the Vietnamese Communists decided to increase the number of troops in Cambodia. By April 22, North Vietnamese forces had managed to occupy one-fourth of the national territory of Cambodia.

On April 20, 1970, President Nixon announced his decision to withdraw 150,000 U.S. troops over the next year in an action that represented the second phase of the Vietnamization process. However, the president apparently perceived that large numbers of North Vietnamese military forces in territory adjacent to South Vietnam's western borders threatened Cambodian independence. Moreover, once the number of American troops reached a sufficiently low level, Saigon would become vulnerable to an attack from the west. Not only would South Vietnam be pressured on two fronts, but the lives of the remaining American troops would be increasingly endangered. This situation appeared unacceptable to the president (Nixon, 1978:488).

On April 26, the decision to launch an incursion was completed. The purpose of the intervention was twofold: first, to eliminate the sanctuaries, and second, to destroy the mobile Communist command post, the Central Office of South Vietnam (COSVN). The incursion was conducted simultaneously on two fronts. The first was led exclusively by members of the Army of the Republic of Vietnam (ARVN). This force attacked a section of Cambodia jutting into South Vietnam known as the "Parrot's Beak," which reaches to within 33 miles of Saigon. The other front was opened in an area called the "Fishhook," approximately 50 miles northwest of Saigon. This latter force consisted of a joint effort on the part of American and ARVN troops. COSVN was believed to exist in the Fishhook.

On April 30, 1970, President Nixon appeared on American national television to announce the decision to intervene in Cambodia. The next day, Nixon visited the Pentagon to receive firsthand military information concerning the operation. Before leaving the Pentagon, Nixon authorized the elimination of all sanctuaries (Nixon, 1978:454).

As a result of the incursion, the domestic political situation in the United States became critical; it might even be appropriate to describe it as an internal crisis caused by an international event. Many university students and faculty conducted protest strikes, and a good deal of violence erupted. A total of 450 colleges and universities were closed. The National Guard was called out twenty-four times at twenty-one campuses in sixteen states. Many students were injured and four were killed at Kent State University. Within the Nixon Administration, considerable opposition was voiced, and three key aides of national security advisor Henry Kissinger resigned.

The operation in Cambodia continued through the month of May. In a May 30 conference with General Abrams, the president was informed that enough equipment had been captured to arm 110 battalions and that the sanctuaries had been destroyed (Simon, 1974:109). By the second week of June, the administration began to withdraw American troops. On June 30, a report was released from San Clemente, California, stating that all American troops had been withdrawn (Committee on the Judiciary, 1974:48).

After the troops were withdrawn, the bombing raids that had provided air support for the ground operations continued. The administration explained the extension of the bombing as a means to prevent the reestablishment of the sanctuaries by Communist troops. The air effort continued through 1973.

The results of the Cambodian incursion were mixed. On the one hand, the sanctuaries were destroyed, American troop casualties were reduced, and enormous quantities of arms were captured. On the other hand, as a result of the invasion, the North Vietnamese troops simply fell back further into Cambodian territory, away from the border and critically closer to Phnom Penh. And, the war in Vietnam continued.

Bibliography

Allison, G. T. (1971) *Essence of Decision: Explaining the Cuban Missile Crisis*. Boston: Little, Brown.

Axelrod, R. (1976) "The Cognitive Mapping Approach to Decision Making," in R. Axelrod, ed., *Structure of Decision: The Cognitive Maps of Political Elites*. Princeton: Princeton University Press.

Bell, A. D., Jr. (1981) "The PSE: A Decade of Controversy." *Security Management* March: 63–73.

Bell, A. D., Jr., W. H. Ford, and C. R. Mcquiston (1974) "Physiological Response Analysis Method and Apparatus." Canadian patent No. 943230, issued March 5, 1974, and U.S. patent No. 3,971,034, issued July 20, 1976.

Bell, D. V. J. (1975) *Power, Influence, and Authority*. New York: Oxford University Press.

Benjamin, G., ed. (1982) *The Communications Revolution in Politics*. Proceedings of the Academy of Political Science 34, 4.

Bernstein, Basil (1971) *Class, Codes and Control*. 2 vols. London: Routledge & Kegan Paul.

Bessinger, R. C., and W. W. Suojanen, eds. (1983) *Management and the Brain: An Integrative Approach to Organizational Behavior*. Atlanta: Business Publishing Division, Georgia State University.

Borgen, L., and L. Goodman (n.d.) "Audio Stress Analysis, Anxiety and Anti-Anxiety Drugs: A Pilot Study." Unpublished manuscript.

Bormann, E. G. (1973) "The Eagleton Affair: A Fantasy Theme Analysis." *Quarterly Journal of Speech* 59, 2:143–159.

Brecher, M. (1978) "A Theoretical Approach to International Crisis Behavior." In M. Brecher, ed., *Studies in Crisis Behavior*. New Brunswick, N.J.: Transaction Books, pp. 5–24.

Brenner, M. (1974) "Stagefright and Stevens' Law." Paper presented at meeting of Eastern Psychological Association, April.

Brenner, M., H. Branscomb, and G. E. Schwartz (1979) "Psychological Stress Evaluator— Two Tests of a Vocal Measure." *Psychophysiology* 16, 4:351–357.

Brown, R. (1973) "Development of Language in Children." In G. Miller, ed., *Communication, Language and Meaning*. New York: Basic Books.

Burke, K. (1966) *Language as Symbolic Action*. Berkeley: University of California Press.

——— (1976) "Dramatism." In J. Combs and M. Mansfield, eds., *Drama in Life: The Uses of Communication in Society*. New York: Hastings House.

Carney, T. F. (1972) *Content Analysis: A Technique for Systematic Inference from Communications*. Winnepeg, Canada: University of Manitoba Press.

Cassirer, E. (1946) *Language & Myth*. New York: Harper.

Center for Biopolitical Research (1980) *Remote Psychophysiological Assessment of Elites during International Crises*. DeKalb, Ill. ONR Contract No. N00014-79-C-0028.

Center for Strategic Studies, Georgetown University (1966) *Dominican Action—1965: Intervention or Cooperation*. Washington, D.C., July.

Cherry, C. (1978) *On Human Communication*. 3d ed. Cambridge: MIT Press.

Chomsky, N. (1957) *Syntactic Structures*. The Hague: Mouton.

—— (1968) *Language and Mind*. New York: Harcourt.

Committee on the Judiciary, Statement of Information (1974) *Bombing of Cambodia*. House of Representatives. 93 Cong., 2d sess. Book XI. Washington, D.C.: Government Printing Office.

Connally, W. E. (1974) *The Terms of Political Discourse*. Lexington, Mass.: D.C. Heath.

Corning, P. A. (1983) *The Synergism Hypothesis: A Theory of Progressive Evolution*. New York: McGraw-Hill.

Cragan, J. F., and D. C. Shields (1977) "Foreign Policy Communications Dramas: How Mediated Rhetoric Played in Peoria in Campaign '76." *Quarterly Journal of Speech* 63, 3:274–289.

Daly, J. A., and S. J. Andriole (1979) "Problems of Applied Monitoring and Warning: Illustrations from the Middle East." *Jerusalem Journal of International Relations* 4, 2:31–74.

Davitz, J. R. (1969) *The Language of Emotion*. New York: Academic Press.

Dektor CIS, Inc. (1972) *Psychological Stress Evaluator*. (Sales brochure), Springfield, Va.

De Rivera, J. (1968) *The Psychological Dimension of Foreign Policy*. Columbus, Ohio: Merrill.

Deutsch, K. (1963) *The Nerves of Government: Models of Political Communication and Control*. New York: Free Press.

Draper, T. (1968) *The Dominican Revolt*. New York: Commentary Publishers.

Druckman, D., R. M. Rozelle, and J. C. Baxter (1982) *Nonverbal Communication: Survey, Theory, and Research*. Beverly Hills, Calif.: Sage Publications.

Ealy, S. D. (1981) *Communication, Speech, and Politics*. Washington, D.C.: University Press of America.

Edelman, M. (1964) *The Symbolic Uses of Politics*. Urbana: University of Illinois Press.

—— (1977) *Political Language: Words That Succeed and Policies That Fail*. New York: Academic Press.

Ekman, P., and W. V. Friesen (1969) "Non-Verbal Leakage and Clues to Deception," *Psychiatry* February:88–105.

—— (1975) *Unmasking the Face: A Guide to Recognizing Emotions from Facial Clues*. Englewood Cliffs, N.J.: Prentice-Hall.

Eliot, R. S., and D. L. Breo (1984) *Is It Worth Dying for?* New York: Bantam Books.

Emmert, P., and W. D. Brooks, eds. (1970) *Methods of Research in Communication*. Boston: Houghton Mifflin.

Fagen, R. R. (1966) *Politics and Communication*. Boston: Little, Brown.

Falkowski, L. (1979) *Psychological Models in International Politics*. Boulder, Colo.: Westview Press.

Fishman, J. A. (1972) *The Sociology of Language*. Rowley, Mass.: Newbury House.

Fodor, J. A., and J. J. Katy (1964) *The Structure of Language: Readings in the Philosophy of Language*. Englewood Cliffs, N.J.: Prentice-Hall.

Frank, J. D. (1967) *Sanity and Survival: Psychological Aspects of War and Peace.* New York: Vintage.

Fry, D. B. (1979) *The Physics of Speech.* Cambridge: Cambridge University Press.

George, A. L., and R. Smoke (1974) *Deterrence in American Foreign Policy.* New York: Columbia University Press.

Gerbner, G., ed. (1969) *The Analysis of Communication Content.* New York: John Wiley.

Godden, R., and R. Maidment (1980) "Anger, Language, and Politics: John F. Kennedy and the Steel Crisis." *Presidential Studies Quarterly* X, 3, Summer: 317–331.

Goodin, R. E. (1980) *Manipulatory Politics.* New Haven: Yale University Press.

Graber, D. A. (1976) *Verbal Behavior and Politics.* Urbana: University of Illinois Press.

Gregor, A. J. (1971) *An Introduction to Metapolitics.* New York: Free Press.

Grings, W. W., and M. E. Dawson (1978) *Emotions and Bodily Responses.* New York: Academic Press.

Hermann, C. F. (1969) *Crises in Foreign Policy: A Simulation Analysis.* Indianapolis: Bobbs-Merrill.

———, ed. (1972) *International Crises: Insights from Behavioral Research.* New York: Free Press.

Hermann, C. F., and L. P. Brady (1972) "Alternative Models of International Crisis Behavior." In C. F. Hermann, ed., *International Crises: Insights from Behavioral Research.* New York: Free Press.

Hermann, M. G. (1977) "Verbal Behavior of Negotiators in Periods of High and Low Stress: The 1965–66 New York City Transit Negotiations." In M. G. Hermann, ed., *A Psychological Examination of Political Leaders.* New York: Free Press.

——— (1979) "Indicators of Stress in Policymakers during Foreign Policy Crises." *Political Psychology* 1.1, Spring: 27–46.

Hertzler, J. O. (1965) *A Sociology of Language.* New York: Random House.

Hess, E. H. (1965) "Attitude and Pupil Size." *Scientific American* 212: 46–54.

Hilton, G. (1971) "An Algorithm for Detecting Differences between Transition Probability Matrices." *Journal of the Royal Statistical Society* Series C, April.

——— (1976) *Intermediate Politimetrics.* New York: Columbia University Press.

Hirsch, L., and T. C. Wiegele (1981) "Methodological Aspects of Voice Stress Analysis." In M. Watts, ed., *Biopolitics: Ethological and Physiological Approaches.* San Francisco: Jossey-Bass, pp. 89–103.

Holsti, O. R. (1969) *Content Analysis for the Social Sciences and Humanities.* Reading, Mass.: Addison-Wesley.

——— (1972) *Crisis Escalation War.* Montreal: McGill-Queen's University Press.

——— (1976) "Cognitive Process Approaches to Decision-Making: Foreign Policy Actors Viewed Psychologically." *American Behavioral Scientist* 20, 1, September/October: 11–32.

Holsti, O. R., and A. L. George (1975) "The Effects of Stress on the Performance of Foreign Policy Makers." In C. P. Cotter, ed., *Political Science Annual* VI. Indianapolis: Bobbs-Merrill.

Hopple, G. W. (1980) *Political Psychology and Biopolitics: Assessing and Predicting Elite Behavior in Foreign Policy Crises.* Boulder, Colo.: Westview Press.

Horvath, F. (1978) "An Experimental Comparison of the Psychological Stress Evaluator and the Galvanic Skin Response in Detection of Deception." *Journal of Applied Psychology* 63, 3: 338–344.

Johnson, J. B. (1978) "Stress Reactions of Various Judging Groups to the Child Dental Patient." Unpublished master's thesis. University of Iowa, Iowa City.

Johnson, L. B. (1971) *The Vantage Point: Perspectives of the Presidency, 1963–1969.* New York: Holt, Rinehart, and Winston.

Kaplan, H. M. (1960) *Anatomy and Physiology of Speech.* New York: McGraw-Hill.

Kegley, C. W., Jr. (1973) "A General Empirical Typology of Foreign Policy Behavior." *International Studies Series 2.* Beverly Hills: Sage Publications.

Kennedy, J. F. (1961) "Radio and Television Report to the American People on the Berlin Crisis, July 25, 1961." *Public Papers of the President.*

Kess, J. F. (1976) *Psycholinguistics: Introductory Perspectives.* New York: Academic Press.

Kissinger, H. A. (1979) *White House Years.* Boston: Little, Brown.

Kobasa, S. C. (1982) "Commitment and Coping in Stress-Resistance among Lawyers." *Journal of Personality and Social Psychology* 42:707–717.

Lacey, J. I. (1967) "Somatic Response Patterning and Stress: Some Revisions of Activation Theory." In M. H. Appley and R. Trumbull, *Psychological Stress: Issues in Research.* New York: Appleton-Century-Crofts, pp. 14–42.

Laffal, J. (1965) *Pathological and Normal Language.* New York: Atherton Press.

Lasswell, H. D., and N. Leites, eds. (1949) *Language of Politics.* Cambridge: MIT Press.

Lazarus, R. S. (1966) *Psychological Stress and the Coping Process.* New York: McGraw-Hill.

Lee, D. G., W. C. Johnson, and J. M. Beld (1979) "The Rhetorical Challenge of the Carter Transition: To Build a Governing Majority." In D. Nimmo, ed., *Communication Yearbook 3.* New Brunswick, N.J.: International Communication Association.

Leng, R. J., and S. G. Walker (1982) "Comparing Two Studies of Crisis Bargaining: Confrontation, Coercion, and Reciprocity." *Journal of Conflict Resolution* 26, 4:571–591.

Leng, R. J., and H. G. Wheeler (1979) "Influence Strategies, Success, and War." *Journal of Conflict Resolution* 23:655–684.

Levi-Strauss, C. (1967) *Structural Anthropology.* Garden City, N.Y.: Doubleday.

Lewis, B. J., and J. W. Worth (1975) "Transfer of Stress through Verbal and Written Communication." Unpublished manuscript.

Lindesmith, A. R., and A. L. Strauss (1968) *Social Psychology.* 3d ed. New York: Holt, Rinehart, and Winston.

Lowenthal, A. F. (1972) *The Dominican Intervention.* Cambridge, Mass.: Harvard University Press.

Lykken, D. (1974) "Psychology and the Lie Detector Industry." *American Psychologist* 29, 10:725–739.

Maher, B. A., K. O. McKean, and B. McLaughlin (1966) "Studies in Psychotic Language." In P. J. Stone, D. C. Dunphy, M. S. Smith, and D. M. Ogilvie, *The General Inquirer: A Computer Approach to Content Analysis.* Cambridge, Mass.: MIT Press.

Martin, J. B. (1966) *Overtaken by Events.* Garden City, N.Y.: Doubleday.

Matson, F. W., and A. Montage, eds. (1967) *The Human Dialogue.* New York: Free Press.

McGlone, R. (1975) "Test of the Psychological Stress Evaluator (PSE) as a Lie and Stress Detector." Paper presented at the Carnahan Conference on Crime Countermeasures, Lexington, Ky.

McGlone, R., and H. Hollien (1976) "Partial Analysis of Acoustic Signal of Stressed and Unstressed Speech." Unpublished manuscript.

Meadow, R. G. (1980) *Politics as Communication.* Norwood, N.J.: Ablex Publishing.

Meisel, J. (1982) "Communications and Crisis: A Preliminary Mapping." In D. Frei, ed., *Managing International Crises*. Beverly Hills, Calif.: Sage Publications.

Merritt, R. L. (1982) "Improbable Events and Expected Behavior." In D. Frei, ed., *Managing International Crises*. Beverly Hills, Calif.: Sage Publications, pp. 77–86.

Miller, G. A. (1951) *Language and Communication*. New York: McGraw-Hill.

——— (1973) *Communication, Language and Meaning*. New York: Basic Books.

New Century Dictionary (1956) New York: Appleton-Century-Crofts.

Nixon, R. M. (1978) *The Memoirs of Richard Nixon*. New York: Grosset & Dunlap.

Oneal, J. R. (1982) *Foreign Policy Making in Times of Crisis*. Columbus, Ohio: Ohio State University Press.

Osborne, L. L. (1980) "Rhetorical Patterns in President Kennedy's Major Speeches: A Case Study." *Presidential Studies Quarterly* X, 3, Summer: 332–335.

Osgood, C. E. (1963) "On Understanding and Creating Sentences." *American Psychologist* 18: 735–775.

Osgood, C. E., G. G. Suci, and P. H. Tannenbaum (1957) *The Measurement of Meaning*. Urbana: University of Illinois Press.

Paige, G. D. (1968) *The Korean Decision: June 24–30, 1950*. New York: Free Press.

Paige, J. M. (1966) "Letters from Jenny: An Approach to the Clinical Analysis of Personality by Computer." In P. J. Stone, D. C. Dunphy, M. S. Smith, and D. M. Ogilvie, *The General Inquirer: A Computer Approach to Content Analysis*. Cambridge, Mass.: MIT Press.

Peterson, S. A. (1982) "The Human Brain and Hypostatizing." Paper presented to the annual convention of the International Society of Political Psychology, Washington, D.C., June.

Pitkin, H. F. (1966) *Cartesian Linguistics*. New York: Harper and Row.

——— (1972) *Wittgenstein and Justice: On the Significance of Ludwig Wittgenstein for Social and Political Thought*. Berkeley: University of California Press.

Pocock, J. G. A. (1971) *Politics, Language and Time*. New York: Atheneum.

Price, V. A. (1982) *Type A Behavior Pattern: A Model for Research and Practice*. New York: Academic Press.

Public Papers of the President: Lyndon B. Johnson, 1965. Washington, D.C.: Government Printing Office.

Public Papers of the President: John F. Kennedy, 1961. Washington, D.C.: Government Printing Office.

Public Papers of the President: Richard M. Nixon, 1970. Washington, D.C.: Government Printing Office.

Raphael, T. D. (1982) "Integrative Complexity Theory and Forecasting International Crises." *Journal of Conflict Resolution* 26, 3, September: 423–450.

Reber, A. S. (1973) "On Psycholinguistic Paradigms." *Journal of Psycholinguistic Research* 2: 289–319.

Reeves, T. E. (1976) "The Measurement and Treatment of Stress through Electronic Analysis of Subaudible Voice Stress Patterns and Rationalemotive Therapy." Unpublished doctoral dissertation, Walden University.

Robinson, J. A. (1972) "Crisis: An Appraisal of Concepts and Theories." In C. F. Hermann, ed., *International Crises: Insights from Behavioral Research*. New York: Free Press, pp. 20–35.

Schick, J. M. (1971) *The Berlin Crisis 1958–1962*. Philadelphia: University of Pennsylvania Press.

Schiflett, S. G., and G. J. Loikith (1980) "Voice Stress Analysis as a Measure of Operator Workload." Technical Memorandum #TM 7-3SY, Patuxent River, Md.: Naval Air Test Center.

Schlesinger, A. M., Jr. (1965) *A Thousand Days: John F. Kennedy in the White House*. Boston: Houghton Mifflin; and Cambridge, Mass.: The Riverside Press.

Schramm, W., and D. F. Roberts, eds. (1971) *The Process and Effects of Mass Communication*. Rev. ed. Urbana: University of Illinois Press.

Schubert, G. (1981) "Brain Science and Political Thinking." Paper presented to the annual convention of the International Society of Political Psychology, Mannheim, Federal Republic of Germany, August.

Schwartz, S. (1982) "Is There a Schizophrenic Language?" *The Behavioral and Brain Sciences* 5, 4, December: 579–626.

Scott, R., and A. Howard (1970) "Models of Stress." In S. Levine and N. A. Scotch, eds., *Social Stress*. Chicago: Aldine, pp. 259–278.

Selye, H. (1956) *Stress of Life*. New York: McGraw-Hill.

Shapiro, M. J. (1981) *Language and Political Understanding*. New Haven: Yale University Press.

Shapiro, M. J., and G. M. Bonham (1973) "Cognitive Process and Foreign Policy Decision-Making." *International Studies Quarterly* 17, 2, June: 147–173.

Shapiro, T. (1979) *Clinical Psycholinguistics*. New York: Plenum Press.

Shearer, W., and T. C. Wiegele (1977) "A Comparison of Vocal Stress Analysis and Skin Responses." Paper presented at the annual convention of the American Speech and Hearing Association, Chicago, November.

Simon, S. W. (1974) *War and Politics in Cambodia: A Communication Analysis*. Durham, N.C.: Duke University Press.

Skinner, B. F. (1948) *Verbal Behavior*. New York: Macmillan.

———— (1957) *Verbal Behavior*. New York: Appleton-Century-Crofts.

Slusser, R. M. (1973) *The Berlin Crisis of 1961*. Baltimore and London: The Johns Hopkins University Press.

Smith, A. G., ed. (1966) *Communication and Culture: Readings in the Codes of Human Interaction*. New York: Holt, Rinehart, and Winston.

Smith, G. (1973) "Analysis of the Voice." Unpublished manuscript.

———— (1977) "Voice Analysis for the Measurement of Anxiety." *British Journal of Medical Psychology* 60, 4, December: 367–373.

———— (n.d.) "Lie Detection by Voice Analysis: The Problem of Reliability." Unpublished manuscript.

Snyder, R. C., H. W. Bruck, and B. Sapin, eds. (1962) *Foreign Policy Decision-Making: An Approach to the Study of International Politics*. Glencoe, Ill.: Free Press.

Snyder, G. H., and P. Diesing (1977) *Conflict among Nations: Bargaining, Decision Making, and System Structure in International Crises*. Princeton: Princeton University Press.

Somit, A., ed. (1976) *Biology and Politics*. Paris: Mouton.

Sorensen, T. C. (1965) *Kennedy*. New York: Harper and Row.

Stephenson, W. (1953) *The Study of Behavior: A Technique and Its Methodology*. Chicago: University of Chicago Press.

Stone, P. J., D. C. Dunphy, M. S. Smith, and D. M. Ogilvie (1966) *The General Inquirer: A Computer Approach to Content Analysis.* Cambridge, Mass.: MIT Press.

Tanner, O. (1976) *Stress.* New York: Time-Life Books.

Tanter, R. (1974) *Modelling and Managing International Conflicts: The Berlin Crisis.* Sage Library of Social Research 6, Beverly Hills, Calif.: Sage Publications.

Thatcher, R. W., and E. R. John (1977) *Foundations of Cognitive Processes.* New York: John Wiley.

U.S. Senate, Committee on Foreign Relations (1961) *Documents on Germany 1944–1961.* 87 Cong., 1st sess., 1961.

Usdin, E., and I. Hanin, eds. (1982) *Biological Markers in Psychiatry and Neurology.* New York: Pergamon Press.

Watson, J. B. (1924) *Behaviorism.* New York: W. W. Norton.

Watts, M., ed (1981) *Biopolitics: Ethological and Physiological Approaches.* San Francisco: Jossey-Bass.

Weintraub, W. (1981) *Verbal Behavior: Adaptation and Psychopathology.* New York: Springer Publishing.

White, E., ed. (1981) *Sociobiology and Human Politics.* Lexington, Mass.: D. C. Heath.

—— (1982) "Clouds, Clocks, Brains, and Political Learning." *Micropolitics* 2, 3:279–309.

Whitehead, A. N. (1958) *Symbolism: Its Meaning and Effect.* New York: Macmillan.

Wiegele, T. C. (1973) "Decision-Making in an International Crisis: Some Biological Factors." *International Studies Quarterly* 17, 3:295–336.

—— (1976a) "Health and Stress during International Crisis: Neglected Input Variables in the Foreign Policy Decision-Making Process." *Journal of Political Science* 3, 2:139–144.

—— (1976b) "Voice Stress Analysis: The Application of a Physiological Measurement Technique to the Study of the Cuban Missile Crisis." Paper presented to the International Studies Association, Toronto.

—— (1977) "Models of Stress and Disturbances in Elite Political Behaviors: Psychological Variables and Political Decision Making." In R. S. Robins, ed., *Psychopathology and Political Leadership.* New Orleans: Tulane Studies in Political Science.

—— (1978a) "Physiologically-Based Content Analysis: An Application in Political Communication." In B. D. Ruben, ed., *Communication Yearbook 2.* New Brunswick, N.J.: Transaction Books.

—— (1978b) "The Psychophysiology of Elite Stress in Five International Crises: A Preliminary Test of a Voice Measurement Technique." *International Studies Quarterly* 22, 4, December.

—— (1979a) *Biopolitics: Search for a More Human Political Science.* Boulder, Colo.: Westview Press.

—— (1979b) "Signal Leakage and the Remote Psychological Assessment of Foreign Policy Elites." In L. S. Falkowski, ed., *Psychological Models in International Politics.* Boulder, Colo.: Westview Press, pp. 71–93.

—— (1980a) *Psycholinguistic Analyses of Physiological Stress during International Crises.* DeKalb, Ill.: Center for Biopolitical Research.

—— (1980b) "Remote Psychophysiological Assessment of Elites during International Crises." Report prepared for the Cybernetics Technology Office, Advanced Research Projects Agency, January.

——, ed. (1982) *Biology and the Social Sciences: An Emerging Revolution.* Boulder, Colo.: Westview Press.

———— (1984) "Coronary-Prone Behavior and Political Decision Making." Paper presented to the International Conference on Ethological Contributions to Research in Political Science, Tutzing, Federal Republic of Germany, June.

———— (1985) "Psychophysiology and Politics." *Political Behavior Annual*. Boulder, Colo.: Westview Press.

Wiegele, T. C., and S. Plowman (1974) "Stress Tolerance and International Crisis: The Significance of Biologically Oriented Experimental Research to the Behavior of Political Decision Makers." *Experimental Study of Politics* 8, 3:63–92.

Wiggins, S. L., M. McCrainie, and P. Bailey (1975) "Assessment of Voice Stress in Children." *Journal of Nervous and Mental Disease* 160, 6:402–408.

Windsor, P. (1963) *City on Leave: A History of Berlin 1945–1962*. New York: Praeger.

Wittgenstein, L. (1966) *Tractatus Logico-Philosophicus*. New York: Humanities Press.

———— (1968) *Philosophical Investigations*. 3d ed. New York: Macmillan.

Worth, J., and B. Lewis (1975) "Presence of the Dentist: A Stress-Evoking Cue?" *Virginia Dental Journal* 52, 5:23–27.

Young, R. A. (1977) *Internationa. Crisis: Progress and Prospects for Applied Forecasting and Management*. A special issue of *International Studies Quarterly*, March.

Zinnes, D. A. (1968) "The Expression and Perception of Hostility in Pre-War Crisis: 1914." In J. D. Singer, ed., *Quantitative International Politics: Insights and Evidence*. New York: Free Press.

Zipf, F. K. (1949) *Human Behavior and the Principle of Least Effort*. Cambridge, Mass.: Addison-Wesley.

Index

Author Biographies

Thomas C. Wiegele, Professor of Political Science and Director of the Program for Biosocial Research at Northern Illinois University, has published numerous items of a biobehavioral nature. Those publications include *Biopolitics: Search for a More Human Political Science* and *Biology and the Social Sciences: An Emerging Revolution*.

Gordon Hilton is Associate Professor of Political Science at Northern Illinois University. Among his writings are *Intermediate Politometrics, The Dimensionality of Nations Project*, as well as articles in anthologies and scholarly journals.

Kent Layne Oots received his Ph.D. in political science from Northern Illinois University. His previous research has focused on interest groups and transnational terrorism.

Susan V. Kisiel is a Ph.D. candidate in International Studies at the University of South Carolina in Columbia. Her research interests include Western European politics and foreign policies, international crisis decision making, international relations theory, and biopolitics.